INSTITUTIONAL STRUCTURE and CONFLICT IN NIGERIA

By Ekwueme Felix Okoli

Copyright © 1980 by

University Press of America,™ Inc.

4720 Boston Way
Lanham, MD 20706

3 Henrietta Street
London WC2E 8LU England

All rights reserved
Printed in the United States of America

ISBN (Perfect): 0-8191-0888-4
LCN): 79-3425

**THIS BOOK IS DEDICATED TO
MY FATHER CHIEF JAMES EGBUEJE OKOLI
AND
MY MOTHER ELIZABETH NEBECHI OKOLI**

PREFACE

No one doubts the existence of ethnic particularism in Nigeria. It is equally clear that ethnicity or tribalism has exercised a rather unwholesome influence on Nigerian politics. But it is largely misleading to blame the ills of Nigerian political system solely and essentially on tribalism.

Every configuration of power, be it a state or a confederation of states necessarily revolves around a center of power which controls the allocation of valued resources. This center of power has invariably a number of groups peripheral to it. These groups may be regional, ethnic or religious. In many cases the cleavages caused by these groups reinforce each other in varying degrees of combination.

Nigeria is therefore not unique by virtue of its ethnic pluralism. Infact a casual survey of the states that make up the world shows that more than 90% of them are multi-ethnic. Yet a sizeable proportion of these states has been able to put a lead on ethnic particularism. Switzerland is a prize example of a multi-ethnic state which has been signally successful in containing ethnic cross-pressures. Great Britain which ruled Nigeria as part of a vast empire is a vivid example that ethnic particularism could be contained. While the Empire waxed strong, there were enough political relevant values to satisfy the English, the Welsh and the Scotts. Each took a justifiable pride in the achievements and perquisites of empire. Now that the empire has shrunk to a tiny little island and the politically valued resources have become increasingly scarce, we hear audible rumblings of the movement for Scottish and Welsh home rule. Tribalism, the peculiar disease of the underdeveloped countries has suddenly become the problem of sophisticated and highly developed Britain. It is therefore clear that ethnicity or tribalism becomes politically relevant during the period when crippling economic pressures provoke a readjustment to life style, or when the collapse of imperial system has placed a serious strain on the institutions designed to mediate the allocation of political values within a state. It is at this time when the institutional mechanism can no longer mediate effectively the allocation of politically relevant values that personal and parochial interests assert themselves.

The extent to which these personal and parochial interests become politically relevant depends on the willingness of the politically relevant elite to make personal, parochial or ethnic criteria the basis for the allocation of politically relevant values. It is therefore the actors in the political system who activate, accentuate and reinforce ethnic awareness. Consequently, even in an economically strong state ethnicity or parochialism becomes politically relevant when they are used as basis for the allocation of politically relevant values within a polity.

The problem with Nigeria is two fold. In the first place, from 1947 to 1960, while the regional institutions were gaining influence and power, no action was taken to create a central power base that would be independent of the regions. This situation arose because the center was at this time under the control of the British colonial authority. As the British authority was gradually deemphasized centrifugal forces set in. As these forces tended to reinforce regional autonomy, it became increasingly difficult to set up a competing and independent power at the central level. This problem was complicated by the fact that the emphasis of the constitutional architects in Nigeria was not on the development of a strong central institution but on the devolution of as much power as possible to the regions.

Secondly, as the regions gained greater autonomy in the economic and political spheres; they became for the ambitious as well as for the ordinary citizens, the most relevant political entity. For the political elite, the region became in fact the state and therefore the most significant setting within which he could attain his political as well as socio-economic goals. Regional politics by delimiting the rights and roles of the individuals both within the regions and in federal institutions made the regional government the embodiment of the sum total of individual rights and duties.

Sectional ties including regional or ethnic particularism tend to grow in intensity not because of any absolute import attributed to the ties themselves but because of the sense of security and the gratification of personal needs and ambitions which they provide.

There is scarcely any doubt that it is the individual's need to identify with an entity and his confidence that his needs will be most effectively met within an entity that compels his loyalty and devotion to that entity.

In essence, the compelling attraction of ethnic or regional ties stems from the fact that what serves the interest of the ethnic group or region serves the interest of those within it. Thus the constitutional arrangements in Nigeria, by regionalizing political power regionalized at the same time, the rights, interests and loyalties of Nigerians and made it impossible for the federal government to develop that superordinate loyalty without which a state cannot endure for long.

Therefore, the conflicts and crises in the First Republic in Nigeria were not caused wholly and solely by ethnic particularism or tribalism. Ethnic cleavages only served to reinforce regional sectionalism when the institutional mechanism designed to mediate inter-ethnic rivalry proved too weak to stem the tide of rising regional conflict.

This preface cannot be complete without an acknowledgement of my deep gratitude to the many scholars who have influenced my intellectual development. First and foremost I must express my deep and sincere gratitude to Dr. Adamantia Pollis, my supervisor, for her encouragement, guidance and support. To Dr. Francis Botchway and Dr. C. Neale Ronning, members of my doctoral committee, I owe a depth of gratitude for their unflinching support, critical comments and encouragement.

I am also greatly indebted to Raymond F. Johnson, who inspite of a crippling kidney disease, spared neither time nor energy in typing, correcting and editing the final copy. To Dr. Ifeanyi Ezissi for his support and encouragement in moments of despair; to my wife Sybil and my children, Tagbo, Igwebuike and Ijeoma for their patience, understanding and forbearance in the trying circumstances under which this study was done. Finally I am grateful to the Graduate Faculty of The New School for Social Research under whose auspices this study was done in partial fulfillment of the requirements for the degree of Doctor of Philosophy.

I must not forget to mention the staff of the Black News of Brooklyn, New York who diligently type-set the manuscript for publication. Special thanks go to Segun Shabaka and his assistant Muslimah Mashariki for their untiring effort and patient care in the arduous task of type-setting and correcting the script.

CHAPTER I

INSTITUTIONAL STRUCTURE AND CONFLICT IN NIGERIA:

A Case Study of Conflict in a Multi-Ethnic State from 1946-1966

Introduction

The study addresses itself to the crucial role of the institutional structure in delimiting and mediating conflict generation and conflict resolution in the multi-ethnic state of Nigeria. Its basic premise is that the institutionalization of devolutionary regionalism in Nigeria from 1967 intensified the existing ethnic cleavages; stunted the growth of federal political institutions with an existence independent of regional governments, and thus stifled the emergence of national consciousness and national loyalty.

It is contended, therefore, that the constitutional arrangements which led to the creation of the Nigerian Federation in 1954 precluded the emergence of strong and independent political institutions at the central level. Furthermore, that in the absence of such central institution independent of the regional groups, which could make authoritative and binding decisions and enforce those decisions in all of the regions, the groups play for total stakes and, therefore, create conditions which increase the likelihood of violent conflict and crisis.

Political institution is here defined as a set of clearly stipulated normative patterns, designed to determine the mode of political interaction within a polity and to regulate, in an authoritative and recurrent manner, the roles of the political actors in the system. By conflict, is meant a sharp disagreement over the policies and practices governing the attainment of political objectives within a polity. The conflict reaches crisis proportions when the institutional framework designed to mediate it fails to resolve the conflict within the ambit of the policies and practices, norms and values of that particular polity.

It is our belief that by analyzing the internal dynamics of political interaction in crisis situations within the Nigerian institutional setting, we can spotlight those factors which prevented the federal institutions from mediating inter-regional conflicts and compelling the performance of legally binding roles needed to achieve national political goals. To put it in the words of Eisenstadt, our aim is to find:

> To what extent...the different evolving political institutions provide an adequate framework for the development of the consensus needed for the implementation of the societal goals? It is well known that in many European countries, before the beginning of the modern era, the development of central political institutions preceeded and greatly facilitated the development of such consensus. Can we find a similar process here? Can we not find the development of political institutions which are able to regulate the relations between the government and the various social groups, the distribution of rights and obligations, and to mediate between different groups according to some common norms and within an accepted framework of values?[1]

In Nigeria the emphasis of each constitutional arrangment since 1947 had been on the devolution of power from the central government to the regional governments, not on the development of a powerful central institution able to regulate relations among the regions. This has led to the increasing autonomy of the regional governments. The emphasis was on regional rights on the one hand, and on Federal obligations to the regions on the other. There was no mutuality between the two. The accent was on sharing the national pie, but none of the regions was willing to help in the baking. The result has been the loyalties and commitments of individuals, including the federal legislators, tended to gravitate to the regions of their origins, and only peripherally to the federal government. As Sir Tafawa Balewa, the former Prime Minister, said at the Conference on the Nigerian Constitution in 1950:

> There have been arguments that when we go to the Legislative Council, we don't go as Regional Representatives and that is quite right, but at the same time if my region sends me to the Legislative Council, and I put aside its interests, well I do not know what I can call myself. The interests of Nigeria as well as the regional interest must go side by side...Some friends of mine also tell me that in many matters the North never lacked friends--that is true, but Mr. Chairman, though I know the East and the West and the North and though I know how easily in the present Legislative Council we joined hands, still there are times when cats and mice become friends.[2]

The metaphor of cats and mice is particularly pertinent. It has unmuffled overtones of mistrust and fear. This uneasy mood of suspicion dominated the thinking of the regional delegations to the Legislative Council, and to the Constitutional Conferences. It became the measure and the mold of regional interaction in the central institutions in independent Nigeria. It created a situation in which any region which controlled the center became in fact the "cat," and others had to reconcile themselves to the roles of the "mice." The underlying mood of suspicion incidental to the relations between cats and mice smothered any feelings of trust, mutual confidence, and mutual involvement. In the absence of these feelings of mutual involvement in a common enterprise, any sense of commitment to a common entity is impossible.

Without mutual trust and confidence, any institutional framework, however, carefully constructed, would buckle under the intense heat of inter-group conflict. Where mutual trust and confidence are absent, a community cannot emerge; for in the words of de Jouvenel, a community is nothing but the "the institutionalization of trust."[3] Not just blind unreasoning trust; not just that belief that finds justification in the fear of the unknown; but that belief and trust which derive their strength and vitality from mutual predictability of behavior within an institutional setting. This relationship between institutional structure and behavior patterns is regarded by Heinz Eulau as being "necessarily complementary."[4] He emphasized that "institutional arrangements, norms and functions express behavior patterns that have been stabilized through passage of time."[5] He adds that, "In turn current behavior is necessarily circumscribed and direced by the past patterns we call institutions."[6]

While we do not share with Huntington the unqualified view that "the capacity to create political institutions is the capacity to create public interest,"[7] there is no doubt that Heinz Eulau was correct when he said that it is within an institutional setting that "man rules and obeys, persuades and compromises, bargains, coerces and represents, fights and fears."[8]

This complementarity between behavior expectations and institutional structure is particularly stressed by Talcott Parsons and Edward Shils. In their concept of patterns variables they singled out three "major modal aspects" of the frame of reference which are invariably involved in actions. These aspects are: 1) motivational orientation; 2) value orientation; and 3) the structure of institutions.[9] The structure of institutions is therefore an indespensable determinant of political action and consequently the nature of institutional structure exercises a dominating influence on the actions of the political elite and on the nature and scope of political interaction within a polity.

In a country dominated by a colonial power such as Nigeria, the norms, values, and authority of the central institutional structure necessarily derived their power and legitimacy from the imperial power. A dissolution or partial dissolution of this power invariably caused a definite break in the repetitive and habitual patterns of behavior, and consequently, the actors in the changed institution lose what Eulau calls the Environmental frame of reference."[10]

The success or failure of those in charge of the central institution in re-establishing this environmental frame of reference and in reestablishing the authority, power and legitimacy of the central institutions is the measure of the success of failure of political interaction within the polity. As the Governor of Nigeria pointed out in March, 1953:

2

> No sensible person ever disregarded the difficulties of making a success of the constitution...there were bound to be stresses and strains in a young country of such a size and diversity growing up so quickly. I myself said publicly, before the constitution came into being, that it was *at the Center that the machinery of our constitution would meets its severest test* (emphasis *mine*)...The Council of Ministers is the principal instrument of policy in and for Nigeria. But the method of selection of the Central Ministers made it very difficult for them always to feel that their responsibility was towards the Center, and not towards the Regions from which they came.[11]

This ambivalence of feeling on the part of the central ministers was the result of the accentuation of regional autonomy at the expense of the central government's power and authority. As the British gradually withdrew the support of the imperial authority, which shored up the Federal institutional structure, and as the regions gained increasing autonomy, the political actors came to depend more and more on the measure of support that they received from the regions. As a consequence, both their loyalty and interests became inextricably tied to the regions, to which they looked for reward and reappointment. The eventual result was the regionalization of the interests and loyalties of the members of the central legislature and the progressive weakening of their commitment to the center. This situation was described by Professor Cole as follows:

> ...The trend in the last decade and a half had been towards separation rather than unity; that there has been no real emergence of symbols which would attract loyalties, or even the attention of the illiterate and impoverished masses; that increasing urbanization, economic development and social mobility have not as yet resulted in a new social setting in which a national consciousness can be grounded, that political parties and other groups fail to accept the common interests on which ties of national unity can rest; and without the existence of such ties of unity, a central government in a Nigerian Federal system must either remain a weak (institution) or disappear entirely.[12]

In fact, throughout the life of the self-governing Nigerian Parliamentary System (1960-1966), the federal government remained a weak institution manipulated by over-mighty regions. There is no doubt, according to Wheare, that "emergency powers are given to the Parliament of Nigeria, which when invoked, suspend the division of legislative powers between the general and regional governments."[13] However, it is not so much the bare provision of the constitution as the spirit with which it is exercised that imparts strength and legitimacy to the regime as exercised in 1961, these provisions led to the suspension of the government of Western Region and the imposition of emergency administration under the Federal Government.

As our brief discussion on the Western Regional Crisis of 1962-3 will show it was when the two regions (Northern and Eastern), backed up the federal government that the central government was able to implement the emergency measures. It was rather the interests of these two regions in destroying the power of the opposition by destroying its base in the Western Region, which dictated the course of the emergency administration in the Western Region. It was perfectly true at that time, as Wheare pointed out, that "in the handling of the Western Regional Crisis of 1962-3 Nigerian Federal Cabinet" illustrated the strength of the emergency provisions more than the strength of federalism."[14]

Here we must draw a clear distinction between a constitutional provision and the power to translate the provision into action. The Federal Government of Nigeria had undoubted plenary emergency powers; but without the active support of the Northern and Eastern Regions and the coalition party controlled by these two regions at the central level, the federal government could not have implemented the emergency measures. It had neither legitimacy nor a well defined sense of national interests to back its actions. It was essentially the institutionalization of regional separation and the conflict between these regions that dominated the politics of the emergency administration in the Western Region. Far from exhibiting the strength of the federal structure, it showed in the most glaring fashion how central institutions could be perverted to serve purely regional interests. The eventual result was the elimination of the Western Region as a force in the struggle for regional dominance at the center.

Once the Western Region was eliminated as a powerful element in the competition, the struggle for dominance became the main preoccupation of the Eastern and Northern Regions. It was this struggle that led to the eventual collapse of the Federation of Nigeria. The weakness of the federal institutions became progressively clear as the two regions struggled to build country-wide coalitions. The very fact that the institutional mechanism of the Nigerian Federation was so constructed that the North, by virtue of its population alone, was much more powerful than the other regions combined, made it impossible to actualize what John Stuart Mill called the essentials of a federal system. He stressed that it is essential in a federation that:

> There should not be any one state so much more powerful than the rest as to be capable of vying in strength with many of them combined. If, therefore, there be such a one, it will insist on being master at the joint deliberations; if there are two, they will be irresistible when they agree; and whenever they differ everything will be decided by a struggle for ascendency between the rivals.[15]

This prediction was realized in its entirety in the Nigerian Federation. The North sought and achieved parity with the South in the institutional structure. When this parity was threatened by the destruction of the Action Group's power in the Western Region, and the consequent coalition of parties built by the National Council of Nigerian Citizens in the Eastern and Western Regions, a struggle developed for ascendency between the North and the East. The federal insitution was too weak to mediate this struggle, and consequently, the Nigerian constitutional structure collapsed under the strains imposed by this conflict. It was the institutional arrangement more than anything else which sowed the seeds of disaster.

Even if Nigeria had been ethnically and culturally homogeneous, the institutionalization of regional autonomy without the development of a central power, both independent of the regions and coordinate with them in its respective area of competence, would none-the-less have created serious dysfunctional stress. But because Nigeria is multi-ethnic, once institutional arrangements had failed to mediate political conflict, ethnic factors came into sharp focus and reinforced the conflict arising from institutional dysfunction. There is therefore some merit to the statement by Melson and Wolpe that, "it is probably more accurate to support the idea that conflict produces tribalism, than to argue that tribalism is the cause of conflicts."[16]

If ethnic (tribal) rivalry is caused by conflicts, what then are the root causes of the conflicts? It is our contention that it is the institutionalization of regional separation and the consequent weakness of the federal institutional structure which were the sources of conflict. Regional autonomy is by no means an evil; in fact it is an indispensable prerequisite of a sound federal system. As Wheare pointed out:

> People must have an established government to which they can be attached, but that attachment *must not be too strong* (emphasis *mine*). Therein lies always a possible weakness of a Federal government--that state loyalty may prevail over general loyalty. More particularly is this likely to be true where state boundaries coincide with racial, linguistic or national boundaries...But the danger is that in time of conflict the union will fall apart. It is the continual problem of statesmanship in a Federation to avoid this clash of rival loyalties. That the two loyalties must be there is the prerequisite of a Federal government, but that the one should not overpower the other is also a prerequisite.[17]

It was the institutional arrangement which made loyalty to the region more salient than loyalty to the central government, which in the words of the Govenor of Nigeria, "made it difficult" for the central ministers and central legislature "to feel that their responsibility," as well as their loyalty, "was towards the center, and not towards the regions from which they came."[18]

Therefore, to get at the roots of the conflicts and crisis that plagued the First Republic in Nigeria, we must subject actual crisis to critical analysis. Without a systematic analysis of the causes and courses of the various crisis of the First Republic, it would be extremely difficult to uncover the underlying motive. It is an acknowledged fact that crisis situations are by nature both unstructured and complex. As such, they give full scope to the interplay of power and personality, factionalism and ethnicity, as they expose individuals to conflicting pressures. Furthermore, it is during periods of crisis tha the constraints of institutional norms, patterns and modes of action are subjected to searing stresses.

It is, therefore, the intent of this work to subject three major crisis which came to a head at diferent periods between 1962 and 1964, to critical analysis. The objective is to find out to what extent the institutional arrangements made under the various instsruments which went into the making of the Nigerian Constitution affected the ability of the central institutions and Nigerian elites to resolve conflicts, to mediate authroitatively the allocation of values, and to delimit the scope and magnitude of political conflict within the federation.

Three conflicts which developed into crisis have been selected for detailed analysis. These are: 1) the election conflict which culminated in the crisis of 1964; 2) the revenue conflict, a continuing source of controversy and tension, reached crisis proportions in 1964; and, 3) the census conflict which underlay the various struggles for power in Nigeria from 1947 to 1964   erupted into a full-scale crisis in 1964.

These crisis merely brought into sharp focus the stresses and strains which had been gathering momentum since the beginning of the constitutional experiment in Nigeria in 1946. It is, therefore, necessary to review the constitutional developments of Nigeria from is amalgamation in 1914 to the end of parliamentary government in 1966.

Consequently the first chapter deals with constitutional developments in Nigeria from 1914 to 1960. As Joseph La Palombara said, "a nation's constitution...may be viewed as the totality of its political institutional arrangements, which are the tools for the exercise of power."[19] The brief analysis of the constitutional arrangements is intended to show how these political institutional arrangements determined the nature the configuration of political conflict in Nigeria.

The second chapter traces in broad outline the constitutional problem of Nigeria from 1947 to its independence in 1960. Two minor crises, the Eastern Regional crisis of 1953 and the crisis over the motion for independence in 1953, are discussed briefly in this chapter to illustsrate the crippling effect of faulty institutional arrangement.

The third chapter discusses the interaction in independent Nigeria from 1960-1965. In this chapter the Western Regional Crisis of 1962-1965 is given the prominence that it deserves.

The fourth chapter deals with the census conflict and crisis. It is preeminetly the regional distribution of population in Nigeria which had provided the most intractable obstacle to the equitable allocation of the politically relevant values within the federation. Of all these problems, the issue of revenue allocation has been the most thorny and the fifth chapter deals in extensive detail with this problem of revenue allocation. In turn, the problem of revenue allocation is intricately interwoven with the problem of control of the central power structure. It is the control of the central power structure which gave rise to the conflict and crisis over the federal election of 1963-1964. This election crisis is dealt with in the sixth chapter of this study.

In conclusion, the various issues raised in these crisis are placed in the context of the mainstream theories of conflict and ethnicity in a multi-ethnic plural society. As no discussion of the conflicts and crisis in in Nigeria would be complete without a recognition of the role of the military, in the concluding analysis, we shall deal with the increasing role of the military in these crises which led to the eventual coup d'etat by the military establishment.

Finally, we must emphasize that the written sources on the conflicts and crisis in Nigeria are perplexing rather than enlightening. For one thing the present state of theorizing about Nigeria reveals serious ambiguities and a measure of confusion. It is certainly correct, as Peter Waterman stressed, that the Nigerian situation "by its very complexity" presents a "case which tests the explanatory power of contemporary social theory" and that there is "a growing conviction that the existing body of theory is found wanting."[20] This growing conviction has resulted in increasing dissatisfaction on the part of certain committed scholars and in an apparent reluctance of other experts on Nigeria to risk their reputations in an attempt to theorize on the causes of political conflict in Nigeria.[21]

What, in fact, are the mainstream theories about Nigeria, whose failure has led to this unsatisfactory state of affairs? The first school of thought sees Nigerian problems in terms of tribalisms (ethnicity). This group, represented by Walter Schwarz, John Hatch, and Ulf Himmelstrand,[22] sees the crisis in Nigeria purely in terms of conflicts between the various tribal groups. Their position is that "Nigeria is a collection of mutually antagonistic tribal groups only recently and artificially constructed into a state without regard for ethnic and culutral differences and jealousies."[23]

A casual glance at the political and cultural histories of these various groups prior to the consolidation of British power shows that there was a discernible, if not a vibrant interaction between the various groups that make up modern Nigeria. The pattern resembled a mosaic. Conflicts existed but these were not unrelieved, at times they were resolved by peaceful contacts. As the commission empaneled to inquire into the fears of minorities in 1958 observed: "In considering the problem within each region, we were impressed by the fact that it is seldom possible to draw a clean boundary which does not create fresh minorities."[24]

Other scholars such as Robert Melson and Howard Wolpe, as well as Kenneth Post and Michael Vickers,[25] paint a picture of Nigeria as a conglomerate society. Following the theory of Clifford Geertz in "The Integrative Revolution," they posit the theory that the main 'cause of conflict in Nigeria is what Geertz terms 'primordial attachments'," that is, "the assumed givens of social existence." According to Geertz:

> These congruities of blood, speech, custom and so on, are seen to have an ineffable and at some times overpowering, coerciveness in and of themselves. One is bound to one's kinsman, one's neighbour, one's fellow believer, ipso facto; as the result not merely of personal affection, practical necessity, common interest, or incurred obligation, but at least in great part by virtue of some unaccountable absolute import, attributed to the very tie itself.[26]

Yet in Nigeria, as our discussion of the various crisis will show, intra-ethnic conflicts were unil the civil war as rampant, and in fact more bloody, than the inter-ethnic conflicts. In particular, the crisis in the Western Region in 1961-62 and 1964-65 were essentially between the same ethnic groups living in the same locality. There, neighbor fought against neighbor, irrespective of the ineffable ties of blood, speech and custom. The crisis in the Eastern Region in 1953, as we will show in the relevant section, was essentially, but not entirely, beween members of the same ethnic group. Ethnicity or tribalism per se cannot explain the conflicts and crisis in Nigeria. Richard Sklar, in a subsection entitled 'If This Be Tribalism,' cast grave doubts on the idea that conflicts are caused by tribalism. He concluded that, "If the struggle within the National Council of Nigerian Citizens can be attributed to a structural contradiction it was the inconsistency of a unitary party within a federal state."[27]

Political power was centered in the regions because the super-structure at the central level was eliminated "without the substitution of a political structure which links the major components in the plural society,"[28] and which like the colonial power structure, had the power, authority, and legitimacy to make binding decisions affecting the various regions. In other words, the problem of Nigeria is the problem of its institutional structure.

Edward Feit, pointing to the comparatively easy overthrow of the Governments of Nigeria and Ghana by the military stressed:

That small armies were able, with so little difficulty, to set aside the regimes that had ruled their countries must indicate that these regimes had little substance to them, that they were little more than shadows. But if this is indeed so, then where were the substantive institutions? What are, in truth, the political institutions of Africa.[29]

Here again the problem is seen in institutional terms. Quoting Huntington's definition of institution as "stable, valued, recurring patterns of behavior,"[30] he noted:

> The only institutions in Africa that meet this definition are the traditional African systems, the tribes and the administrative institutions introduced by the colonial power. The significance of the coups can therefore be made clear only if institutional interaction with other forms of political organizations both before and after independence are outlined.[31]

The analysis of traditional African systems in Nigeria has been the preoccupation of anthropologists and does not concern us here. The problem of the term 'tribe' is equally outside the scope of this study. It is, however, our reasoned belief that the problem in Nigeria is to a large extent institutional and that only by analyzing political interaction within the institutional setting can one probe the depth and dimensions of the issues which surrounded the crisis in Nigeria.

Of all the written sources which recognize the importance of the institutional structure, only *Structure and Conflict,* written by Kenneth Post and Michael Vicers, has attempted to analyze the Nigerian crisis in structural context. Their thesis is that:

> Modern Nigeria is a conglomerate society, that is, one made up by the grouping together of peoples of different cultures. Given that the differences are sufficient to lead to conflict between these peoples as a result of contact between them, such societies can only exist if there are forces extraneous to the cultural groups acting to hold them together. In immediate terms, this implies the existence of a political and administrative 'grid' superimposed on these different groups with sufficient force at its disposal to coerce them if necessary.[32]

Certain issues raised by this thesis deserve comment. Admittedly, Nigeria is a conglomerate society, but the very fact that Nigeria is a multi-ethnic community is not of itself a vitiating factor. According to Walker Connor, a survey of the 132 states that constituted the international community in 1967 revealed that only 12 (9.1%) are homogeneous from the ethnic standpoint, 25 have dominant ethnic groups accounting for more than 90 percent of their populations, and 25 other states contain majority ethnic groups ranging from 79 to 87 percent of their total populations.[33]

The remainder consist of a number of ethnic groups varying in strength of population. Multi-ethnicity is therefore not peculiar to Nigeria, consequently ethnicity alone cannot provide a satisfactory explanation to the Nigerian problems.

The second point made by Post and Vickers which needs comment is their argument for a political and administrative grid. If by this they mean the existence of a federal governmental structure with sufficient force at its disposal to coerce if necessary, then it must be observed, as Wheare has noted, that the federal government of Nigeria had emergency powers which could enable it to coerce the regions. The problem with Nigeria was that the federal legislators owed their positions at the center, not to the Nigerian citizens, but to the regions as corporate entities. Like the American confederation of 1777, distribution of power, values and interests in the First Republic in Nigeria was to the regions in "their corporate or collective capacities and as contradistinguished from the individuals of whom they consist."[34]

So pervasive is the corporate power of the region over the individual in Nigeria that wherever a person may reside, the natal region remains the home. However long he may dwell in another region, he remains a perpetual pariah, even in his own country.

He can only stand election in his own region. Therefore, his interests, his rights, and his values are circumscribed by his region. As the regions gained greater autonomy in the economic and political sectors, it became for the ambitious, as well as for the ordinary citizen, the most relevant political entity--the sum total of his rights, his duties, and his loyalties.

As such, the region became the institutional setting within which the individual could "move in established patterns of human relations confident of the actions expected of him and the responses that his actions will evoke."[35] It is this confident assurance that strengthens and secures the chords of solidarity, sentiment, and loyalty to that group. As Grodzins said, "One is loyal to the group that provides gratification because what serves the group serves the self. What threatens the group threatens the self."[36] It is the reinforcement of regional sentiment by regionalizing the rights, interests and politically relevant values in Nigeria that primarily made it possible for the regions to overawe the central institutional structure and to claim the primary loyalty of the individual.

Sectional interest including regional particularism tends to grow in intensity, not because of any absolute import attributed to the tie itself, but because of the existence of competing loyalties of the same general order without the moderating influence of the superordinate loyalty to an all embracing national entity. In Nigeria, the center never had a chance to develop this superordinate loyalty. From 1947 to 1960, while the regions were growing in power and influence no action was taken to create a central power base independent of the regions. This situation arose at this time because the center was tightly controlled by the British Colonial Authority. Its power and legitimacy depended on the authority of the imperial government.

As the British authority at the center was gradually de-emphasized, centrifugal forces set in. As these forces reinforced regional autonomy, it became increasingly difficult to set up a compelling and independent power at the central level. The relevant organizing unit was regional rather than ethnic, for example, even though the North had fifty percent of the seats in the central legislature, it is by no means a monolithic group. According to the 1963 Census, the Hausa-Fulani, the largest single ethnic group, constituted only 32.97 percent of the Nigerian population. According to the 1952 Census, which reputedly contained the most reliable census figures for the North, the Hausas constituted 38.6 percent of the Northern population, the Fulanis accounted for 18 percent, the Kanuris, 7 percent. There are, in fact, over 200 ethnic groups in the North.[37] The greatest problem of the Northern Region had been the problem of holding all these ethnic groups together in order to present a united front against the South. In the East the Ibos, the second largest ethnic group, constituted roughly 62 percent of the regional population and about 22 percent of the total population of Nigeria.

It is evident that no ethnic group could dominate the central legislature without forming coalitions with other ethnic groups. The contest for the control of the center had always involved cross-ethnic coalitions and inter-regional cooperation. All the federal legislative cabinets in Nigeria from 1951 to the end of the First Republic had been multi-ethnic and trans-regional in composition.

The language of the conflict had been cast predominantly in regional terms. It was only when the conflict reached crisis proportions that the ethnic component assumed discernible dimensions. The crucial issue had been which region could establish a coalition at the center that it could control so as to preserve its own interests, power, and autonomy. The discussion of the various crises over the census, revenue allocation, and the 1964 election will shed light on these issues.

The method which we have adopted here is a structural functional analysis of the development of these crises, their origins, and their escalation from the conflictual stage to full blown crisis. This necessarily involves a historical analysis of the factors and forces which shaped and reinforced the conflict and finally led to the crises. In discussing each crisis, we have emphasized the following points:

The relations between the center and the regions as regards the increasing encroachment of the regional institutions on the power of the central government as the British super-structure was gradually replaced by an indigenous parliamentary system. This situation led to the inability of the central institutional structure to mediate authoritatively regional competition for power, resources and patronage within the federation as a whole.

As the central authority passed into the hands of Nigerian legislators, the centers of authority gravitated to the regions. Effective and responsive communication between the units was stymied by multiple and discordant cues. This was because these cues had their sources in the three regional headquarters and not in the center, which tended to take instructions from their party superiors in the regions. Where the party boss was not at the same time the regional leader, lines of authority became hazy and the consequent failure of communication resulted in constitutional crisis. This was the case in the Eastern Region in 1953 when Dr. Azikiwe, the leader of the National Council of Nigerian Citizens, wanted to control both the cabinet, as well as the Leader of government business in the region, even though he was not a member of the regional parliament.

The same situation occurred in the Western Regional crisis of 1961-1962 when Chief Awolowo, as the leader of the Action Group, wanted to control the Akintola cabinet of the Western Region, even though he was neither the leader of that cabinet nor a member of it. The lines of authority between the party leader and the parliamentary leader of the party crossed in each of these two instances and the result in each case was serious institutional crisis.

Overemphasis on regional autonomy also erected barriers to informal relations between the regional elites. It crystalized a sense of competition between the regions. Where political competition between regions ruled the relations of politicians, informal relations between them became suspect. Free and frank exchange, which is the basis of informal relations, was throttled and suspicion and anxiety reigned supreme, in the First Republic of Nigeria.

Within a period of 16 years Nigerians had engaged in five experiments in constitution making. At each of these conferences such intractable issues as revenue allocation, the power of the regions, and the composition and power of the federal government were continually reopened. It is obvious that under such conditions continuity of policy is impossible and the source of the determination of that policy becomes at best problematic. Consequently, the institutional structure of the federal government was not able to acquire any legitimacy. This was particularly in evidence during the election of 1964 when the electoral commission, with all the powers conferred on it by the constitution, had neither the authority nor the legitimacy to make binding and authoritative decisions.

Throughout the various constitutional experiments in Nigeria the most problematic issue was the nature and role of the federal government as an institution and its relation with regional authorities. The resulting political system was a hybrid between a federation and a confederation in the fiscal field, an ingenious mixture of a unitary system with emergency powers, and a federal system with maximum autonomy for the regions. All of these issues are dealt with in the following pages.

CHAPTER II

INSTITUTIONAL STRUCTURE AND CONFLICT IN NIGERIA -

A HISTORICAL ANALYSIS

The problems that beset the First Republic of Nigeria can best be understood within the context of its institutional setting. A schematic analysis of the main stages in its institutional development, is therefore, a prerequisite to the understanding of the structural basis of the conflict and crises that destroyed the First Republic in Nigeria. This chapter addresses itself to that issue.

The political entity known as Nigeria is made up of territories acquired by the British along the confluence of the Niger and Benue rivers during the later half of the 19th century. This acquisition was accomplished in successive stages through a slow process of commercial and cultural penetration coupled with occasional military expedition.

British contact with the area now known as Nigeria began as early as 1553 when a British captain known as Windham first ventured into the harbor of Benin on the Guinea Coast in quest of trade. From that period until the middle of the 19th century emphasis was on commercial penetration and cultural imperialism based essentially on Christian education.[1] To this imperial motive, the abolition of the slave trade in 1807 added a moral dimension. From that moment, the British government, characterized by Dame Margery Perham as "poacher turned game-keeper"[2] sent naval squadrons to patrol the Guinea Coast, British trading companies to make trade pacts with the principalities on the Niger delta and expeditions to explore the inland areas. These traders and explorers did not scruple to use force where it would be effective. In 1851 a British naval force attacked Lagos and took it by storm. In a tersely worded dispatch it was stated with a note of imperial condescension that:

> It is not without some reluctance that Her Majestey's government have determined by the occupation of Lagos, to extend the number of British dependencies on the African coast.[3]

In 1861, Lagos was made a Crown Colony, becoming the bridgehead of British imperial expansion in the area known as Nigeria. If, therefore, the British Empire in Nigeria was "acquired in a fit of absentmindedness" there was, indeed, a method in that fit of absentmindedness. This method became increasingly evident, when as a prelude to the Berlin Conference, 1884-1885, British agents scoured the length and breadth of what eventually became Nigeria, signing treaties of protection[4] with African chiefs and kings. As a consequence of the Berlin Conference, British claims on the Niger-Benue area were acknowledged by other European states and as a result of the treaties made in that conference, the boundary of the area known as Nigeria was visible in its bare outlines.

In 1886, the British government gave a charter to the British Royal Niger Company empowering it "to administer, make treaties, levy customs and trade in all territories in the basin of the Niger and its affluents."[5] The company took over all rights, obligations and privileges already exercised by the British in the area. Equipped with this power the company under the leadership of Sir George Goldie concluded a series of treaties of commerce and protection with the kings and chiefs in the area. In 1897, the British government supplied the company with money and officers to from the West African Frontier Force. This force, under the command of Captain Frederick Lugard (later Lord Frederick Lugard), settled the Western and Northern boundaries of Nigeria with the French. Thus, in 1899, when the British government revoked the charter of the Royal Niger Company, the political boundaries of Nigeria were clearly defined. In 1900, the British government assumed direct administrative and military control. The Royal Niger Company, however, continued its commercial activities and became part of the United African Company.

11

Between 1900 and 1914 the area known as Nigeria was administered as three separate entities - The Colony, the Protectorate of Southern Nigeria and the Protectorate of Northern Nigeria. The headquarters of Northern Nigeria was Zungru, while that of the South was in Calabar. The administrative institutions established by the British in the two areas were different, one based on direct British administration, the other administered by the British through the regional elite.

In 1906, the Protectorate of Southern Nigeria was amalgamated with the Colony of Lagos and became known as the Colony and Protectorate of Southern Nigeria. A legislative council composed of British colonial officials (10 official members), three Africans nominated by the colonial governor and three Europeans representing mercantile interests, was established by Letters Patent of 28 February, 1906. The six nominated members (three Africans and three Europeans) constituted the unofficial members. In the southeastern part, it was stated that because there "was no higher unit of government that the commune or small groups of continuous villages, the British system of administration had, therefore, to be direct."[6] Even in the southwestern part of Nigeria where there had been a long history of centralized government, the British policy was towards direct control fo the local government system, leaving the Obas in control of their own ceremonial laws and functions. For example, F.A. Atanda noted with respect to the Alafin of Oyo that laws dealing with the "the observance of traditional religious festivals, religious and social taboos originated from the Alafin on the advice of his officials or the chiefs in charge of such matters" while "laws regarded as vital to the establishment of sound local government, such as taxation, communal labor for public works...", originated from the political officer (British), but were "promulgated in the name of the Alafin."[7] In short, the British political officer ruled while the Alafin reigned.

In the Protectorate of Northern Nigeria, a different institutional policy informed the establishment of British power after 1900. Sir Frederick Lugard, who as the British Commissioner in the North, determined the format of colonial super-structure in the North, elucidated that policy in an address to the Sultan of Sokoto in 1903. After explaining that henceforth the Sultans and Emirs (Kings) of Northern Nigeria were to be appointed by the British High Commissioner, subject to the usual laws of succession, he declared that, "the Emirs who are approved will rule over their people as of old time and take such taxes as are approved by the Commissioner, the Alkalis (Muslim Court Judges) and the Emirs will hold the courts as of old..."[8] This policy of minimum interference with the status quo became the cardinal principle of British administration over Northern Nigeria and received the enchanting title of *Indirect Rule*(emphasis *mine*).

Differential incorporation of political structures was clearly evident in the policies which informed the establishment of British rule in the Northen and Southern Regions of Nigeria. And, according to C.K. Wheare,the absence of similarity of political institutions is one of the greatest obstacles to both the desire and the capacity for union.[9] Even the 'British imperial control, the only factors common to all the different units remained' highly rudimentary. In fact, an official publication of the Nigerian Federal Ministry of information pointed out that:

> ...though a protectorate existed on paper no great administrative steps were taken to consolidate control even when the company's flag was hauled down and the british government formerly assumed protectorate powers over southern and Northern Nigeria. In 1900 no steps were taken to create a (real) legislature government being by direct decree of the Governor.[10]

Circumstances, however, dictated the amalgamation of Southern and Northern Nigeria in 1914. The overriding consideration was economic.[11] From the proclamation of the British protectorate over Nigeria, the colonial super structure in the South (Southeastern and Southwest) was financed from revenue derived from duties on spirits imported and consumed in Southern Nigeria. The Northern Region being mostly Muslim largely abstained from the consumption of alcohol. Thus, the

Southern Regions paid for the cost of British administration indirectly through the payment of duties on liquor.

The Northern Region, on the other, had maintained a complicated system of bureaucracy known as emirate through an indigenous system of taxation (jangali). When the colonial superstructure was imposed, 50% of this tax went to support the colonial super structure. Even though seven percent of the duties collected in the Southern ports was sent to the North to help to pay the cost of British administration the revenue from the North was grossly inadequate to meet the cost of both the indigenous bureaucracy and the superimposed colonial administration. As John R. Hicks and Sydney Phillipson pointed out:

> Throughout the whole of this period (1901-1914) Northern Nigeria was dependent on outside assistance in order to balance its budgets. Each year it received a large grant from the Imperial Government. Without these grants it would not have been able to pay its way.[12]

Even if the Imperial Treasury had been willing to continue such grants-in-aid, the financial burden of the preparation for World War 1 made continued subvention from the crown at best a problematic proposition. It was these considerations that provided the real incentive for the amalgamation of Southern and Northern Nigeria in 1914. It was, indeed, as Margery Perham astutely remarked, "a merging of three British administrations and not an amalgamation of three different regional populations."[13]

The political institution designed to control this new entity known as the Colony and Protectorate of Nigeria leaves no doubt that it was in law and fact a British administration. On January 1, 1914, Sir Frederick Lugard became the Governor General. By an order-in-council he established a Nigerian Council of 36 members. Twenty-three (23) of these were colonial civil servants (officials). These officials formed the Executive Council. In addition, there were seven Europeans who were unofficial members (not civil servants) nominated by the Governor General to represent the Chambers of Commerce, shipping, banking and mining. Siox were Nigerian unofficial members nominated by the Governor General. These included two Emirs (chiefs) from the North, the Alafin of Oyo, one member from Lagos, one from Calabar and one from the Warri-Benin area.[14]

The order-in-council which created the council stipulated that they must meet once a year and that "no resolution passed by the council shall have any legislative or executive authority, and the governor shall not be required to give effect to any such resolution unless he thinks fit and is authorized to do so."[15]
This was, in fact, an undiluted crown colony system. Such a despotism, however benevolent, could not but evoke vocal protests froom the colonials. Such was the reaction of Africans educated in Britain and resident in Nigeria at this period (1914). As the First World War drew to a close, it became obvious that government by imperial decrees could no longer flourish unchallenged nor could the demands of educated Africans for meaningful participation in their government be ignored with impunity. In the words of the *Lagos Weekly Record,* "the cry for political franchise rings out first and foremost throughout West Africa, especially in the Gold Coast, Sierra Leone and Nigeria."[16]

In the face of mounting criticism and concern, a new constitution was promulgated by the colonial office in 1922. This constitution marked the beginning of representative government in Nigeria. In fact, it was the first constitution in British Tropical Africa to include provisions for elected African representatives;[17] the events leading up to its enactment and its general provisions deserve some comment.

The Constitution of 1922

Agitation by educated Africans quickened the tempo of institutional political development in Nigeria and left disernible imprints on both its form and content. It was obvious that the colonial officials were painfully aware of this growing opposition to alien rule and were clearly disturbed by the development. This concern finds undeniable echoes in a speech made by the Governor of Nigeria, Sir Hugh Clifford, in 1920. He observed that:

> There has been during the last few months a great deal of loose and gaseous talks on the subject of popular election of members of council in Nigeria--talk which has for the most part emanated from a self-selected and selfappointed congregation of educated African gentlemen who collectively style themselves the"West African National Congress.[18]

The importance of this group and their effect on the 1922 constitutional proposal for Nigeria is borne out, not only by the Governor's reference to it soon after its formation, but more particularly, in his obvious attempt to deny any influence on their part in its development. In an address delivered in Octoober, 1923, he took pains to stress that:

> The institution of this council, and the grant of the franchise to Lagos and Calabar, represent a very real advance in the political history of Nigeria; and I, who have strongly advocated these innovations, and have felt no less strongly that the time has come when adequate machinery must be provided for the representation of unofficial interests, for the expression of public opinion, and for the scrutiny of the policy and actions of the Government by spokesmen of those whose affairs are entrusted to this charge, are sanguine that the changes which are today inaugurated will ultimately make for better administration of Nigeria.[19]

To what extent did the Constitution of 1922 provide for the expression of public opinion? To what extent did it give scope for scrutiny of the policy and actions of the government by spokesmen of those whose affairs were entrusted in this charge? Who, in the opinion of the British, were the spokesmen of the Nigerian people at this time? It is with these questions in mind that we will consider the various strands that went into the making of the 1922 Constitution of Nigeria.

An unmistakable indication of the official British attitude towards the above questions is contained in a speech made by Sir Hugh Clifford in the Nigerian Council on December 29, 1920. The gist of the speech can be summarized as follows:

1. Nigeria as a nation did not exist and could not be created. It was inconceivable that:

> ...this collection of self-contained and mutually independent native states, separated from one another as many of them are, by great distances, by differences of history and traditions and by ethnological, racial, tribal, political, social, and religious barriers, were indeed capable of being welded into a homogeneous nation...[20]

It can be seen that official British policy on Nigeria was, therefore, predicated on the assumption that there did not exist and could not exist a disernible Nigerian public whose opinion could be ascertained or expressed. Therefore, that "self-selected and self-appointed congregation of educated African gentlemen," could by no stretch of the imagination claim to represent any identifiable public.

2. National self-government for a medley of groups so different in their history and tradition was an impractical proposition, consequently the British were not only opposed to the concept of a Nigerian nation, but were definitely against its development

3. The British Government was prepared to concede and foster "the right for example of the people of Egbaland"[22] or those of the "great emirate of the North" to national self-determination. But any thought of a selfgoverning super structure binding

all these disparate units into a single nation was outside the realm of practical politics.

4. The concept of national self-government was applicable only to "self-contained and mutually independent native states."[24] Its application to the congeries of nationalities that made up Nigeria would strike:

> ...a deadly blow at the very root of national self-government in Nigeria which secures to each separately the right to maintain its identity, its individuality, its own chosen form of government, and the peculiar political and social institutions which have been evolved for it by the wisdom and by the accumulated experience of generaltion of its forebears.[25]

These calculations determined the form and content of British constitutional experiments in Nigeria, not only in 1922, but in subsequent years. John P. Mackintosh had argued that:

> Considering the British approach first, it is hard to establish or describe as there were few statements of intention or policy. Indeed, it may be doubted whether either the colonial office or senior members of the service in Nigeria ever thought very far ahead. Most of their decisions appear to have been reactions to immediate problems rather than part of a scheme designed to introduce any particular kind of self-government by any particular date.[26]

Since the Report of the Parliamentary Committee on West Africa in 1865[27] Britain had talked of ultimate self-government for the "native tribes." But it is arguable whether there was any serious intention to grant real and meaningful self-government to the Nigerians or to other West African settlements. None the less, there was a settled policy on the nature of political advance which the British envisaged for West Africa, in general, and for Nigeria in particular. It was to be a gradual process of apprenticeship in which any political reform "should always be based upon their original institutions," extracting from them "as many features as possible of the old customs and principles," as were consistent with British institutional ideas and principles. Any such experiment must secure to each of the different peoples, not only the right to "maintain its identity and its nationality," but also its "chosen form of government" and its "peculiar political and social institutions."[28] Ambitious plans such as self-governing Nigerian nations were definitely outside the scheme of things. Balkanization rather that the fostering of a sense of community was the overall determinant of a British constitutional experiment in Nigeria.

It is with these ideas in mind that the British colonial administration in 1922 devised the institutional structure for Nigeria. Here again different institutional arrangements were made for the South and the North. In the Southern Regions a legislative council consisting of 46 members was established. Twenty-seven [27] of these members (including the governor) were British colonial officials (known as official members); of the remaining 19 unofficial members, 15 were nominated by the governor and four were elected - three from Lagos and one from Calabar - under a limited subjects (naturalized Africans) or natives of the protectorate "who had a residential qualification of 12 months and gross income of 100 pounds per annum."[29] Here it is necessary to observe that Nigerians born in the Colony of Lagos were classed as British subjects; so were naturalized Africans from other British colonies such as the Gold Coast (Ghana) and Sierra Leone. Nigerians born outside the Colony of Lagos were regarded as natives of the protectorate.

The 1922 Constitution made it clear that the legislative council would only legislate for Lagos and the Southern Regions. British interests in the North, were however, fully represented in the council by the Lieutenant Governor of the North (Political Officers) who were all members of the executive council. British commercial interests in North were represented in the council by a member of the Kano Chamber of Commerce and a representative of the mining industry in the North (tin mines in Jos). The constitution left no doubt that the governor had the supreme responsibility and authority to legislate for the whole of Nigeria. He was empowered to exercise, on behalf of His Britannic Magesty, all such powers ordained or to be ordained by the Colonial Office.[30] Both the legislative and executive powers over the whole country, including the prerogative of mercy and the power to grant land, were vested in him.[31] The Constitution gave the Governor power to govern the country with the advice of an executive council consisting mainly of the heads of the colonial civil service. It was stipulated that in the exercise of his powers "he shall in all cases consult with the executive council, except in cases of extreme urgency when he must inform the council as soon as possible."[32] To ensure that his power was pre-eminent, he was not only the presiding officer, but had the power to nominate other official members subject to the consent of the Secretary of State. He had also the power to appoint extraordinary members to tender special advice as occasion required.[33] He was empowered to promulgate on his own initiative ordinances on a list of subjects specified in a Letter of Instructions issued to him by the Colonial Office. These subjects include currency, or the issue of bank notes; the power of Banking Associations; treaty-making powers; the control and discipline of the armed forces; and the imposition of various duties.

The order establishing the council empowered the governor, with the advice and consent of the council, to make all laws necessary for the peace, order, and good government of the Colony and Protectorate of Southern Nigeria. To ensure that "advise and consent" did not assume the connotation of enforced command, the following specific provisions were embodied in the constitutional instrument: As the President of the council, the Governor was equipped with a veto power over all acts of the council. The power of the council was further circumscribed by the provision that its ordinances were not to be prejudicial to treaty rights, nor must they violate native law concerning civil relations, unless these were "incompatible with due exercise of his majesty's powers and jurisdictions or clearly injurious to the welfare of the said natives."[34]

With respect to the Protectorate of Northern Nigeria, legislative power was vested exclusively in the Governor. He was empowered to legislate by proclamation. The only limitation was that the "sanctioning of the council (legislative) shall also be required for all expenditure out of the funds and revenues of Nigeria in respect of that portion of the Pretectorate of Nigeria known as the Northern Provinces."[35] This was little more than a formality. In practice all motions relating to money bills introduced in the council were cleared with him and received his prior consent. Furthermore, colonial regulations applicable to all British colonies circumscribed the financial powers of the legislative council.[36]

The approval of the Secretary of State for the colonies was required on all annual estimates of revenue and expenditure and all supplementary estimates. As estimates on important public works projects were subject to his prior approval before they could be introduced into the legislative council.[37]

As far as Northern Nigeria was concerned, British policy was from the start, one of minimum interference with the indigenous political system, and of isolation of the North from the South. According to Perham:

> Great efforts were made to dispense with Southern labor and to train local clerks and artisans. The Northern people were encouraged in their natural desire to resist external influences whether upon their religion, dress, architecture, or way of life generally.[38]

This policy strongly influenced the provisions of the 1922 Constitution with reference to the North. The only express link which the Constitution established between the North and South was financial. The legislative council was only empowered to sanction expenditures out of the funds and revenues of Nigeria in the Northern Provinces. As in 1914, when the North was amalgamated with the South, the dominant rationale was fiscal. In political matters the Governor was vested with exclusive power to legislate for the North. If, as Sir Hugh Clifford had declared, "time had come when adequate machinery must be provided for the representation of unofficial interests,"[39] why was the interest of the North not represented in the council which the governor declared would "ultimately make for the better administration of Nigeria"?[40]

In fact, Sir Bernard Bourdillon hinted broadly that this isolation of the North from the South was a policy dictated in the main by colonial officials. He noted that:

> As regards representation of the North, I was told again and again that the North was not interested, that the Northern Emirs would not come to Lagos and were only concerned to manage their affairs without interference from the South. I know that some at any rate of them were distinctly isolationist in their ideas, but I suspected that some of their administrative officers (British officers) were still more so...[41]

There was little doubt that the "decision politically to separate the two Protectorates of Nigeria was consciously taken," and that the avowed intention was to preserve the "special identity"[42] of the North. Considerations other than the preservation of the special identity of the North also influenced this policy. There was an ingrained fear on the part of the British that there was a potential threat of a Mahdist* uprising, and that this possibility posed a danger to British interests in the North. It was, therefore, in the manifest interest of the British to adopt a policy of minimum interference in the affairs of the Emirate. The loyalty of the Emirs during the Satiru** Revolt of 1905 not only confirmed the wisdom of the policy, but also revealed the extent of Islamic political propaganda in the North,[43] which must be reckoned with in any institutional arrangement for the control of the North.

In the South, on the other hand, British officials regarded the educated Africans, not just as a threat, but as a veritable menace. In fact, as far back as 1885, A.W.L. Hemming, head of the African department in the colonial office, had dubbed educated natives "the curse of the West Coast."[44] Even the Secretary of State for the colonies expressed the opinion that it would be advisable to have "nothing to do with educated natives as a body."[44] That this policy was adopted in Nigeria is evidenced by a statement by Hutton Mills, an educated African. He told the Governor of Nigeria, Sir Hugh Clifford, that prior to his arrival "the educated natives, especially the lawyers, entertained the frustrating feeling that they were not wanted in the country."[45]

It was, therefore, the objective of the "British to isolate the problem of Islamic political propaganda and agitation in the North from the problem posed by the agitation of edcuated in the South. Furthermore, by differntial incorporation of the political institutional structure of the two sections, the British officials hoped to institutionalize the special identities and interests of the North and the South. They knew only too well that once these interests were canalized in regional political structures, their preservation would be the preoccupation of each region. The ensuing conflict of interests would embroil the two sections in a bitter political controversy. Thus, embroiled, the two sections would divert their energies to interregional power and prestige. This would, in turn, diffuse the attack on the colonial authority.

As time went on, it became clear that this policy of divide and rule could not work effectively unless a measure of political interaction between the two regions was built into the system. The British officials certainly realized that the problem was institutional. However, their solution called not for institutional similarity but for a gradual removal of the barriers to political interaction between the two sections. As Sir Donald Cameron observed:

> ...the policy accepted for some considerable time that the Moslem administration should be sheltered as far as possible from contact with the world--the century-old doctrine of political untouchability...could not be expected to stand up against the natural forces of Western civilization that was gradually but quite perceptible creeping further

and further North in Nigeria; a curtain being drawn between the Native Administration in the North and the outer world...But we have advanced now to the stage that the curtain is being gradually withdrawn and, I hope, will be fully withdrawn within a comparatively brief period.[46]

Here is a clear and unequivocal statment by a British Governor that it had been a century-old policy to shelter the North from contact with the world, including the South. The development of differential institutional structures in the North and South was, therefore, the result of British official policy.

If an effort had been made to reverse the process in the 1922 Constitution and a common forum in which the North and South could interact and exchange views had been established the ground would have been prepared for the development of consociational political style in Nigeria. But the British knew very well that these two sections were rather equal in land mass and population. They also realized in the words of John Stuart Mill that these two regions would be "irresistible when they agreed" on any issue.

Therefore, should they agree on a common policy toward the colonial power, the days of British power and dominance in Nigeria would be brief, indeed. To avoid this unpalatable prospect the British decided to divide the Southern Region into parts. Consequently, in 1939, the Protectorate of Southern Nigeria (Southern Region) was divided into Eastern and Western Regions. The institutional rearrangement had a decisive effect on Nigerian political development. The division of the South into two distinct regions led to the development of two regional political institutions each with its own identity and with the institutional support to perpetuate that identity; each jealous of its rights and hostile to any intrusion by the other in its internal political affairs; each anxious to legitimize its position by emphasizing its own culutral and ethnic percularity.

Thus, while the North regarded the South as one undifferentiated Christian group, the Southeast and the Southwest viewed each other as potential enemies and rivals for politically relevant values at the center. Although both the Southeast and the Southwest were, at this time, as multi-ethnic in composition as the North, their Christian persuasion did not provide them with the same type of organizing ideals and ideologies as the Islamic religion did for the North. To the Muslims of the North, Islam is a total way of life and permeates the social and the political, the cultural as well as voluntary associations. What is more, Muslims regard all associations with non-Muslims as an expedient, if not a detestable' evil. According to Sidney R. Waldman:

> "another situation not conducive to exchange of support occurs when the various parties to the conflict feel that compromise on potentially tradable issues is compromise with evil and thus, evil...In this case, the decision system will be characterized by deadlock if no majorities (or decision-dominating coalition) exist, given the initial distribution of interest.[48]

The Muslim North felt that association with the largely Christian South was undesirable unless it had the majority to control that association. It had, therefore, insisted that all politiclly relevant values be divided equally between the South and the North. Although the South had been divided into Southeast and Southwest the North continued to regard the two sections as non-Muslim and as such potential enemies of the Muslims. For this reason, when it served the interest of the North, it cast its language in terms of North-South confrontation. When it desired to play the East against the West it would attack the East and consequently the Ibo, the predominant ethnic group in the East.

Under such a situation it was impossible to develop a sense of common involvement in the enterprise of building the institutional foundation for a strong and united Nigeria. Coleman was, therefore, correct when he stated that:

before 1947 there was little opportunity for a Nigerian to feel that he was under a common government which commanded his obedience, allegiance, and loyalty."⁴⁹

What then caused the radical change in the British official policy of shielding the North from outside influence? What led to the eventual development of a common government and common central institutions for the North and the South in 1947? We have noted earlier the statement by Sir Donald Cameron that the century-old defenses built aroundd the North had been breached by the irreversible tide of time. But is the on-rush of what he called "the natural forces of Western civilization" solely responsible for the union of the North and the South under a common central legislative system in 1947? It is perfectly clear that other reasons contributed to the institutional engineering from 1947 onward aimed at the establishment of a common political framework for Nigeria in which Nigerians would participate in a *meaningful way* in the government of their country.⁵⁰

These factors include the profound changes in world politics brought about by the two world wars; the rise to self-asertion by colonial peoples all over the world and changed fortunes of the imperial powers who found their power and prestige dwindling in the face of technological advances and the rise of the two super powers (United States and Russia). All these, inaddition to the rising tide of anti-colonial agitation in Nigeria led to the realization by the British colonial authorities that a radical reordering of British policy in Nigeria was absolutely essential in order to stem the swelling tide of dissent.

The ranks of dissenters increased to an alarming degree as ex-service men, unable to find meaningful jobs, threw in their lot with nationalists. To quote Coleman:

> Army life was not confined to white troops; more than 100,000 Nigerians served in the military forces during the war. Two divisions with more than 30,000 men had experience in the Middle East, East Africa, Burma and India. For large numbers the army became a school where they learned new skills and trades, as well as the English language. The necessities of effective command, battle discipline and communication required a common language; except for the Hausa contingents,⁵¹ this had to be the English langage. While in the army, most men enjoyed a standard of living higher than they had ever experienced before - regular money income, clothing, food and medical care. They also were taught combativeness and violence. It is, therefore, not surprising to find ex-servicemen among the most militant leaders in the nationalist movement during the post-war period.⁵²

The cumulative effect of these various developments was a definite decision by the colonial authorities that the policy of gradualism in the constitutional advance of the colonies was ill-suited to the changing pace of post-war political realities in Nigeria. It was believed that only a constitution which gave as meaningful role to the colonial elite could blunt the edge of discontent and still give the British a firm hold on Nigeria. The Richards Constitution of 1947 was, in fact, promulgated to serve these ends.

The Richards Constitution of 1947

The fatal flaw of the Richards constitution of 1947 was that it was a reactive document. It was an ingenious attempt at stemming the tide of internal and external criticism of the British colonial structure. Internally it sought to mollify demands for meaningful participation in government without weakening British power over the central power structure. In the international arena it sought to create the impression that constructive efforts were being made to ensure ultimate self-government for the colonies. It was, therefore, not a forward-looking document, nor was it capable for growth and adaptation to the socio-political developments of the post-war period.

Institutionally, it was faced with the task of integrating the North and the South into a centralized political structure, in which the indigenous elite of the two sections would interact and share in the decision-making process with the colonial officials. Events in the country had proved that the relative isolation of the North from the central decision-making process was indeed shortsighted. But any meaningful association of the North and South posed the potential danger that if the elites of the two sections were to achieve any measure of consensus, the days of British control of the Nigerian power structure would certainly be numbereed. If this consensus were attained, the indigenous elite would constitute themselves into a permanent opposition bloc. "An opposition in perpetual majority"[54] would make a mockery of the concept of parliamentary government.

The alternative to this would be to create an institution in which the colonial officals were in a permanent majority. But,

> ...an official majority in a colonial legislature, bound to vote as they are instructed and therefore, bound to carry any measure that the Governor wishes, must, even if it is never used, induce a feeling of frustration and impotence in the minds of the unofficials. Nor is the position really a happy one for the officials themselves. On the other hand an official majority, when the executive is irremovable represents that political anathema, power without responsibility.[55]

The happy solution was to design a constitutional structure in which the unofficials (nominated or elected non-government officials) were in a majority but in which *the actual* power resided in a *small* cadre of colonial civil servants who would hold their seats in the legislature by virtue of thier appointment to posts in the colonial bureaucracy. This could be accomplished by assigning the unofficial legislative seats on regional lines and creating conflicting regional interests which would put one region against the other. One embroiled in inter-regional conflict the unofficial members would be unable to combine and constitute themsleves into a monolithic bloc of opposition.

Sir Bernard Bourdillin certainly felt that:

> The obvious eventual answer to the problem is a measure of responsible government (by) a body in which the unofficials are in a majority but in which they have not formed the habit of considering themselves as an opposition.[56]

The optimum condition was to be attained by establishing Regional Councils based "firmly and squarely on the already established Native Administrations of Nigeria..."[57] The members of these regional councils were to be selected "by and from the Native Administration of the regions concerned."[58] This arrangement, as it was envisaged, would possess two distinct merits for the British. It would ensure the preservation and perpetuation of the Native Authority System, which was regarded as the "most important political achievement of British Administration in Nigeria..."[59] It would also ensure the integration of the educated Africans into the native authority system and thus ensure the "policy of gradual development through local government."[60] The integration of the educated element into the native authority stems, controlled by the traditional elite, would certainly prevent these educated elements from pre-empting the scene and dominating the central political structure.

With these considerations in mind, Sir Arthur Richards, the Governor of Nigerial from 1943 to 1947, drew up a constitution which has passed into Nigerian constitutional history as the "Richards Constitution." It provided for a central structure known as the Legislative Council of Nigeria; and three deliberative regional assemblies, one for the North, one for the East, and one for the West. In addition, it created a second chamber in the Northern Region called the Northern House of Chiefs. The principal features of each institution are adumbrated below.

The Legislative Council

The legislative council was made up of the Governor (who was the president of the council), 20 official members, and 29 unofficial members. Four of these 29 unofficial members were Emirs, selected by the Northern House of Chiefs. Two were chiefs from the Western Region, nominated by the Governor. Each of the regional councils selected from among its members a certain number of regional representatives to the central legislature. They were as follows: five from the Northern Region; four from the Western Region; and four from the Eastern Region. The constitution empowered the Governor, after consultations with the native authorities, to nominate one member to represent the Colony of Lagos, and one member each to represent four special interest, e.g., banking, shipping, industry and commerce, and mining. (The four special interest representatives were all Europeans.)

The legislative council was empowered to enact laws for the whole of Nigeria. Its legislative power was, however, purely deliberative - the real legislative power was vested in the Governor, since he was empowered to nominate most members. He had, in addition, a casting vote and veto power, and the power to issue a special warrant to authorize expenditures if the financial committee of the council failed to approve the budget. All legislative bills, except such as were purely formal or introduced under a certificate of urgency, must be introduced by regional legislature and debated in the regional councils before being submitted to the central legislature, with such amendments as were desired by the regional councils.[61]

The Regional Councils

The composition of the regional councils varied with each region. Thus, from the start the basis of the institutional system violated the requisite that for a federal system to operate efficiently there should be a measure of similarity between the socio-political institutions of the component units. Even though it was the avowed intention of the Richasrds Constitution to lay the foundation of a federal system,[62] no attempt was made to adhere to the general principles of federalism. If the constitutional experiment was, indeed, a first step in the direction of the establishment of a federal structure, it was surely an erroneous first step. For one thing, all legislative and executive powers were vested in the central government. The regions were neither coordinate with the central government nor were they independent within any sphere of government activity. They were in law and in fact subordinate to the central authority. Furthermore, the consititution provides that the central government could not act on individuals except indirectly through the regions. Individual rights and duties were derived only through the regions and not by virtue of membership in an entity known as Nigeria.

In the North provisions were made for a provincial assembly. This assembly was made up of 19 official members and 20 unofficial members. Fourteen of these unofficial members were chosen by the members of the native authorities from among those of their ranks who were not major chiefs. The remaining unofficial members were nominee of the Governor who were mainly chosen from the non-Moslem communities in the Northern Region to represent the Sabon-Gari,[63] industry, commerce, and various other groups. The senior resident, who was one of the 19 official members, presided over the provincial assembly. The constitution also made provision for a second chamber known as the Northern House of Chiefs. The membership of this upper house consisted of 13 chiefs who were recognized by the colonial authorities as first-class chiefs and 10 second-class chiefs who were selected from the non-Moslem provinces in the Northern Region. The Chief Commissioner of the Northern Region, a colonial civil servant, presided over the House of Chiefs. The official language of these two chambers was Hausa.

In the Western Region the constitution provided for a single chamber assembly (as opposed to the House of Chiefs and the House of the Assembly in the North) known as the Western Regional Provincial Assembly. The membership of this assembly consisted of 14 official members and 15 unofficial members. The Chief Commissioner of the Western Region, who was one of the 14 official members, officiated as the president of the assembly. Of the 15 unofficial members, three were chiefs nominated by the Governor after consultation with the chiefs of the Western Region. Seven of the unofficial members were selected by and from the members of the native authorities. The council's other unofficial members were nominated by the Governor from interests not otherwise represented. (These were mostly Europeans and religious leaders.)

In the Eastern Region the constitution provided for a single chamber assembly consisting of 14 official members and 15 unofficial members. As in the Western Region, the Chief Commissioner, who was one of the 14 official members, presided over the assembly. Ten members were selected by the members of the native authorities from their own ranks. Five were nominated by the Governor to represent a variety of interests.

It is clear from this brief analysis that there was no pretense of building parallel institutions for the North and South (East and West). The objective was not to achieve compatibility in political institutional structures - it was pre-eminently a device to ensure that the "diverse elements may progress at varying speeds amicably and smoothly, towards a more closely integrated economic, social and political unity, without sacrificing the principles and ideals inherent in their divergent ways of life."[64] There was indeed a conscious policy designed to perpetuate institutional dissimilarity among the component parts. According to Coleman:

> Broadly speaking, official planners held two views regarding future relations among native authorities, the artificial administrative regions and the central superstructure. 'One school composed mainly of officials in Northern Nigeria who had experience with large emirates, urged that the native authorities be given progressively wider powers until they become self-governing, presumably with an attenuated British superstructure holding them together in a loose confederation. Some members of this school advocated complete separation of Northern Nigeria from the rest of the country so as to permit it to pursue its own independent constitutional development.[65]

But the immediate objections to the provisions of the Richards Constitution did not stem from its inherent separatist institutional structure: the main focus of attack was the provision relating to the powers and functions of the legislative council and the regional assemblies. The provisions of the Richards Constitution can be summarized as follows: in financial matters, official grip on the purse strings was both pervasive and prevailing. The finance committee of the legislative council was presided over by the Chief Secretary to the Colonial Government, with the Financial Secretary as the Vice Chairman. The main body of the committee, except for these two officers, consisted of all the unofficial members of the legislative council. All estimates and supplementary estimates for the whole of Nigeria had to be referred to it before being presented to the whole council. In principle, the majority of the finance committee consisted of African unofficial members. However, no money bills were sent to the committee without the prior consent of the Governor. Furthermore, it was provided that the Governor had power to issue a special warrant, "if the finance committee does not approve expenditure which he considered necessary."[66] Here we see a clear example of an official majority whose wishes could be thwarted by the fiat of a colonial governor. It was not just a case of power without responsibility it was a flagrant perversion of the majoritarian principle of democracy (representative government).

As far as the regional or provincial assemblies were concerned, their most important duties were "connected with finance."⁶⁷ Each regional council was provided with its own budget. The costs of all government services within the region, including the salaries of government officials, would be included in the regional estimates. Each region would "debate its estimates in detail before passing them with such amendments as they desired to suggest. In the Northern Provinces the estimates would also be considered by the House of Chiefs which had the power to delete or amend items but not to insert new ones."⁶⁸ The estimates thus approved by the regional councils were submitted to the Governor, who had the power to amend them "if he thought this necessary in the public interest."⁶⁹ The elected and nominated representatives of the people in the legislative council were "to be discouraged from discussing details of the regional estimates."⁷⁰

It is necessary to emphasize the complete and pervasive control of the financial affairs of Nigeria by the Governor and the British colonial officials because one of the greatest impediments to inter-regional cooperation and harmony was the charge that the North had been cheated out of receiving its fair share of national revenue.⁷¹

It is evident from the earlier discussions of fiscal control that any inequity was attributable to the Governor, his Chief Secretary, and the Financial Secretary. They held the purse strings firmly in their hands. Any disbursement to the regions could not have been made without their knowledge and full consent.

The most sweeping criticism levelled against the Richards Constitution was, in the words of Chief Awolowo, "that it retains some of the objectionable features of the old, contains unsavory characteristics of its own, and falls short of expectations."⁷² In legislative, as well as fiscal matters, it was business as usual, with the colonial officials firmly in the saddle. In fact, Sir Bernard Bourdillon specifically stated that "the function of the legislative council will be the same as at present, with the essential difference that it will legislate for the whole of Nigeria."⁷³ The most important change of the Richards Constitution was, therefore, the fact that the North and the South were for the first time represented in a single body which had the power to "legislate" for the whole country.

Even in this legislative sphere, "discussion seemed the crux of the principle. There was neither the intension nor the pretension to secure greater participation by the Africans in the direct management or control of their affairs."⁷⁴ Neither before nor after the introduction of the Richards Constitution could it be said that the South had any measure of legislative or fiscal authority. Therefore, the idea of fairness in revenue allocation, which seemed to have been the greatest point of disagreement between the North and South (see Chapter 5), was a political issue, designed more to divide than to unite. The conflict and crisis over revenue allocation are dealt with in Chapter 5 and need not detain us here.

What was perhaps the most damaging criticism of the ʿRichards Constitution was directed at the provisions characterized by Nigerians as the obnoxious ordinances. These ordinances were the Minerals Ordinance, which vested the title of all minerals found in Nigeria in the Crown: The Public Land Acquisition Ordinance; and the Crown Lands (amendment) Ordinance of 1947, which designated as Crown Lands all lands acquired or to be acquired by the government for public purposes; and the Appointment and Deposition of Chiefs (amendment) Ordinance, which gave the governor the power to appoint and depose chiefs subject to his own discretion. Criticism levelled at these ordinances thoroughly discredited the Richards Constitution and led to its replacement by the Macpherson Constitution of 1951.

The Macpherson Constitution

The Richards Constitution had been imposed on the country without any attempt to consult the people over whose political destinies the constitution was intended to preside. Even Sir Bernard Bourdillon felt that the high-handed manner in which the constitution was imposed was unfortunate. He noted that:

> Generally speaking, I believe that the Nigerian proposals conform to the ideas. But I have one regret in connection with them, and it is rather a serious one. I have suggested that the people themselves

should have a considerable say in shaping their own constitution.[75]

To remedy this obvious shortcoming, a Constitutional Conference was called at Ibadan in Western Nigeria to decide the form and content of a new constitution, which was called the Macpherson Constitution (named after the British Governor of Nigeria, Sir John Macpherson). The short, but highly eventful life of the Richards Constitution had dramatized the fact that the days of the policy of gradual development in the constitutional history of British colonies were far spent. What the Richards Constitution had envisaged was a debating society society in which Africans would be given the opportunity for greater participation in the discussion of their affairs.
Thus, through a long process of tutelage in the art of parliamentary government. But the avalanche of criticism levelled against the Richards Constitution, and the spirited political controversy which it engendered showed that the governor had thoroughly misjudged the tempo and temper of Nigerian politics. Nigerian politicians by undertaking a country-wide tour, to protest against the Richards Constitution, and through a deputation sent to London under the auspices of the National Council of Nigerian and the Cameroons made it aboundantly clear that what they wanted was not participation in discussion, but participation in the management of their own political institutions and processes.

The prospect of participation by Africans in the political process raised anew the problem of how best to deter the educated element from upsetting the imperial apple cart. The warning of Dame Margerry Perham, that while the British should attempt to integrate the educated elements into the native administrative structure they must not attempt to give them a role in the central superstructure, kept reverberating in the ears of the colonial officials. It was no longer a question of whether Africans would be given a meaningful share in the management of their own affairs, but rather, how to ensure that their participation in the process did not result in "an unexpected rate of development."[76]

The most effective way to muffle the increasing audible demand for responsible self-government was to channel meaningful political power through the regional institutions, to democratize the native authority system,[77] and make it the gateway to all political roles in the central structure. Once the native authorities were made the channels through which central political offices could be attained, the educated elements would be permitted to advance indirectly through the native authority to the higher councils.

This proposal was supposed to have two merits from the British perspective. It was intended to set up competition between the educated elite and the traditional elite. Since the traditional elite dominated the native authority system, its influence would dilute, if it did not eclipse, the influence of the educated element. Secondly, since the Macpherson Constitution envisaged the grant of increasing autonomy to the regional councils, the competition for the control of the central legislature by those regional assemblies would unleash a struggle for power between the regions. In the ensuing struggle the colonial establishment could comfortably pose as mediator between the contending parties.

But if competition between region and region and between the traditional and educated elites, was to be kept within manageable limits, a way had to be found to ensure that the educated elements and their supporters did not gain control of the regional houses. The country-wide tour of the delegation of the National Council of Nigeria and the Cameroons in 1947 had shown how easily a band of dedicated nationalists could mobilize popular support against the colonial power. Four steps were therefore taken by the British to safeguard against this eventuality.

1. The North had to be encouraged, not only to show keen interest in the affairs of the center, but also to seek parity (equal representation) with the South in the central legislature. Sir Bernard Bourdillon was admittedly instrumental in convincing the Northern political elite to adopt this policy. In a speech delivered before the United Empire Society, he recalled as follows;

I suggested to them that the intelligent attitude for them to take was not: 'We will not have the Southerners interfering in our affairs,' but 'We ought to have at least an equal say with the Southerners in advising the Governor as to the affairs of the whole country.' Without a single exception they saw the point, and agreed.[78]

Thus, the idea of parity in representation between the North and the South became, for the Northerners, a shibboleth. Before this catchword, all other political considerations had to yield pride of place. To drum up support in the Northern Regions for this view, the Northern politicians decided to politicize the question of parity (equal representation) between the North and the South. The Sultan of Sokoto issued a call for "Money to help the North."[79] The aim was to use the money thus collected to send a delegation to England to press for equal representation. All this was done to mobilize political opinion in the North in favor of equal representation between the North and the South. When Southern politicians suggested that the North be given 45 seats, the East and the West 33 seats each, the North threatened to secede. The issue was then referred to the old legislative council established under the Richards Constitution. That council ruled in favor of equal representation between the North and the South (East and West combined).

2. An intricate system of indirect elections had to be devised to ensure that election to the central legislature was weighted in favor of the traditional elite who controlled the native authority system. For this reason the Macpherson Constitution provided for indirect elections through tiers of electoral colleges. In the East and West the electoral system was divided into three stages - the primary, intermediate, and final electoral colleges. Suffrage in the final electoral college was linked to adult taxpayers. Voting was by secret ballot. In the North the electoral college was divided into four or five stages. To quote Richard L. Sklar:

> In the Northern Region, special techniques were devised to weigh the vote in favor of traditional and conservative elements in early elections. In 1951, every native authority, typically an emir, 'was permitted to "nominate" number of persons equal to 10 percent of the final electoral college who were injected into the college.[80]

Not only was the membership of the central legislature weighted in favor of the North, but no effort was spared to ensure that the traditional rulers had effective control of the selection process.

3. Another step taken to muzzle the political power of the educated element was the provision in the Macpherson Constitution for merging Lagos, the capital of Nigeria, with the Western Region. Lagos had been the hot-bed of political agitation in Nigeria: it also had the greatest concentration of educated Nigerians. By merging Lagos with the West, the constitution ensured that the influence of the educated in Lagos would be neutralized by that of the traditional elite in the West, who would outnumber the Lagos-based politicians.

4. The final and perhaps the most destructive impediment to the development of Nigerian-wide political organizations was the inclusion in the constitution (the adoption) of a Northern proposal that election to the Northern House of Assembly should be open only to Northern Nigeria indigenes, 25 years or over, who had been residents in the region for at least three years. This had the effect of excluding from active political participation in the Northern Region of all those whose parents were not indigenous to Northern Nigeria - that is, those who were not born and bred in Northern Nigeria by parents who were indigenous to the North. This was not only devised to balkanize political allegiance, but was certainly calculated to exclude, not only the educated elements, but virtually all Southerners, from effective participation in Northern Nigerian politics. It also had the baneful and highly disruptive effect of regionalizing citizenship rights, obligation and duties. It made certain Nigerians aliens in their own country and created that most distasteful of legal statuses, the citizen with responsibilities, but without rights.

As Eyo Ita aptly stated:

> I have already pointed out the urgent necessity of complete equalisation of all opportunities as the basis of unity and franchise. I have also shown the evil of citizenship status and equal franchise to African "aliens" born or resident in villages and towns outside their own clans, tribes or regions. I believe in complete Nigerianization of all citizens. I plead most earnestly that at first opportunity a legislation should be created giving every citizen irrespective of tribe, sex, or creed equal political status and equal opportunity in all economic, cultural and social rights and privileges.[81]

Without this equalization of opportunities, rights and duties, the sense of a common nationality could scarcely emerge. The institutions were in fact not designed to foster such a community of feelings. Moreover, the Macpherson Constitution was designed to prevent the emergence of such common identity and this to stifle the rising tide of political agitation against continued imperial control, led by the educated elements.

Once these safeguards were built into the system, the 1951 constitution (the Macpherson Constitution) did introduce a measure of representative responsible government into Nigeria. The major changes introduced by the new constitution were as follows. The Regional Houses of Assembly, whose functions had been purely deliberative under the Richards Constitution, now acquired legislative powers within their respective regions. In each region an executive council, with specified powers over certain govermental functions, was established and members of the Regional Executive Council were given ministerial responsibility over these functions. Each Regional Executive Council was presided over by a 'Lieutenant Governor appointed by the colonial establishment. In addition, the imperial interest was represented by six official members in each regional assembly. 'In the North and West provisions were made for a second chamber known as the Regional House of Chiefs.

The constitution also provided for a Central House of Representatives with both legislative and executive powers. Membership in the central legislature was made up of 68 representatives from the North and 34 representatives each from the Eastern and Western Regions. The 'Northern Region had 50 percent of the membership of the Central House of Representatives based exclusively on its population. The East and the West had equal representation irrespective of the disparity in their numbers.

Thus, not only did the constitution ensure control of the general legislature by the North, but every effort was made to guarantee that regional consideration was paramount. For instance, membership in the House of Representatives was open to members of the Regional House. Aspirants to the Federal House had to seek the support of leaders of the Regional Houses of Assembly. The Regional House became, in practice, if not in principle, the party and electorate for those aspiring to be federal legislators. Thus began the consolidation and primacy of regional interests in the affairs of the Central House of Representatives. Politicians quickly learned that to reach the Central House, one must not only belong to the party in power, but must also be in the good graces of the regional establishment. Party interests reinforced regional interests and in the process they became indistinguishable. Thus, those who controlled the regional legislatures also controlled the parties in the regions. Election to the Central House of Representatives became little more than a reward for allegiance and devotion to the region.

It is, therefore, little wonder that the leader of the Northern People's Congress (the party in power in the North), and the leader of the Action Group (the party in power in the West)[82] decided to seek election to the Regional Houses of Assembly while their lieutenants were sent to the Central House of Representatives. This decision had the effect of stunting the growth of a strong and independent House of Representatives. The concentration of the energies of the Northern People's Congress (NPC - Northern Region) and the Action Group (Western Region) in building up regional power diverted the attention of the political elite in both regions from the central political institutions to those of the regions. The development of any powerful political interest devoted to the strengthening of a pan-Nigerian central institution was thus precluded.

Only the leader of the National Council of Nigerian Citizens (NCNC - Eastern Region), who was then resident in Lagos, the capital of Nigeria, sought to gain election into the central organ. As we noted earlier, Lagos, the capital of Nigeria, was merged with the Western Region to muzzle the power of the highly vocal educated Africans in Lagos. This institutional arrangement had a devastating effect on the NCNC, the only party that was pan-Nigerian in outlook. Dr. Nnamdi Azikiwe, the leader of the NCNC, had hoped to win election to the House of Representatives and consequently to the Council of 'Ministers at the central level. The presence of the leader of a major political party at the Central Council of Ministers would have given that institution the power, prestige and organizational base necessary for the development of a pan-Nigerian national outlook at the central level.

Dr. Azikiwe (Zik) did win election from Lagos to the Western Regional House of Assembly. However, because of the institutional mechanism for election to the Central House of Representatives, he was unsuccessful in gaining a seat in the Federal House of Representatives. The events in the Western House of Assembly, discussed below, which led to the exclusion of Dr. Azikiwe from the Central House of Representatives showed how institutional arrangements could be designed to stutify the democratic process.

The general electin of 1951 was conducted through a three-tiered electoral college in the Western Region. It began with elections at the local government or native authority level. Although the platform was the local authority, there were two political parties - the NCNC and the Action Group - vying for control of local institutions. In Lagos, which was incorporated into the Western Region, the election was contested by the Action Group and the National Council of Nigeria and the Cameroons (NCNC). There, where the election was contested on party lines, the NCNC won all five seats. In the remainder of the Western Region, where the election was conducted not on party platforms but throught the local government council (members were identified by this local council, not by parties) districts as electoral platforms, the strengths of the parties were in doubt. Each party waited for the first meeting of the Western House to determine its strength.

At this point ethnic considerations came into play. The NCNC was headed at the national level by Dr. Nnamki Azikiwe, an Ibo. The membership in the Western House was mainly composed by Yorubas. The Action Group was essentially a Yoruba party, designed to further the interests of the Yorubas. Both its leadership and membership were predominantly Yoruba. Therefore, any person who supported the NCNC was viewed as anti-Yoruba and pro-Ibo. When the Western House of Assembly met on January 7, 1952, a number of members who had been supporters of the NCNC crossed the line and joined the Action Group. Of the 75 members of the Western House of Assembly, 49 declared for the Action Group; only 26 identified with the NCNC.[83]

By the provisions of the 1951 constitution, a specified number of representatives for each administrative district was to be elected by the members of the Regional House to the House of Representatives. Lagos, being one of these administrative districts, was entitled to two members in the House of Representatives. As all the elected members from Lagos were members of the NCNC, it was Dr. Azikiwe's hope that as the leader of the NCNC delegation from Lagos he would be elected to the House. However, the Action Group, which controlled a majority in the Western House, was not prepared to vote for him. In the ensuing election, two members of the Yoruba ethnic group - Dr. Olorun-Nimbe and Prince Adeleka Adedoyin - were elected to the House of Representatives to represent the Lagos district. Dr. Azikiwe had to reconcile himself to the leadership of the opposition in the Western House of Assembly.

The events in the Western House had a highly disruptive effect on the development of political parties in Nigeria. It became obvious that the region and not the party was the focus of political power in Nigeria. It drove home the point that regionalism, reinforced by ethnic division, was inconsistent with the development of a pan-Nigerian political party. It demonstrated clearly that for a political party to survive, it must have a regional base. It accentuated regional sentiment and shattered the fragile national feeling, which the struggle against imperial domination was beginning to forge. By excluding Dr. Azikiwe from the House, it deprived that body of the presence, power, and prestige of the leader of a major political party. The other two leaders had by choice remained leaders of their respective regional assemblies. The House of Representatives, therefore, was composed of lieutenants of the three political parties, who were under the direction, leadership, and control of the party leadership in the region. Thus, the House of Representatives became subordinate to, rather than coordinate with, the Regional Houses of Assembly.[84]

The effect of this arrangement on the NCNC was as dramatic as it was damaging. It contributed directly to the first institutional crisis in the history of representative government in Nigeria. James S. Coleman noted that:

> After hardly more than one brief year of operation (1952) the Macpherson Constitution proved unworkable, not only because of its manifest deficiencies and structural anomalies, but also because important political elements became increasingly determined that it should be immediately and drastically revised.[85]

The structural anomalies of the Macpherson Constitution more than any other defect left an enduring mark on the institutional development of political parties, especially in the Eastern Region. It led to the Eastern Regional crisis of 1953. It also caused an open split in the ranks of the NCNC.

The Eastern Regional Crisis, 1952-1953

The institutional arrangement under the Macpherson Constitution was, in the words of Richard L. Sklar, "the kind that invites trouble and is virtually made to collapse."[86] Although the constitution had provided for four minsterial portfolios in the central legislature to be selected by the party in power in each region, these ministers were neither responsible to the parties that elected them to office, nor to the regional assembly which they were supposed to represent. They were removable only by a two-thirds vote of the members of the House of Representatives. A regional party which could not muster a two-thirds vote in the House had no way of disciplining dissident ministers. In the Regional House of Assembly, the executive, made up of officials and ministers appointed by the party in power, could not be dismissed from office except by a two-thirds vote of members. Compounding all these there was no institutional mechanism provided in the constitution for the dissolution of the legislature of a single region.[87]

In the Eastern Region the issue was whether to experiment with the Macpherson Constitution or reject it outright. Dr. Azikiwe, the president of NCNC, and members of the Central Working Committee of the party, concluded that the Macpherson Constitution contained many objectionable features and should, therefore, be scrapped. The constitutional conflict involving the NCNC cast doubt on the contention that the conflicts in Nigeria were caused by ethnic differences since of the four federal ministers expelled by the NCNC, three were Ibos and one was an Efik. The majority of the Eastern Regional Ministers were Ibos. Yet all of them stood together in their defiance of the order of the leader of the NCNC, Dr. Zik (himself an Ibo). The conflict was, therefore, essentially intraregional (all the parties to the dispute were from the Eastern Region) and largely intra-ethnic. A majority on both sides of the conflict were Ibos.

In October, 1952, a meeting of the national executive of the NCNC was summoned at Port Harcourt to consider a motion to boycott the Macpherson Constitution. This motion was defeated by a majority of the party parliamentarians, led by the regional and central ministers, appointed by the party. According to Sklar:

> Two distinct but related issues were at stake: the policy of the party with respect to the Constitution, and the authority of the National President vis-a-vis the parliamentary leaders in the Eastern and central government.[88]

The clash was between two key institutions of the parliamentary democracy - the party system and the parliamentary system. The crucial issue was whether the party which appointed the ministers had any leverage with which to remove them from office. The question was answered in the affirmative by the Central Working Committee of the NCNC, which met in Jos in December, 1952. At that convention the President of the NCNC declared in no uncertain terms that ministers appointed by the party must "toe the party line or be disciplined."[89] As a warning to other parliamentarians, four NCNC ministers in the Central House were dismissed from the party.[90]

The Jos decision was received with shock and dismay by the executive council of the Eastern Region, which was controlled by the National Council of Nigeria and the Cameroons (NCNC). Professor Eyo Ito, the parliamentary leader of the party in the Eastern Region, called an emergency meeting to consider what steps the Parliamentary Committee would take in the ensuing crisis. The President of the party, Dr. Azikiwe, summoned a joing meeting of the same Parliamentary Committee and the party's National Executive Committee at the same hour and on the same day. At the meeting he asserted his power to reshuffle the portfolios of the Eastern Regional ministers. All nine of the Eastern Regional ministers were asked to tender their resignations so that the cabinet could be reshuffled. They all did. However, six of them secretly sent letters to the Lieutenant Governor withdrawing their resignations before they were ever submitted by the national president of the party. When the national president submitted the resignations to the Lieutenant Governor, he found to his chagrin that six of the ministers had reneged on their promises to resign. The six, moreover, maintained that they had been coerced into resigning.

Whatever might have been the real story, there was no doubt that a full-blown constitutional crisis had developed. Constitutionally the Eastern House could not be dissolved unless the central legislature and all other Regional Houses OF Assembly were at the same time dissolved. The convention that the leader of the party can reshuffle the cabinet made up of party members could not apply because the constitution provided that the ministers could only be removed by a two-thirds majority of the House of Assembly. However, the majority of assemblymen in the House were definitely in sympathy with the attempt of the national leader to reshuffle the cabinet. It did not matter that the leader of the party was not a member of the Eastern House of Assembly, and consequently, not the constitutional leader of the cabinet in the Eastern Region. But of course, the constitutional instrument made no provision for a parliamentary leader - the Lieutenant Governor was the de facto leader of government business and the repository of colonial power and authority.

Consequently, when the Eastern House of Assembly passed a vote of no confidence in the Eastern Regional Government by a wide margin of 60 to 13, the six ministers who had withdrawn their resignations refused to resign. They were dubbed 'sit-tight ministers' and the phrase passed into the repertoire of Nigerian political terms. They sat tight because they had the backing of the colonial establishment.

The crisis in the Eastern Region had shown that the Macpherson Constitution was neither parliamentary nor democratic in spirit. However just their case, (and there was no doubt that their party had treated them in a shoddy, if not unconventional, manner), the ministers had lost the confidence of the assembly. The Lieutenant Governor could not safely countenance their contempt for the democratic process and expect that process to emerge untarnished. It was true that the regional appropriation bill had to be passed, as he claimed, but it was obvious that no bill emanating from the government would be passed by that House, and in fact the House consistently voted down the appropriation bill. The Governor was, therefore, compelled to use his reserve power to legislate for the region and decree the appropriation bill into law.[91]

It was not just in the Eastern Region that the facade of parliamentary democracy crumbled under the stresses and strains of institutional dysfunction. In both the Western House of Assembly and the Central House of Representatives, the deficiencies of the constitutional instrument stood revealed at every turn. In the Western Region the leader of the Action Group, Chief Obafemi Awolowo, complained that the Macpherson Constitution, as construed by the British government, was totally inconsistent with the Action Group's conception of the "spirit or convention of the constitution."[92] A motion of non-fraternization with Sir John Macpherson was introduced by an Action

Group member from the Ishan ethnic group. It was passed at a conference held by the Action Group in Warri in December, 1952.[93]

The crisis in the Eastern Region exposed the "inadequacies" of the Macpherson Constitution even at the federal level. Debates in the Federal House over the issues raised by the Eastern Regional crisis revealed that the constitution made no provision for separate dissolution of the various Houses of Assembly. There were four Houses of Assembly - The House of Representatives, the Eastern, Northern and Western Houses of Assembly. Constitutionally, none of these legislative assemblies could be dissolved separately. It was therefore by a constitutional amendment at the federal level that provisions were made for the dissolution of the Eastern House so to resolve the crisis.

As the crisis was being resolved, a new one developed in the central legislature itself centering around a motion for independence from Great Britain in 1956. The motion was tabled by Anthony Enahoro (the same Action Group member who introduced the motion of non-fraternization with Governor Macpherson) in March, 1953. Nevertheless, the motion put unbearable strain on the already tottering institutions devised by the Macpherson Constitution.

The Northern Region expressed implacable opposition to the motion. The Northern delegates made a counter-motion calling for independence "as soon as practicable."[94] By sheer weight of numbers, the Northern delegation exercised virtual veto over any action by the House of Representatives which it did not favor. Most of the Southern politicians, in the face of the overwhelming Northern majority, walked out of the House. The Nigerian newspapers, most of them based in the South, were uncharitable towards the North in their coverage of the events and heaped unrestrained epithets, to say the least, on them. In addition, the Lagos crowds subjected the Northern legislators to a barrage of insults.

The humiliation proved a bitter pill for the Northern leaders and was perhaps the most damaging blow to the fragile relations between the North and the South. The North immediately issued an eigth-point program calling for "complete legislative and executive autonomy in all matters except defense, external affairs, customs, and certain research institutions organized on a West African basis."[95] This was certainly a call for disengagement. The South, on the other hand, persisted in hoping that the common people in the North could be convinced to desert their leaders and join in a Nigerian federation embracing the North and the South. It was in pursuit of this policy that Chief S.L.Akintola, a Yoruba and one of the leaders of the Action Group, decided to go to the North to campaign for the support of the common people to endorse the idea of self government in 1956.

The reaction of the North to this intrusion was instantaneous and violent. A protest riot broke out in Kano. When the dust settled the casualties numbered 277; 15 Northerners and 21 Southerners had lost their lives.[96] This incident evidences our contention that it was only when the institutional mechanism designed to mediate political disputes failed that ethnic factors emerged and reinforced the conflict. Mallam Inuwa Wada, the Information Officer for the Native Authority, put the North's case as follows:

> Having abused us in the South, these very Southerners have decided to come over to the North to abuse us, but we have determined to retaliate the treatment given us in the South. We have therefore organized about 1,000 men ready in the city to meet force with force; those men will parade all Kano tomorrow, singing and shouting that the delegates are not wanted at Kano and that no lecture or meeting will be delivered by them.[97]

The ethnic ramifications of the Kano riot defy logical explanation. In the speech quoted above, Inuwa Wada's anger was directed against the South in general. The delegation which provoked the riot was an Action Group detegation and predominantly Yoruba. Although most of the members of the Action Group in Kano who were supposed to welcome the delegation were Yorubas, the violence that erupted was directed, not against the Yorubas, but against the Ibos. If, according to the official explaination, the riot was the result of tribal (ethnic) tensions,[98] then the conflict would have been between the Yoruba ethnic group, which had organized and sponsored the delegation and the Hausas. But the riot assumed pronounced overtones of a Hausa-Ibo conflict.[99] Richard Sklar has suggested that there was a strong element of political partisanship in the conflict. He noted that:

> The (official) report neglected to mention that Hausas who were sympathetic to the Northern Element Progressive Union, an ally of the NCNC, rendered great assistance to the beleagured Southerners, a statement that was frequently repeated to the writer by persons of Northern and non-Northern origin in Kano. Several informants who lived through the tragedy expressed the view that political partisanship was a more fundamental cause of the explosion than the official report allows. Some of them suggested that the officials were inclined to emphasize the tribalistic aspect of the rioting because it might appear as more 'primitive' type of behavior and therefore reflect adversely on the ability of the people to govern themselves in a modern state.[100]

Of course there was no doubt that the Kano disturbance had political overtones. The Northern People's Congress (NPC) had realized early that the NCNC constituted the greatest threat to Northern domination of that center. Furthermore, the NCNC country-wide tour of 1947 had given a fillip to anti-establishment elements in the North. Both the Northern Elements Progressive Union and the Bornu Youth Movement, which were opposed to the NPC, were at this time allies of the NCNC. Moreover, at the time of the Kano riot, the Action Group was engaged in secret negotiations with the NPC on the possibility of an alliance between the two parties to pursue a common policy in the regions and in the center.[101] The negotiations culminated in an agreement which was concluded by the two parties in February, 1953, just three months before the Kano riots. The conflict over the independence debate in March, 1953, apparently did not disturb that understanding, for the first meeting of the alliance was held in Lagos in the very month of March.[102]

Clearly, there was a political understanding between the NPC and the Action Group to combine forces and eliminate the NCNC as a force in Nigerian politics. As the majority of the members and leaders of the NCNC were Ibos, NPC's anger was directed against the Ibos, even though the Yoruba dominated Action Group organized the Kano rally that precipitated the riot.

Again, as with the conflict which led to the military coup d'etat in 1966, events which had their origins in the Western Region were instrumental in bringing the political conflict in Nigeria, in this case the Kano riot, to the brink of violence. But in the ensuing conflict, it was the Eastern Region, which predominantly Ibo, and the Northern Region, which is predominantly Hausa-Fulani, that were the chief protagonists in the violent confrontation.

Here again it can be seen that the ethnic conflicts which complicated the constitutional crisis over the provisions of the Macpherson Constitution were a by-product of the institutional dysfunction and not the cause of it. In the Eastern Region it was not until a constitutional crisis had erupted that ethnic overtones became audible. When the news of the expulsion of the central ministers, who were members of the NCNC, reached Enugu, capital of the Eastern Region, Professor Eyo Ita, a member of the Efik ethnic minority in the Eastern Region, openly condemned the expulsion. His stand against the high-handed action of the NCNC part leadership evoked personal attactks on him. It was the virulence of this personal attack which offended the Efiks and crystallized a distinctly Efik opposition against the NCNC and its leadership.

Whatever might have been some of the underlying issues which led to the Kano riots, had the institutional arrangements designed to mediate political competition, both at the central and regional levels, been able to mediate the conflict over goals and policies, factors such as ethnicity and regionalism would not have come into play. Even the British authorities saw the problem as an institutional one, although they felt that the solution lay in greater decentralization. As the colonial secretary stated in retrospect, "Nigeria if it was to be a nation must be a federation, with as few subjects reserved for the Central Government as would preserve national unity."[103]

It was the conviction that the root cause of the problem was institutional that led to the statement that "recent events in Nigeria had shown that it is impossible for the regions to work effectively in a federation so closely knit as that provided by the present constitution."[104] Based on this assumption, the Colonial Secretary called a conference of Nigerian leaders to meet in July, 1953 to devise a new institutional structure for Nigeria. The result was the Lyttleton Constitution of 1954 (named after Sir Oliver Lyttleton, the British Secretary of State for the colonies).

The Lyttleton Constitution of 1954

The Lyttleton Constitution of 1954 has been termed "the Regionalist Constitution" by Richard L. Sklar.[105] Without question the constitution canalized and entrenched the forces of regional autarchy, evident since the beginning of constitutional experiment in Nigeria in the Richards Constitution of 1947. The constitutional provisions from 1947 to 1954 had been an ingeneous mixture of the unitary and the federal constitutional structures. It was the 1954 constitution which completely "transformed the structure of the Nigerian government from unitary foundations to the existing bases of Federalism"[106] under the First Republic. It is contended herein that this enthronement of regional autarchy prevented the emergence of a strong central government independent of the regional government, and able to mediate authoritatively between their conflicting demands and desparate policies.

What then were the major provisions of the constitution which gave rise to governmental impotence? Space does not permit us to discuss the constitution in detail - only the most salient aspects of its provisions will be dealt with here. Under the constitution of 1954, Nigeria became a federation. The federal structure was made up of a central legislature and three self-governing regions with residual powers. The regions were endowed with full legislative and executive powers on all matters except for a specified list of Exclusive Subjects, which were reserved for the Federal Government. This provision transferred the major responsibility for policy making from the colonial governor to the indigenous legislator in all internal matters. Certain categories of subjects were placed on a concurrent legislative list of both the federal and regional legislatures. Although each of the regional Houses was presided over by a British governor, the governor had no power to stop the House from debating any issue or passing any law within the area of its competence. The governor was constrained by law to give his assent to any bill passed by the House. However, he could reserve a bill for Her Majesty's pleasure if, in his opinion, the bill contravened the obligations of any treaty in force or was in any way inconsistent with Royal prerogatives or was prejudicial to the rights of property of British subjects who were not resident in Nigeria. A bill could also be reserved for Her Majesty's pleasure, if it was prejudicial to trade, transport or communication in any part of the British commonwealth or if it was likely to imperil the continuance of the federation.

As far as the Northern House was concerned, the constitution specified that any bill passed by the House could be reserved for Her Majesty's pleasure if it would be in any way prejudicial to the peace, order and good government of Northern Cameroons - a trust territory which was administered as an integeral part of the Northern Region.[107]

An executive council, made up of elected officials, was established with the Premier of the region as the President. Official members were eliminated from the executive council, except in the Northern Region, where the Attorney General was made a member. In the other two regions, the post of Attorney General was filled by appointees of the Regional 'Premiers. The governors of the various regions had to seek and follow the advice of the executive council in the exercise of their powers under the constitution, except as provided in the Nigerian (Constitution) Orders in Council, 1954.

Provisions were made for separate dissolution of each House of Assembly to avoid the most glaring pitfall of the Macpherson Constitution. The constitution also provided for separate registration of voters in each region, and for separate elections for the House of Representatives and for the Regional 'Houses of Assembly. However, the framers of the council declined to provide for a uniform electoral system.

In the Eastern Region provisions were made for universal adult suffrage. Women as well as men were eligible to vote. In the West the franchise was limited to adult tax-payers. In the North the election was by indirect electoral college. Women were precluded from voting and only male taxpayers were entitled to that privilege. Nigerians who were not indegenes of Northern region were not allowed to contest election. By a special provision which was applicable only to the Northern Region, any ten members of the final electoral college had the power to nominate non-members of the electoral college as candidates for final election to the Regional House. Richard Sklar pointed out as a matter of record that:

> It is the experience of NEPU (a minority part of the same Hausa-Fulani ethnic group) that their candidates who won at the primary and intermediate stage have to contest at the final stage against their defeated opponents. This happens because the electoral laws of the Region provided that any person whether or not he had gone through the first two stages may be nominated to stand at the final stage by anyone who had passed through the primary supported by nine other members of the same final electoral college...This also makes it possible for any person who may never have fought the elections at all to be nominated at the final stage as a candidate even in his absence.[108]

Here it is clearly evident that differential electoral arrangements were made in the various regions. Free and fair elections are a test of democratic institutions, but it can be seen that the electoral system of the 1954 Constitution was a far cry from the Westminster model. This conscious creation of dissimilar institutional structures rode roughshod on what Professor Wheare considers the most important prerequisite of a federal constitution; that is, similarity of social and political institutions.[109]

It was not just in the provisions regarding elections that the Constitution of 1954 furthered the process of eventual disintegration of Nigeria. In its financial and economic provisions, the constitution placed emphasis on the maximum possible autonomy for the regions. Thus, the Nigeria Commodity Marketing Boards, whose task was the stabilization of prices of primary products, were regionalized. The amount of 75.5 million pounds which had been accumulated by the boards was distributed among the regions on the principle of derivation. The uncommitted reserves of the country, amounting to 40.12 million pounds, were also distributed among the regions on the basis of derivation. 'Not to leave anything to chance, a formula was devised for sharing future export and import revenues.

In addition, the constitution of 1954 made far-reaching provisions which materially affected the development of complementary institutional structures in the regions; for example, it provided for full internal self-government in 1956 to any region which so desired. The Western Region opted for internal self-government in 1956; so did the Eastern Region. The Northern Region hinted broadly that it might demand self-government in 1959. Again, this provision set the pace for differential arrangements for the Northern Region and the two Southern Regions, East and West.

As soon as this constitution came into force on the 1st of October, 1954, all the regional elites braced themselves for the election to the Federal House. It was the assumption of all political observers of the Nigerian political scene that each regional party "would secure a majority of the federal seats in that region."[110] To everyone's surprise, the National Council of Nigeria and the Cameroons won a majority of the seats in the two Southern Regions (East and West).

The victory of the NCNC in the Eastern and Western regions frightened the other two regional parties - the Action Group in the Western region and the Northern Peoples Congress in the Northern Region. As the NCNC was the only party with national pretentions, emphasis was laid by the other two regional parties, that it was an Ibo dominated party and the threat of Ibo domination became audible. It must however, be observed that the successful NCNC members in the Western region were mainly Yorubas, Benis and Itshakiri. This perceived threat coupled with the approaching internal self-government in 1956 gave a new lease on life to regionalist sentiments. Party maneuvering for the control of the regional power structure was intensified. The provision in the 1954 Constitution, that another constitutional conference would be held in 1956, made it increasingly urgent for the regional parties to secure their hold on their respective regions to enhance their bargaining power at the conference table. Regional interest reinforced by party interest overrode any consideration of the overall national interest.

Prelude to Independence

The Constitutional Conference which was scheduled in 1956 to explore the possibility of a target date for Nigerian Independence, was postponed because of a crisis in the Eastern Region. The crisis stemmed from a motion introduced in the Eastern House by Mr. E.O. Eyo, accusing Dr. Azikiwe (Premier of the Eastern Region) of gross abuse of public office. The substance of the charge was that Dr. Azikiwe had channelled 200,000 pounds of public funds into the African Continental bank. It was alleged that this bank, in which his family had financial interest, was operating at a loss, and that he knowingly funneled public money to prop up a failing bank. A commission, headed by Sir Stafford Foster Sutton, a British Chief Justice of the Nigerian Federation, found him guilty of conduct which fell short "of the expectations of honest reasonable people."[111]

Because of this inquiry, the British government decided that regional internal self-government which was promised under the 1954 Constitution, would not be granted to any region in 1956. The Constitutional Conference which was to have been held in the same year (1956) was rescheduled for 1957.

The 1957 Constitutional Conference which laid the foundation for the Independence Constitution of 1960, was held in London in May. This conference is particularly important because it raised a number of fundamental issues. Foremost among these issues were the fears of the minorities, and the means of allaying them. As this issue was felt to be extremely important, a commission under the chairmanship of Sir Henry Willink, Master of Magdalene College, Cambridge, England was appointed to inquire into the fears of the minorities and to suggest the means for allaying them. Two other commissions, one on Revenue Allocation, and another on Constituency Delimitation, were appointed. Having appointed these commissions and having laid the groundwork for the Independence Constitution, the conference adjourned to enable the commissions to complete their tasks.

The Minorities Commission, 1957-1958

Of all the commission set by the 1957 conference, the minorities commission was the most significant because it revealed the fear surrounding the impending dissolution of the imperial institution engendered in the minds of the poeple, especially the minorities. In August 1958, it published its findings. The commission pointed out that the fears of the minorities were mainly directed against the power of the regional government."[112] They referred to the opinion prevalent among the minorities that the majorities within each region "would always seek to use power to their exclusive advantage and that the federation would continue to play the comparatively minor part in the Nigerian scene, which it does today."[113] Here again, it is the strong power of the regions and the powerlessness of the federal government arising from its control by one politically predominant region that has created this endemic fear. The suggestion by the various minorities weas, invariably, that the only solution to their problem would be the creation of more states."[114] However, the commission felt that:

34

> In considering the problem within each region, we were impressed by the fact that it is seldom possible to draw a clean boundry which does not create a fresh minority. The proposed state had in each case, become very small by the time it had been paired down to an area, in which it was possible to assert with confidence, that it was desired. This was in every case an important factor in our recommendation, but, it was not the only consideration which we took into account. The powers left to the regions by the decision of 1953 (embodied in the 1954 Constitution) are considerable, and as we have said elsewhere, we do not regard it as realistic to suppose that any of the regions will forego the powers they now have."[115]

The commission, therefore, recommended that no new regions should be created, that provisions should be made in the constitution "for human rights, in general, and the rights of the minorities within the existing regions."[116] This decision was predicated on the strength of regional opposition to the creation of more states. This opposition spearheaded by the Northern Region which is multi-ethnic shows how the ethnic factor was subordinated to regional consideration.

In September, 1958, the constitutional conference was reconvened in London to consider the reports of the commissions appointed in 1957. The report of the commission on constituency delimitation was adopted without amendment. The report on revenue allocation (Raisman Commission) is discussed in Chapter 5 of this essay. As far as the report of the Minorities Commission was concerned, the delegates to the conference accepted in principle that a new region could be created. However, the complicated machinery which they set up, made it virtually impossible for a new state to be created without the consent of the region, out of which the regions would be carved.[117]

The Federal Election of 1959

As a result of the London Constitutional Conference of 1958, it was agreed (a) that a new federal election would be held in Nigeria in 1959, (b) that Her Majesty's Government would entertain a resolution seeking independence for Nigeria if such a resolution was passed in the Federal Parliament to be elected in 1959.[118] This election deserves a brief comment, as it set the tone of subsequent political development in Nigeria.

The election was, indeed, a popular outpouring of emotional support for independence. Close to 80 percent of 9 million registered voters turned out to vote for the legislature that was to pass a resolution for their independence from Britain. According to Kenneth Post, "the election was relatively free and fair. It was only where administrative and legal structures were already open to political pressures - the native administrations in the North being the most obvious examples - were there abuses?"[119] Although Post credited the British authorities with the responsibility for the relative fairness of the election, these officials were powerless to prevent the "administrative and legal structures" of the North from abusing the electoral process.

It was, indeed, to use the words of Post, "the last great act of the British Raj."[120] Not only did the British look askance at the institutionalized oppression in the North, the Governor-General, Sir James Robertson, upset the democratic process of post election coalition formation by appointing Sir Abubakar Tafawa Balewa as Prime Minister even before all the results of the election were received. This, in fact, made it imperative for the Southern political parties to form a coalition with the NPC since its leader at the federal level had been asked to form a government. These irregularities condoned by the British set the tone for post independence election practices, especially in the Northern Region. It was, in fact, the inability of achieving orderly transfer of power through elections that contributed most to the military take over in 1966.

The federal parliament elected in 1959 met in January, 1960. In the presence of Mr. Harold Macmillan, the British Prime Minister, Sir Abubakar Tafawa Balewa, moved a resolution, asking Her Majesty's government to grant self-government to Nigeria on October 1, 1960. The resolution was carried unanimously. Her Majesty's government, thereafter, introduced the necessary legislation in the United Kingdom Parliament and on October 1, 1960, Nigeria became independent and was admitted as a member of the British Commonwealth of Nations.

CHAPTER III

INDEPENDENCE CONSTITUTION AND GROWING PAINS OF NATIONAL INDEPENDENCE

The previous chapter closed with a discussion of the 1959 constitutional conference and the final motion for Nigerian independence passed by the Nigerian Federal 'Parliament in 1960. The motion was made as a result of the decision reached at the conference. This chapter will trace, in brief outline, the basic changes made by the independence constitution and the problems raised by those changes. The discussion of the problems raised by Nigerian independence is centered around the conviction that the failure of 'Nigerian politicians to transcend built-in regional loyalties and develop transcendental national loyalty prevented the development of federal institutions with the capacity ot mediate effectively and impartially political interaction and orderly transfer of political power within the federation.

The independence constitution itself was the culmination of years of experiment in devolutionary federalism dating from 1946. What emerged out of this experiment was loose federation. The division of powers between the regions and the federation was the same as that under the 1954 Constitution.[1] However, a number of safeguards were written into the independence Constitution, because of fears expressed by certain groups, especially the minorities in Nigeria.

Among these safeguards were **guarantees of freedom of association,** freedom of conscience, and freedom of ecpression. These fundamental human rights, including freedom of movement, were entrenched in the constitution. In addition, certain institutions were created with constitutional safeguards which insulated them from political control. Among these were the Judicial Service Commission, the Federal Electoral Commission and the post of a direstor of Public Prosecution.

Two of these institutional safeguards were abolished within three years from the date of independence. The post of Director of Public Prosecution was abolished in 1961. In 1963, when Nigeria became a republic the constitution was amended. As part of this amendment, the Judicial Service Commission was abolished. The appointment of judges which was the major function of that body was in the future to be made by the President on the advice and consent of the Prime Minister. Freedom of expression was curtailed but not abolished by a Press bill passed in 1964 which made any person who knowingly spread false rumors liable to a fine of 200 pounds or imprisonment for a term of one year. A measure of restraint is certainly an indispensable prerequisite of responsible reporting. But what made this provision a dangerous weapon for any government bent on curbing dissent is the provision that "it shall be no defense to a charge under this section that he did not know or did not have reason to believe that the statement, rumors or reports were false unless he proves that prior to the publication he took reasonable measures to verify the accuracy of such statements, rumors or reports."[2] The elasticity of the term, "reasonable measures," certainly imports an element of uncertainity.

All this erosion of fundamental safeguards are symtomatic of institutional dysfunction issuing from a low level legitimacy. They corrode confidence that social problems could be resolved by institutionalized and predictable procedures. According to Huntington, "predictability requires regularized and institutionalized patterns of behavior." He emphasized that, "without strong political institutions, society lacks the means to defend and realize its common interests." In Nigeria, in particular, the weakness of the instutional structures has a direct bearing on the conflict and crises that were endemic to the First Republic. As James O'Connell pointed out, with respect to Nigeria, "a consciousness of the fragility of their legitimacy tends to spur governments to over-react to every threat that they discern."[5] Over-reaction by government breeds repression and repression courts resistance. And where the institutionalized force of the government becomes repressive, resistance is apt to take on a violent cast.

In Nigeria revolt against governmental autocracy was a constant phenomenon. As colonel Ojukwu noted:

"The five years immediately after that date (date of Nigerian Independence, October 1,1960) were marked by successive crises; notably the Tiv riots of 1960-1966, the Western Nigerian Emergency of 1962, the national census controversy of 1962-1963, the federal election crisis of 1964-1965, and the Western Election Crisis of 1965-1966. By January, 1966, it became clear that unless the situation was arrested, the successive crises experienced by the country before and since independence would certainly lead to unutterable disaster."[6]

The most significant and certainly the most far-reaching of these crises was the Western Regional Crisis of 1962 which led to and reinforced the Western Election Crisis of 1964-5. As these two crises constituted one inter-connected chain of events, they are discussed in this essay as a single crisis which occurred in the Western Region with little intermission from 1962 to 1965.

The Western Regional Crisis of 1962-1965

The Western Regional Crisis of 1962-1965 is acknowledged by scholars to be "the most severe test to which the new Nigerian nation had been put since independence."[7] This crisis, in fact, severely strained the Nigerian institutional structure and proved in a most dramatic fashion the inability of the Nigerian political institutions to mediate, effectively and impartially, peaceful transfer of political power within the federation. It also vitiated the theory that conflict in Nigeria is caused by ethnic (tribal) differences. The conflict was intra-ethnic and intra-party. It was between two factions of the Action Group, the governing party in the Western Region. The conflict was essentially institutional - between the Action Group party leader who was at the time the leader of the opposition in the Federal House and the deputy leader of the Action Group who was then the Premier of the Western Region as well as the Cabinet Chief. In sum, it was a conflict between the party as an institution and the cabinet system of government.

To place the struggle in its proper context, it is necessary to give a brief account of the underlying factors. Chief Obafemi Awolowo, the leader of the Action Group, a party with its base and support in the Western Region had nursed the ambition to be the first Federal Prime Minister of an independent Nigeria. But he could do this only if his party could capture enough votes in the federal election to command a majority of the seats in the federal house. During the 1959 election, the last election before Nigerian independence, he decided to broaden the base of the Action Group by forming alliances with minority parties in the other two regions.

Having concluded these alliances, Chief Awolowo decided to run for the federal election of 1959. But he was, at this time, the Premier of the Western Region. To be eligible to run, he resigned his premiership and recalled Chief S.L. Akintola who was the deputy leader of the Action Group and also a member of the Federal House. Chief Akintola resigned his seat in the Federal House and by a special election became a member of the Western House of Assembly. He was then selected by the party as the Premier of the Western Region to replace Chief Awolowo.

In the 1959 election, the Action Group, under the leadership of Awolowo, made the creation of more states one of the most important items in the party platform in order to attract the votes of the minorities. The minorities in the three regions had stressed to the Willink Commission[8] that the only solution to their fears would be the creation of more regions. His campaign activities in the Northern Region were largely unsuccessful and alienated the Northern Peoples Congress (NPC) which controlled effective political power at the center. Events in the North during and immediately after the campaign seemed to lend weight to the feeling by the NPC that the Action Group campaign had been detrimental to Northern interests. The Action Group had allied itself, during the election (1959), with the United Middle Belt Congress, a party composed mainly of minorities in the North and   particularly   popular among a minor ethnic group in the North known as Tiv. The Tiv people were largely non-Muslims, incorporated into the predominantly Muslim Northern Region by the British authorities in spite of their spirited and sustained resistance to the incorporation.[9] During the 1959 election the UMBC-Action Group alliance won all seven seats and 84 percent of the

38

votes among the Tiv people. Immediately after that election, the Tiv people rose in revolt (March, 1960). This revolt continued with little intermission even during the independence celebration in 1960. In fact, during the first week of independence, casualties as a result of the revolt amounted to twenty people (16 died at the hands of the rioters and 4 were killed by the police). As many as 4,800 people were placed under arrest and 2,830 out of these were convicted.[10] As Frederick A.O. Schwarz, Jr. remarked:

> On the occasion the Northern government charged that the UMBC-Action Group alliance had incited the Tiv to "wage war" in order to compel Great Britain to postpone independence until a middle belt state had been created...the timing of the Tiv riots lent weight to the charge that they were connected with the coming of independence, and the fact that palm brances (the palm being the symbol of the Action Group) were affixed to those huts that were not burned was a further indication that the riots had a political purpose.[11]

It was not only as a result of the UMBC-Action Group alliance that the Action Group incurred the displeasure of the NPC. As the opposition party in the Federal House, the Action Group became highly critical of the federal government. As a result of the Action Group criticism of the defense pact between Nigeria and Britain concluded in 1960, student riots erupted at Ibadan and Lagos Universities. As a consequence, the mutual defense pact with Britain which gave Britain military craft landing rights in Nigeria, was abrogated. The Action Group criticism of the government also exacerbated the conflict between it and the NCNC.

The National Council of Nigeria and the Cameroons (NCNC) which formed a coalition government with the NPC saw the Action Group both as a rival and a threat. The NCNC had a sizeable following in the Western Region and was, in fact, the opposition party in the Western House of Assembly. On the other hand, the Action Group campaigns during the 1959 election among the minorities in the Eastern Region did much to stir minority sentiment against the government of the Eastern Region (controlled by the NCNC) and to spur the movement for creating a new state in the Eastern Region.

It was widely believed and openly asserted by many that the two coalition partners at the center had in consequence of the above mentioned reasons decided to eliminate the Action Group as a major party in Nigerian politics.[12] In fact, it was argued that the federal government's decisions during the emergency in Western Nigeria were largely determined by the objective of the two parties (NPC and NCNC) to destroy the regional base of the Action Group.

However, the immediate cause of the Western Regional Crisis was the internal feud within the Action Group party itself. If the NPC and the NCNC had contemplated the destruction of the Action Group, it was the party itself that opened its flanks to the enemy. The events which led to the split in the Action Group are many and varied. Although Chief Awolowo was no longer a member of the Western Regional House of Assembly and its cabinet, he had insisted, as the party chief of the Action Group and, in fact, its founder, that he had the power to exercise supervisory authority over every facet of the party activities both at the federal house and the Western Regional House. He intervened several times to override decisions of the Western Regional cabinet of which Akintola was the Premier and did, in fact, assert control over the allocation of patronage in the Western Regional House.[13] According to Mackintosh:

> "Chief Akintola fretted under these limitations, especially when his government ran into financial difficulties and he had to take rapid decisions. On the occasions when Chief Akintola met with the other premiers and reached agreements on national issues, he was embarrassed by having then to submit the decisions to Cheif Awolowo or face accusations from his own party. If such a dispute arose, Chief Awolowo had the great advantage of controlling Allied Newspapers Limited through which any criticism of the Western (Regional) Government could be conveyed to Action Group Supporters."[14]

The issue was much more than the personal ambitions of the two leaders. It was the whole complicated and fundamental question of the interplay, coordination and balance of power between the party executive and the legislative cabinet selected by the party hierarchy when the leadership of the cabinet and the leadership of the party executive are not in the same hands. A conflict arising out of this issue has never been satisfactorily solved in Nigeria. In two instances in Nigeria when a conflict had arisen between the party executive and the party cabinet, the conflict had reached a crisis stage.[15]

The issue in the Western Regional crisis was complicated by the fact that the conflict concerned the major areas of the party policy. The party executive under the leadership of Chief Awolowo adopted the concept of "Democratic Socialism," the Action Group Western Cabinet led by Chief Akintola opposed the concept. While the party executives decided on the policy of supporting minorities in other regions in their demand for more states, the party cabinet under Akintola wanted a policy of noninterference in the politics of other regions.

The first open breach in the relationship between the two leaders came over the issue of austerity measures in the Western Region. The world price of cocoa fell in 1961 and, at the same time, the burden of free primary education was placing unbearable strain on the region's economy. Chief Akintola decided to cut the producer price of cocoa and to increase the assessment of local contributions to secondary school fees.

These measures proved highly unpopular with the leaders of the Action Group Executive Committee. Under the leadership of Chief Awolowo these party supporters decided to force the Western Regional Cabinet to cut the allowances and salaries of the cabinet ministers. Their proposal did not sit well with the Akintola cabinet, consequently an open rift developed between the supporters of Chief Akintola and the supporters of Awolowo and the party executive. Vain attempts were made to settle the differences, both by Yoruba "elders" and the governor of the western Region, the Oni of Ife, who was at the same time an Oba and spiritual head of the Yorubas.

The conflict reached crisis stage when the governor of the Western Region dismissed Chief Akintola as premier on the basis of a letter signed by 66 of the 124 members of the Western House of Assembly to the effect that Akintola no longer enjoyed their confidence.[16] This letter was the result of a decision made at the National Convention of the Action Group party in Jos in April, 1962.

Chief Akintola sent a letter to the governor asking for dissolution of the Western House. This was refused. He next wrote to the Speaker of the Western House of Assembly so as to enable him to seek a vote of confidence on the floor of the house for himself and his cabinet. This request was also denied. Instead, the governor appointed Dauda Adegbenro, an Awolowo supporter, as premier. The Western House of Assembly was then called into session on the 25th of May to pass a vote of confidence on the new premier. Chief Akintola and his supporters, contending that he could only be removed by a two-thirds majority vote of the members present in the House showed up in the House.

Scarcely had the motion been initiated, when riots broke out in the House. The police were called in and used tear gas to clear the House. Several people were injured in the melee the mace, and the furniture of the house were destroyed. When a second attempt made the same day (May 25th) to reconvene the House failed, the police stepped in to clear the House. The chamber was subsequently locked.

On the evening of the same day (May 25th), the federal Prime Minister, Sir Abubakar Tafawa Balewa, convened a meeting of the federal Council of Ministers to discuss the situation in the Western Region. After the meeting, he made a nationwide broadcast stating that adequate measures must be taken to arrest "the explosive situation such as that which now exists in the Western Region."[17] Following the broadcast, the federal government declared a state of emergency in the Western Region. The Western House of Assembly was suspended and an administrator was appointed for a period of six months to ensure an orderly return to peace and good government in the region. Dr. Moses Majekodunmi, a senator and Federal Minister of Health, was appointed administrator and given sweeping powers to administer the region.[18]

First, the administrator was empowered to restrict all the leading politicians, as well as many minor politicians, to certain areas in the Western Region outside Ibadan. However, as Mackintosh noted, "By the end of two months virtually all the Akintola group and NCNC men were freed, but the office holders and many principal organizers of the Action Group remained restricted."[19] Such selective punishment could not but lend color to the accusations that the federal government, under the control of the NPC and NCNC, had decided to destroy the Action Group as a party.

Second, Commission of Enquiry, known as the Coker Commission, was set up to inquire into the activities of six public corporations set up by the Action Group government of the Western Region. There was obviously ver little connection between the events which led to the state of emergency and the objectives of the enquiry. What is more, even though Chief Akintola was, until the time of the crisis, the deputy leader of the Action Group, he and his followers - mostly former high ranking members of the Action Group were exonerated from the charge of wrong doing. On the other hand, Awolowo and those of his followers who were still members of the Action Group were severely reprimanded. This undisguised bias lent credence to the charge that the main object of the enquiry was to discredit the Action Group.

Third, if there was any doubt left as to the intentions of the federal government, it was removed by the charge of treason brought against Awolowo and his Action Group followers. The charge was that Awolowo and the 'Tactical Committee' of the Action Group had plotted to overthrow the federal government. The treason trial lasted for nine months, and at the end, twenty-one of the twenty-five people originally charged were found guilty and imprisoned.

Finally, at the conclusion of the Coker Commission of investigation and while the treason trial was in progress, the federal government reinstated Chief Akintola as the Premier of the Western Region. His faction joined with the NCNC members of the former Western House to form a new government. Although the former ministers were dismissed, no attempt was made to hold new elections so that the new government could receive a fresh mandate form the people. As it were, the federal government had arrogated to itself the task of deciding who would govern the Western Region after a state of emergency had been imposed and the parliamentary government suspended.

In the face of all these irregularities, it is hard to dismiss the charges that the federal government was more than a disinterested observer. As Mackintosh pointed out:

> ...the most damage was done to the Action Group not by the Coker Commission Report or by the treason trial, but by the decisions and actions of the Federal Government. The latter had never taken a passive role as a spectator. The most serious accusation was that during the crisis Sir Abubakar Tafawa Balewa and the Federal Government were privy to the plans of the Akintola Group and had assured them that if sufficient row was made in the Western House, the Federal Government would step in.[20]

No one expected the fedaral government to assume a passive role when order and good government were on trial in any part of the federation. What was expected of the federal government was impartiality. Whatever action it took should not have been an excuse for muzzling a vocal and aggressive opposition, but an action in the interest of Nigeria as a whole.

Even though a legally constituted court of law had found that Cheif Akintola's dismissal was legal, the federal government recognized him as Premier, disregarding the decision of the court. When the declaration of emergency was challenged in the court ,the federal government frustrated the legal process by expelling Sir Dingle Foot, a British lawyer, legally regiserted as a member of the Nigerian Bar. There is no Doubt that the federal government had full constituional authority to declare a state of emergency, but the constitution provided in Section 165, subsection (5) that:

> No provision of this Constitution that any person or authority shall not be subject to the direction or control of any other person or authority in exercising any functions under this constitution shall be construed as precluding a court of law from exercising jurisdiction in relation to any question whether that person or authority has performed those functions in accordance with the Constitution or any other law.[21]

There is no exception to this provision; therefore, the declaration of emergency, once imposed, could properly be challenged in court. Action was, in fact, commenced in the federal Supremee Court by the Action Group premier-designate, challenging the constitutionality of the declaration of a state of emergency. The federal Prime Minister, the Attorney-General of the Federation, and the administrator of the Western Region were named as defendants in the suit. But the Prime Minister, by his actions both immediately before and during the crisis, had made it clear that he was not only impatient with the law's delays, but was ready to use high-handed measures to frustrate and intimidate the judiciary. Barely two weeks before the crisis in the Western Region he had protested a suit filed by the Western Nigerian Government to block creation of the Midwestern Region out of the Western Region. He observed with noticeable impatience:

> We were dragged to court on the bank inquiry and now we were being dragged to court on the Midwest. Well if our courts will allow themselves to be used in the way they are being used on any minor thing I am afraid people will make a mockery of our courts...personally, I think that it is wrong for every small constitutional matter to go to the court, people will soon come to laugh at the courts...[22]

If anything, the very fact that Nigerians regarded the court as the ultimate interpreter of constitutional questions should be regarded as a sure sign of their belief in the impartiality of the courts. But it is questionable whether the Prime Minister was willing to see an impartial judiciary acting as a check on the excesses of the government. His actions seem to support the idea that he was more anxious to make the courts an instrument for carrying out government orders. For example, his opponents pointed out that the treason trials should have taken place before Justice Onyeama, but did not "because of the independence of mind he had revealed in giving an anti-government decision in the National Bank Case."[23] He had also expressed strong views on the need for a judiciary free from any pro-government or party bias. As a result, he had been made a Acting Justice of the Supreme Court a few days before the case came up. This rendered him ineligible for the treason trial and the task fell to Justice Sowemimimo, who, it was alleged, was better disposed towards the federal government and who was photographed dancing at a party thrown by one of the ministers during the course of the trial.[24]

Equally revealing was the federal government's expulsion of the British Queen's Council, Mr. Dingle Foot and Mr. Colthorpe (a solicitor from Britain) when they came to represent Alhadji Adegbenro, who had challenged the constitutionality of the declaration of emergency in the Western Region. This was a slap in the face of the Nigerian legal profession, since Mr. Foot was a registered member of the Nigerian Bar. Although the government later relented and allowed Mr. Foot to make his submissions on the constitutionality of the emergency declaration, the harm had been done. The freedom and impartiality of the judiciary had been tarnished in the minds of Nigerians. As an institution designed to be the final arbiter in institutional conflicts, the Supreme Court had been immobilized, both by the unwillingness of the federal executive to give it the necessary support, and the overzealous attempts by contending factions within the Western Region to embroil the court in an intraparty power struggle. This is clear proof that the court as an institution had not acquired the legitimacy to ensure obedience and respect for its legally binding decisions.

Whatever may have been the merits and demerits of the actions taken by the federal government, it cannot be doubted that it was only when the constitutional practices designed to ensure peaceful transfer of power within the Western Region had failed, that the federal government stepped in. As the Prime Minister noted:

> No responsible government of the Federation could allow an explosive situation such as that which now exists in the Western Region to continue without taking adequate measures to ensure that there is an early return to the Region of peace, order and good government.[25]

It must be reiterated that the crisis in the Western Region in 1962 was strictly intra-ethnic and intra-regional in scope and dimension. it was when the Western Nigerian House of Assembly had failed as an institution to mediate succession to political power that the federal government stepped in to salvage the situation. Once the federal government stepped in, the crisis assumed inter-regional and, consequently, inter-ethnic overtones. This constitutes additional evidence that it was when the institutional framework designed to mediate political disputes failed that the regional and ethnic factors assumed discernible dimensions: And because the party leaders of the two coalition parties (the NPC and the NCN) which controlled the federal government had their centers of power in the Northern and Eastern Regions, respectively, the decisive influence in the solution of the Western Regional crisis was exercised by the two regional Premiers.

The crisis could have been averted if one faction of the Action Group in the Western Region had obtained an overwhelming majority in the house. There were 124 seats - 84 of these members were Action Group party members and 35 were NCNC party members. Seven seats were vacant and the rest were held by independents. Of the 84 members of the Action Group, 66 were supporters of the party leader - Chief Awolowo - though only 65 were said to have actually signed a petition seeking the removal of Chief Akintola, the leader of the opposing faction.[26] If the 35 members of NCNC had considered the interests of the region to be above party politics, they would have thrown their weight in support of one faction or the other. Their solid support would have materially affected the outcome of the crisis. But according to Mackintosh:

> The NCNC felt that they held the balance between success or failure in any such attempt and NCNCcircles alleged that they had been offered 40,000 pounds not to aid Akintola's men. They said that they pondered the offer but concluded that since the major enemy was the Action Group, anything that weakened it was too valuable to be given up for money.[27]

It is necessary to observe that the vast majority of the NCNC opposition to the West were members of the same Yoruba ethnic group as were the vast majority of the supporters of the two factions of the Action Group. It was after the NCNC members of the Western House had decided not support any of the Action Group factions that the NCNC party leader, Dr. Okpara, declared that the NCNC would not recognize Alhadji Adegbenro, the Action Group premier designee. He further declared that, "the federal government would be right in declaring a state of emergency in the West."[28]

Once the emergency was declared, the Northern Regional Premier and the Eastern Regional Premier became the main spokesmen for the federal emergency measures. The two regional premiers supported the federal government in its attempt to prevent the court from inquiring into the legality of the declaration of emergency. As the Premier of the Eastern Region put it, "There is an emergency in a part of the country and you don't need to fumble in court in such a situation."[29] The following day the Northern Premier issued a statement in support of the sentiments expressed by the Premier of the Eastern Region.[30]

As soon as these two leaders took a definite stand in the crisis, the struggle in the Western Region took on an inter-ethnic and inter-regional dimension. As Kenneth Post and Michael Vickers pointed out, the feeling gained ground among the Yoruba political and social elite "that the Yoruba were being victimized by the Ibo and the Hausa-Fulani..."[31] The activities of the NPC, a predominantly Hausa-Fulani party, and the NCNC with its Ibo leadership, lent some weight to this charge. The federal coalition formed by these two parties restored the Akintola faction to power at the end of the emergency. The Akintola faction formed a new party known as the United People's Party and promptly formed a coalition with the Western Nigerian wing of the NCNC. The federal government had, in fact, installed a coalition party to govern the Western Region without ascertaining the wished of the Western Regional electorate. Such an action could not but be viewed by the people of the region as an affront to them as well as an attempt to subject the region to the dictates of the other two regions.

The feeling was reinforced by the fact that in June, 1963, barely six months after the end of the emergency administration, the Midwestern Region, consisting of all the ethnic minorities in the Western Region, was carved out of that region. Thus, the Western Region became the first and only region to be split into two parts during the First Republic. From June, 1963, therefore, the Western Region became also the only region in Nigeria that was ethnically homogeneous.

In spite of the fact that it was peopled by one ethnic group (Yoruba), the politics of the region exhibited all the objectionable features of the Nigerian political struggle. The political struggle in the Western Region after 1963 showed in the most glaring fashion that ethnic heterogeneity was not the most important factor in the Nigerian political conflicts. We have discussed the 1964 election as part of the section on the political crisis of 1964.[32] However, certain salient features of the 1964 and 1965 elections in the Western Region deserve some comment.

The coalition formed by Akintola's UPP and the NCNC wing of the Western Region at the end of the state of emergency was as stormy as it was short-lived. In February, 1964, the national president of the NCNC formed an alliance with the Action Group, which was then reduced to a straggling opposition in the Western Region. This action led to the immediate collapse of the UPP-NCNC coalition government. Chief Akintola, the leader of the UPP and the Premier of the Western Region, quickly formed a new party known as the Nigerian National Democratic Party. This party immediately drew into its ranks all the disaffected members of the NCNC and the Action Group. By March 14th, its supporters in the Western House of Assembly numbered about 60. This number was enough to make it the party in power in the region. The new NCNC-Action Group alliance formed the opposition.

This was not just a mere reshuffling of the cabinet. It was, in fact, a dissolution of the party in power which had received a mandate from the people. Without calling for an election to receive a mandate from the people a new party was formed in the heat of the struggle and consequently a new cabinet. Here we have a peculiar parliamentary institution composed of parliamentarians who had lost their mandate when the Western House was dissolved and an emergency declared in the region. It is not clear by what constitutional power the federal government was able to impose a parliamentary government on a region. There was no election; no plebiscite of any sort. In the infinite wisdom of the federal government, Chief Akintola, who had been declared lawfully dismissed by a duly constituted Nigerian court, was made Premier of the region and asked to form a government. It was obvious that this high-handed measures could not go unchallenged - and it did not. During the crisis which bedeviled the federal election of 1964,[33] one of the conditions stated in the Zik-Balewa Pact that resolved that crisis was the dissolution of the government of the West so that the people of that region would have the opportunity to express their will as to who should govern them."[34]

The election which eventually followed (1965) gave rise to another crisis which brought the democratic experiment in Nigeria to a sad pass. This election was in the only ethnically homogeneous region in Nigeria, yet it exhibited in harrowing details all the gross abuses of the electoral system that had previously tarnished the electoral process. It showed beyond all doubt that the problem of political conflict in Nigeria had its source, not so much in the ethnic heterogeneity of the country, as in the inability of the institutional framework to mediate authoritatively the allocation of values within the political system. In the words of Kenneth Post and Michael Vickers:

> The structural importance of the regions in determining what happened in the First Republic was again demonstrated in the last months of 1965, and again in the West. In that year as in 1962, events there pushed the politics of the whole Federation in a new direction...Even as late as mid-1965 it appeared that the structural frame had just succeeded in containing the numerous conflicts, intersectional and otherwise, inherent in the First Republic. In retrospect it was evident that by January 1966 the frame itself was crumbling and would need desperate measures to shore it up; at that point, in fact violence finally took command. It was in the West since 1962 suffering under stress of chronic instability, that the final crisis was centered.[35]

What Post and Vickers called structural frame is, in fact, the institutional framework for authoritive allocation of values within the political system. The following summary by Dr. Ben Nwabueze sheds light on the enormity of the abuse of the electoral system within an ethnically homogeneous region in Nigeria. He noted that:

> The techniques used in the Western Region election of 1965 were more brazen than those of 1964. The returning officers provided the main tool. Many deserted their posts after accepting nomination papers from government party candidates, thereby making it impossible for the opposition candidates to file their own. Or, if a returning officer remained at his post he might refuse to accept an opposition candidate's nomination paper on some alleged technical fault. A returning officer refusing to desert his post might be abducted after having received the government's candidate's nomination. And lastly, returning officers who had accepted nomination papers from opposition candidates and even issued certificates of validity had their appointments revoked, and their successor refused to recognize the validity of such certificates or to accept new nomination papers...Large bundles of papers deposited with the police for safe-keeping...eventually found their way into the boxes of government candidates. Wads of ballot papers were found in the possession of unauthorized persons... Before the election the Regional Premier, Chief Akintola, had boasted that "whether the people voted for them or not, the NNDP would be returned to power." Rather than swallow such an injury to their right to choose who should govern them, the people of western Nigeria took the law into their own hands and launched a regime of violence and arson that held the region in its bloody grip until the military takeover of January 1966 intervened to flush out the politicians.[36]

It was, therefore, violence in the Western Region that precipitated the coup d'etat which ended the short but eventful life of the First Republic. Here again, we see that it was when the institutional framework had failed to mediate political conflict that ethnic factors became relevant. When the military coup d'etat in January, 1966, took place there was jubilation in the streets. The soldiers were hailed as the saviors of their country. But all of a sudden the ethnic composition of the officer corps which masterminded the coup became relevant. It was realized that a majority of them were Ibos. Then the nation was convulsed with a fear of Ibo domination. Ibos were stalked like deer in the streets of the North. The program had begun and when it ended Nigeria was gripped in the throes of a civil war that ushered in an era of military rule.

In conclusion, it must be observed from the foregoing survey of the developments in Nigeria that the institutional framework had neither the legitimacy nor the elasticity to bear the strains imposed on it by political conflicts. The surprising thing is not that it buckled under the strain, but that it was able to bear it for so long. No country within the British Commonwealth had subjected such crucial and fundamental issues to constant discussion and review as was done in the laying of the constitutional foundation of the Nigerian State. From 1947 to 1963, six constitutional instruments were drafted, discussed and implemented in Nigeria. In each of these experiments in constitution-making such intractable problems as revenue allocation and regional representation at the House of Representatives were opened up for discussion.

Even if Nigeria had been culturally and ethnically homogeneous, such continuous reopening of issues could not but erode the legitimacy of the institutional structure. From 1947 through 1963 Nigeria had muddled through one constitutional experiment after another, each raising new issues and exacerbating old ones. The result was a series of crises leading to the final collapse of democratic government in 1966. The remainder of this study will consider three of these crises - the Census Crisis of 1962-63, the Revenue Crisis of 1964, and the Election Crisis of 1964.

CHAPTER IV

THE POLITICS OF CENSUS ENUMERATION IN NIGERIA, 1952-1964

In the last chapter we discussed the growing pains of national independence and the Western Regional crisis of 1962. In this chapter, an attempt is made to assess the conflicts and crises arising from the politicization of census enumeration and to emphasize the crucial importance of the census figures in determining the political balance at the center between the Northern Region and the two Southern Regions (East and West).

The political importance of the census figures is underscored by the fact that the Northern Region staked its claim to fifty percent of the representation at the center on the basis of its population figures. Furthermore, the political conflict over revenue allocation was complicated by the fact that the different commissions appointed to recommend methods of revenue allocation had made population statistics the quantifiable indicator of the relative financial needs of the various regions in the federation.[1]

Moreover, the issue of the creation of more states evoked much heated political controversy because of the effect it would have on the population of the existing regions and, therefore, on the strength of regional representation at the center. It is one of the acknowledged principles of federalism that there must be a "reasonable balance" in population strength[2] so that no one unit can dominate the bargaining process at the central level. In fact, Tarlton singled out equal territory and population as one of the conditions for "an ideal symmetrical federal system."[3] It is interesting to note that Britain initially excluded Singapore from the Malayan Federation because the inclusion of the Chinese dominated island "would jeopardize the delicate distribution of population and control within the federation."[4]

Yet, in Nigeria, this very British colonial power encouraged and supported the creation of a federal institutional structure in which the population of one region was greater than the population of the other two combined. In 1956, the British governor of the Norther Region, Sir Bryan Sharwood Smith, warned the North against the creation of any new region in the North. He asserted that "the greatest danger to the North is fragmentation."[5] He viewed with alarm the agitation for more states in the two Southern Regions and warned that if this movement were allowed to spread it would lead to proliferation of the regions. He prophesied that the eventual outcome of the proliferation of regions would be that "the case for regionalization would disappear and Nigeria would inevitably return to a unitary form of government, on the effect of which, on the North, it is unnecessary to comment."[6]

For both the British and the North, "the case for regionalization" in Nigeria lies in the fact that the North by its great size and population was in the words of Mill in a position of "being master of the joint deliberation"[7] in Nigeria. For the British the predominance of the North would ensure the protection of its interests. Luckman confirmed that, "the existing regions were retained inspite of the disparity in size," for the "British government felt that a Nigerian government controlled by conservative Northern politicians would be more 'stable' and faborable to its interests."[8] The Northern Region being land-locked, needed the federation for economic reasons. But being the least economically developed, it was afraid of being dominated by the south. Its size and population, therefore, became its greatest bargaining strength.

Thus, the interests of the British and the North combined to produce gross inequality in the sizes of regional institutional structures. The desire of the Northern Region to perpetuate this inequality in size and population found expression in the motto of the NPC (the dominant political party in the North) which is, "One North One People Irrespective of Religion, Rank or Tribe."[9]

This desire of the North to preserve its numerical superiority has complicated and politicized the census enumeration and revenue allocation in Nigeria. Hicks and Phillipson warned against this danger as far back as 1950-1951. They forecast that:

> It is a matter of the greatest importance that the population statistics of Nigeria should be improved, though it is going to be exceedingly difficult to improve them very greatly. They will not be improved as much as they could be if particular sections develop a financial interest in producing figures which will support their claims. There have been unfortunate experiences with this sort of thing in other countries. It is, for instance, widely believed that the last Indian census (of 1941) was seriously vitiated, expecially in Bengal, by the desire of both Hindus and Moslems to swell the numbers of their respective communities as much as possible. We do not want that kind of thing to happen in Nigeria. While methods of counting are imperfect as they must be in Nigeria, it is a matter of the first importance to keep the counting as disinterested as possible.[10]

But neither the British nor the politicians in Nigeria had shown any zeal for disinterested census enumeration in Nigeria. The whole history of census enumeration in Nigeria has been colored by the interests of the various groups and those of the imperial power structure. Attempts will be made in this chapter to trace briefly the historical development of the census taking in Nigeria and the conflict and crises arising from it.

The Historical Development of Census Enumeration in Nigeria from 1789-1964

From the first European contact with the area known as Nigeria, information about its population has been fragmentary and largely based on estimates. As far back as 1789, Captain W. Adams, an American sailor, estimated the population of Lagos at 5,000.[11] In 1815, it was estimated at 11,000;[12] in 1855, 20,000.[13] Finally, when the British took possession of Lagos, the population was said to be 30,000.[14] In 1863, an ordinance was passed by the British requiring an annual census of the Colony of Lagos. Under this ordinance, census was taken in Lagos in 1866 and 1868. For some reason the provisions of the ordinance fell into disuse. However, the decennial census was revived in 1871 and repeated in 1881. Lagos' population in 1871 was 29,000 and 37,000 in 1881.

In the area known as the Eastern Region, the situation was similar. Even before the British occupation, the impression that Iboland was densely populated and the extent of that population had been the subject of comments by interested writers. As far back as 1777, G.C.A. Oldendorp, a German pastor of the Moravian Brethren, was convinced from the number of Ibo slaves he found in the Caribbean, that the Ibos were the most populous of all the ethnic groups in West Africa. He, therefore, devoted a great deal of time and research in an attempt to compile an Ibo vocabulary and Ibo anthropological data.[15] Dr. Africanus Horton, son of an Ibo freedman in Sierra Leone, noted in his book that the Ibo mainland, "was numerously populated."[16]

Finally, in 1900, Leonard estimated the population of Iboland at between 10 and 12 million and observed that the country "is both extensive, populous and divided into numberous clans and communities."[17] As for the other ethnic groups in the former Eastern Region, Talbot noted that in 1791, Bonny, a town made up of Ibos and Calabaris, "contained about 20,000 inhabitants who lived principally by trade."[18]

48

However, when census taking actually started in the Southern Region imperial considerations made it impossible to varify the estimates of these writers.

In 1906, the Colony of Lagos was merged with the Protectorate of Southern Nigeria, which then embraced the whole of Southern Nigeria. In 1911, an ordinance was promulgated requiring the taking of census from time to time in the Colony and Protectorate of Southern Nigeria. In that very year an actual attempt was made to enumerate a large area of southern Nigeria. However, the actual enumeration was confined to the main ports. Outside the ports, actual enumeration was made in the main government stations, especially in the Eastern Region. In the Eastern Region, according to S.B. Chambers:

> Most of the inland area was only effectively occupied in the first eleven years of the century, and while the estimates of population then made, some of which were reduced when they reached headquarters, were probably the best that could be obtained at that time, they are of little use for comparative purposes.[19]

Not only were these calculations based on estimates of people on the spot, but for reasons known only to the colonial authority these very estimates were further reduced by officials who had little or no acquaintance with the area. No pretense to accuracy was made, even in the area now known as the Western Region. The figures were estimated on the basis of data available in each district within the area.

As noted in the historical review attached to the 1952 census, "Opinions vary on the degree of accuracy of these estimates, and it must be remembered that in 1911 most of the southern provinces had not yet come under the effective control of government."[20] Even in Northern Nigeria where there had been a long history of tax collection, the same census pattern prevailed. Between 1901 and 1910 estimates of the population of the North varied between 3,000,000 and 6,714,000. As the Administrative Report of 1952 noted, "It was apparent that estimates of the total population made during this period were guesses."[21] The census of Northern Nigeria taken in 1911 showed this tendency at its worst. The estimates were made on one sheet of paper and forwarded to the colonial office. This document gave the population of the North as 8.12 million. This figure was disputed by some local British administrators in the North, who sent a revised estimate which gave the population of the North as 9,274,981.[22] The latter figure became the official population of the North in 1911.

In 1914, the Colony and Protectorate of Southern Nigeria was merged with the Protectorate of Northern Nigeria and became known as the colony and Protectorate of Nigeria. In 1917 a Census Ordinance was passed requiring decennial census of the colony and the Protectorate of Nigeria. Pursuant to this requirement, a census was conducted throughout Nigeria in 1921. At this time there was a realistic attempt to widen the scope of the census, both as to actual enumeration, and as to the nature of the information collected. Dr. P. Amaury Talbot, the census officer, was a thorough and indefatigable worker with a decided interest in ethnographic data. He divided the enumeration under two subheads - Township census and Provincial census. With regard to the Townshiip census, which covered thirteen townships and embraced a population of 150,000, he regarded the enumerations as fairly complete and the result as nearly accurate. With regard to the Provincial census, he stated that the "statistics can only be regarded as approximate."[23]

It was concluded that five percent should be added to the indigenous population in the townships and ten percent to the provincial areas. The reason for this addition was that "owing to the difficulties arising from the hearty dislike which many of the native tribes feel towards enumeration and the shortage of European staff due to the Great War,"[24] the statistics as a whole were largely an approximation. The population of Nigeria, after this adjustment, was given as 18,631,442. Later revisions rounded it out to 18.72 million.[25]

The next census held under the 1917 ordinance was in 1931. Various factors conspired and conjoined to make this census a memorable affair in Nigerian history. With respect to the North, Mr. Brooke, the census officer, commented in his report that the census "could scarcely have been taken under less favourable conditions."[26] Apart from the financial depression which was worldwide at this period, a locust invasion overwhelmed the whole of Norther Nigeria. This emergency resulted in the diversion of much of the time and energy of the limited administrative staff "in anti-locust measures to the detriment of the census plans."[27] In spite of this, the enumeration in the 1931 census in the North was considered relatively satisfactory. The population of the North was given as 11,435,000.

In the South the experience of the 1931 census was traumatic. As the preparation was underway, the women of Eastern Nigeria broke out into open rebellion. This rebellion, known as the Aba Women's Riot of 1929, had two major causes - both of them equally important for an understanding of the events. Firstly, it was a serious breach of Ibo custom to count human beings. In the second place, it was rumored that the census was the first step in a European attempt to tax the women. These two causes reinforced each other and gave rise to a riot that spread like wildfire, even beyond the confines of Iboland to Calabar. As the report of the 1931 census phrased it:

> The Southern Provinces Section has been the Cinderella of the census of Nigeria in 1931. The preliminary arrangements 1929 and 1930 were interrupted by the riots in the Eastern Provinces, one of the main causes of which was said to be the attempts which were being made to enumerate the native tribes. This interruption was discouraging to anyone who anticipated a really thorough census of the population in the Eastern rovinces, and it is not matter for surprise that a general feeling of nervousness arose in connection with enumeration. The consequences was that a scheme for a general census in the Southern Provinces failed to mature; and although certain proposals were discussed and approved, most of them were eventually found to be impracticable, so that the census of the Southern Provinces finally became a mere compilation of existing data, and the results have often only provisional character.[28]

Of course, the Southern provinces, especially the Eastern section, paid no moderate price for this affront to the imperial power. While the 1921 population was estimated at 5,440,000 that of 1931 was estimated at 4,691,000. This represents a loss in population of 749,000. The low estimate which was made of the population of the Southeastern Region had a serious effect on the total population of Southern Nigeria. In 1921 it was 8,371,000 as against 9,998,000 for the North. In 1931 it stood at 8,493,000 as against 11,435,000 for the North.

It is important to note that because of the Second World War the decennial census was not held in 1941. It is equally important to observe that an updated version of the 1931 census was constantly used between 1946 and 1953 to determine the fiscal allocation to the various regions and to apportion seats in the Central Legislature. For example, the official estimate of the population of the different regions of Nigeria in 1950 was given as follows:

```
North                    13,514,000
West (excluding Lagos)    3,977,999
East                      5,243,000.[29]
```

The figures shown here indicate that the Northern population was a little less than twice that of the East and the west combined. That of the North represented a realistic enumeration, while those of the East and the West were grossly inaccurate since they were the outcome of nothing more than hunches, guesses, and broad approximations. Allocations of political value based on such shifting sands are perforce bound to result in political friction. And in Nigeria they have been productive of not just conflicts, but full scale regional conflict and crisis of confidence.

Rightly or wrongly the North had come to accept the census figure as a true reflection of the Nigerian population distribution. Thus, at the Proceedings of the General conference on the Review of the Constitution held at Ibadan in 1950, the North staked its claim on representation at the Central Legislature and fiscal allocation on its alleged population strength. In a speech made at the conference, Mallam Iro Katsina from the North put the Northern case as follows:

> The Northern Regional Conference has strongly recommended that grant from the Central Revenue together with grants from Imperial Funds and loan funds should be divided between regions on a per capita basis of population and that should start at the same time as the other changes in the constitution.[30]

He argued that the North had been cheated in the distribution of revenue for more than forty years and that it would be difficult to explain to the people of the North why their fair demands for equitable revenue allocation were not met. He concluded that the "North is right in asking her rights." Referring to regional representation, he asserted that:

> The North recommends that the number of representatives in the center from Eastern and Western Regions should not together exceed the number of representatives from the North region. North puts its claim on population because there is nothing more reasonable to consider in thinking the number of representatives better than population.[31]

There were allegations that the British had consistently undercounted the Southern population. However, it can certainly be said in defense of the North that the representatives of the East and the West did not address themselves to the population issue. No attempt was made to spotlight the pitfalls of the population figures as presented or to prove that the population of the South was greater than that of the North. But there is no doubt that the relative population strengths based on figures which are of dubious validity had been politicized. And once an issue is politicize, it is difficult to depoliticize it. Neither reasoning nor a realistic attempt at a solution was evident in the debate or the proceedings. As Sir Tafawa Balewa pointed out during the debate on allocation, "it is not a question of financial expert or anything of the kind. It is something rather more political than financial. This question can be easily settled, Mr. Chairman, in a spirit of cooperation within the three regions."[32]

But the spirit of cooperation was noticeably absent. The debates had the appearance of statement or regional representatives presiding over the demise of a federation, rather than that of statesmen building one. Thus, the acrimony of the debates sowed the seeds of distrust and gathered rancor for further conflicts. Mallam Aliyu Makaman Bida expressed the feelings of the North when he complained that the Southern politicians had labelled the Northern representatives as conservatives and that Mr. Prest had advocated that the west and the East should have more members so that they could act as a sort of 'pupil teacher' to teach the Northerns. He wondered aloud "whether those members could think of the weight of those statements on our minds."[33] He pointed out that these statements had revealed what the position of the North "would be should the British leave us. What would happen naturally would be that the pupil teacher would take over automatically from the teacher and again where the pupils demand their rights, they would be regarded as conservative."[34]

The North was obviously convinced that there was a Southern (Eastern and Western) coalition against it, but the Eastern Region and the Western Region had never been able to present a common front against the North. Nonetheless, it made up its mind that because of the Southern threat it must have fifty percent representation at the center on the basis of its population. On the basis of the same population figures, it argued that revenue allocation must be on a per capita basis.

Thus, the population of the various regions became the most important single determinant of the relative political power of the regions. Under such conditions, it was inconceivable that census enumeration could be apprached in a calm, dispassionate manner. Any diminution in the supposed population of a region or any dramatic change in the demographic composition of the regions would alter, not only the power configuration at the center, but the allocation of revenue to the regions for essential services and economic development. One cannot, therefore, escape the impression that the North, when it staked its bid for equal representation and greater percentage of revenue allocation on the basis of population, was fully aware of the importancce of the census.

The Census Enumeration in Nigeria: Arrangements for the Census

The decennial census under the 1917 ordinance was not held in 1941 because of the Second World War. However, in 1950 it was decided to resume the census enumeration under the ordinance of 1917.

The administrative reports of the census from the three regions agree that "population census of a country as large as Nigeria required long and careful planning."[36] It is, therefore, necessary to see how much planning and supervision went into the enumeration of the census in the three regions. on a Nigeria-wide basis, the government statistician was appointed as the Census Superintendent. His department was charged with the responsibility for the organization, planning and preparation of schedule for the whole of Nigeria. British civil servants were appointed to the various regions to oversee the enumeration, but from there on the uniformity breaks down. In the North, provincial census officers were appointed. According to the administrative report from the Northern Region, "it is believed that without them it would have been almost immpossible to have organized the training of the supervisors and enumerators and arrange for the distribution of the forms as efficiently and expeditiously as these tasks were accomplished."[37]

Although the Southern regions were described as "the Cinderella of the census of Nigeria in 1931,"[38] the officials did not think it necessary to make the services of the provincial census officers available to the East and West. According to the administrative report:

> It was decided that the Provincial census officers who had proved themselves an integral part of the Northern Region Organization were not necessary and all arrangements were made with divisional census officers.[39]

In the East the reason was that it was not possible:

> ...to spare officers to provide the provincial census officers who were the mainstay of the census in the Northern Region and the residents were in general far too busy to deal with details of organization.[40]

In the North the district officers who were appointed as census officers were relieved of "as much detailed work as possible, so as to give them time to supervise the tasks undertaken by the native administration."[41]

In the Western Region each division was under a census officer.

In the East, on the other hand, the district officers combined their normal duties with the duties of census officers. Furthermore, "each district officer was asked to make a plan to suit his own division."

In the South the colonial civil servants were absolutely in control of the census enumeration. Even the task of publicizing the census was performed by colonial officials touring from place to place in the East and West. In the West it was stated that:

> Every effort was made to get the people to understand the object of the census. It was discussed with the native authorities at an early date and continuously thereafter. However it is evident from many of the reports from census officers, that the response by some native authorities was poor and that representatives of rural areas on these councils failed in their promise to help publicise the census.[43]

It must not be forgotten that the West has many powerful Obas,[44] and if these colonial officials had involved them, they would have ensured a well informed and intelligent participation on the part of the people.

For some reason known only to colonial administrative officers it was not seen fit to involve the Obas and the native authorities in the East and West. In the East, the rationale was that:

> The native authorities of the Eastern Region are much smaller and more numerous than in the North or West; a single division may contain four or five independent and numerous subordinate authorities. While individual members of their staff were made availavle, it was necessary for district officers to organize the census from their own offices.[45]

Since the district officials' normal duty involved contact with those native authority councils, one would think that it would be a natural combination to invoive those with whom he interacted in his day-to-day functions.

In the North the native authority bureaucrats, and even ministers and legislators, were deeply involved in the organization, scheduling and the enumeration of the census. The Colonial civil servants acted more as advisers, coordinators and supervisors. The following statement by a colonial civil servant from the East who visited the North during the census is highly revealing.

> Both Emirs and district heads personally wield considerable authority by reason of the fact that they belong to families having traditional authority in their areas. The latter are also senior officials of the native administrations, their salaries ranging in this area usually from 450 pounds to 600 pounds, thus they have considerable experience of administration and are men of some koranic culture. In most cases they are also men of intelligence and education. If, as they frequently are, they are also members of the House of Assembly, the fact that they are also elected reinforces their authority. This is true to a greater degree of the Emirs themselves...
>
> The position of the government officers is also different from that which obtains in the East. In theory at any rate, and to a considerable extent in fact, the Emir is the ruler and the administrative officers the advisers and executives, each at his own level...
>
> The people, without any loss of self-respect, accept their position as subjects of the government and although the usual crop of rumors was circulating, were ready to believe a reasonable explanation, either from their own chiefs or from an administrative officer without the reaction of suspicion usual in the East. They are moreover accustomed to being counted.[46]

Equity and fairness would dictate that more elaborate preparation be made in the East and West where, obviously, the people had a deepseated objection to being counted. The two regions had elected representatives who, like the ministers and legislators of the Northern Region, had constituencies who voted for them and who would listen to them as their chosen representatives. Only token use was made of this highly valuable asset. In the East it was openly acknowledged that "There is no doubt that the formation, for the first time, of an elected government gave great satisfaction throughout the region, and it was realized that all propaganda must flow from the House of Assembly and the ministers."[47] Yet, whatever part these representatives played in the census was only peripheral. It was limited to the reading of messages to be printed and circulated with their portraits on them. It was the collection of these messages, and the production of 48,000 pamplets resulting from it, that Dr. Okpara, a minister without portfolio, supervised.[48] It may be argued that at this time there was a constitutional crisis in the Eastern Region which led to the resignation of the ministers in January, 1953, on the very day that these pamphlets came out in print.[49]

It was the official view that in the Eastern Region "about eighty-five percent of the people seven or more years old are illiterate" and, therefore, "a verbal approach is the most important." The approach was to ask the district officers to make special efforts to visit the villages. It was obvious that the administrative officers were not very enthusiastic about undertaking what the census report called "the impossible task of covering four or five hundred villages in a few months in addition to their normal full-time duties."[50] In both the Southeastern and Southwestern Regions, there were at this time elected representatives of the people who knew their areas well and could have, like the legislators and native authorities in the North, educated their own people as to the importance of the census. Moreover, as early as 1951, the British officials noted in their annual report that the new wireless service was "incomparably the most important source of information and publicity, and the strongest cultural influence in the township beside which the press fades into insignificance."[51] As there was constant communication and contact between the remotest villages and their relatives in the townships, these town ship dwellers could have done a lot to dissiminate any messages read over the radio to the people in the villages. Instead, gramophone records and cinema films carried by mobile units were used in areas where transport facilities were poor, if not entirely non-existent.

In the Western Region no publicity was done in areas such as Owo and Ondo provinces.[52] In many areas a concentrated "campaign was conducted immediately before the count... in some cases only the day before the enumerator arrived in the area."[53] These campaigns were delayed ostensibly to allow little time for opposition to grow. The census report noted that a tour of the Ishara area (in the Western Region) just before the census by the Regional Minister without portfolio, the Odemo of Ishara, helped to make the census in the Ishara area a success.[54] This is evidence that had the government taken the elected representatives in the South into their confidence as they did in the North, the result in the South would have been far more reflective of the actual population. Consequently much of the conflict that subsequently surrounded the 1962 and 1963 census figures would have been obviated.

The point we have argued is that the 1952 census was not a true reflection of the actual population of the South. The publicity for the census taking was poorly organized and badly managed. The decision to use colonial officers in the South as publicity agents at a time when the nationalist wave was at its height and the intentions of the colonial officials were particularly suspect, was of dubious validity. In the North the major part of the publicity and enumeration was done by the native authorities and their Emirs. And, as the administrative report of the North states, "'it is a tribute to the efficiency of the representative native administrations that they were able to undertake the task required of them without seriously dislocating their normal routine."[55] In the South (East and West), on the other hand, the administrative report, especially that of the East, pointed out that it was to the district officers, "with their assistant district officers and census instructors, that the credit is due for the success of the census in their divisions."[56]

It is obvious that a spirit of cooperation and a feeling of mutual confidence existed between the Northern colonial officials and the Northern power elite. This was lacking in the South. For example, the budget for conducting the census was exclusively under the control of the native authority in the North.[57] In the South-both East and West - the colonial officers took personal charge of managing the census budget.[58] Also, the choice of enumerators, instructors, and census supervisors in the South was entrusted to the colonial officials.

It could be argued that there was a political crisis in the East, but in the West where there was no crisis, and where there had been a long tradition of native administration, there was also no realistic attempts to make it a part of the census enumeration. In the

North the prestige and traditional influence of such functionaries as the *Ciroma*, the eldest son of the Emir of Kano,[59] were utilized to ensure that the enumerators and the public at large were duly informed about the importance of the census. Training of census enumerators and supervisors was highly coordinated. It was carried out "by a fully trained native administration staff...Classes were arranged at central points for all supervisors."[60] The rationale for making use of native authority was that:

> However high a standard of the vernacular the provincial census officer (British) may have attained, he cannot always be expected to carry out instruction with the same ease and facility as a native of the province speaking his own tongue to his own people.[61]

It is interesting to note, that the indigenous elites in the North were actively involved in the census, while in the Eastern and Western Regions, which were supposed to be more educationally advanced, the British argued that it was difficult to find suitable personnel to fill the various positions in middle management and even in the largely mechanical job of enumeration. In the Eastern Region in particular, it was stated that, "It had been intended to engage and brief a team of propagandists, one for each province."[62] But this proposal was abandoned because "most of the suitable personnel had become involved in the census in other capacities."[63]

Considering the disastrous consequences of the last census in the Southern provinces in 1931, priority should have been given to the dissemination of full and accurate information on the meaning and importance of the census. This is all the more important because during the 1950's there was a world-wide interest in collecting census figures and individual data from all the countries in the world. This interest was the result of a United Nations program - World Census of 1950. During the 1950's the United Nations established a program called World Census to encourage countries to take censuses. It sponsored regional statistical committees which suggested minimum standards and offered technical assistance in planning and conducting enumerations. In spite of the availability of these facilities and the obvious need to correct the undercounting in the South during the 1931 census, no attempt was made to seek the assistance of the United Nations and very little planning and coordination went into the census enumeration in the Southeastern and Southwestern Regions of Nigeria.

It was obvious that census undertaken without sufficient planning and coordination can scarcely be accurate. Yet, at the end of the 1952-1953 census, the administrative report of the West noted that "the count was 90 to 95 percent accurate."[64] The report from the East after observing that "claims to accuracy must be made with diffidence,"[65] estimated that the figures were accurate within three percent. Even though more preparation and effort were put into the census enumeration in the North, the report from the North only claimed that figures were accurate within five percent.[66]

It is difficult to expect comparable results from procedures so differently organized. Moreover, the census was held at different periods between May, 1952, and June 1953, in different parts of Nigeria. In spite of this, adequate attention was not given to the timing of the enumeration in the Southern Regions. As the census report of the Southwestern Region noted:

> The census was taken at the height of the cocoa season - a fact which should be borne in mind in any comparison between the recorded urban and rural populations of the cocoa area. Several houses in Ibadan and Ijebu-Ode were reported to be locked up throughout the census week although they were visited several times.[67]

In the Southeastern Region it was noted that in June many farmers in the Ibo provinces would be away from home and that the rainy season would seriously interfere with census taking in the Cameroons and the Creeks."[68] Yet, "June was retained for all provinces except the Cameroons and the river provinces for which April was chosen so as to get over before the rains set in."[69]

In the North, however, full consideration was given to timing. The enumeration was officially fixed for July 14, 1952. But because it was feared that counting would not be completed in Kano and in Adamawa within the 14 days allowed, counting was begun in Adamawa on July first and in Kano on July seventh.[70] In Benue Province it was decided that because of "the heavy rains and consequent difficulty in moving over large parts of the province usually in July, "the count should be held in May.[71]

The differential treatment given to the various regions in the whole process of enumeration certainly vitiated any comparison between the results attained in the Northern and in the South. When it is realized that in 1931 actual enumeration was only completed in the North and that the Southern figures were mere estimates one wonders why more planning and coordination did not go into the census enumeration in the South. As the government statistician commented, the 1931 census was "slightly defective in the Northern Provinces and much in defect in the Southern Provinces."[72]

The 1952 census was certainly the first realistic attempt to enumerate the whole population in Nigeria. While the Southern politicians had themselves to blame for not seeking or insisting on a meaningful role in the census enumeration of 1952-1953, their charge that the British were partial to the North cannot be totally dismissed as groundless. According to Dr. Aluko:

> Not only the process of the 1950-3 census, but also the results, attracted suspicion and controversy. Of the recorded total of 34.2 million, 16.84 million were in Northern Nigeria. The figures were contested mainly by Southern Nigerian politicians, particularly when they came to be used as an argument for giving Northern Nigeria 50 percent representation in the Federal Legislature. It was freely alleged by Southern politicians that the British administrators had inflated the population figures of the North in order to ensure that political power in the country remained with the Northern politicians, who were regared as more favourably disposed towards them.[73]

Talk of inflating the population figures at this stage can scarcely be substantiated. bit it cannot be denied that the accumulated effect of differences in organization, processes and actual execution of the enumeration program had an impact on the results. For example, the decision to hold the enumeration in Benue Province (Northern Region) in May ratherthan July was revealed, on a sample check in July, to have made a difference of nearly one percent.[74] The levels of preparation, publicity, and organization in the North and the south certainly made a lot of difference. According to the reports, opposition to the census in the South was evident even till the end of the enumeration. The administrative report from the West observed that:

> It was clear from the pilot census that, even when a village had been saturated with publicity of all kinds for a full week, the most important thing was the way in which the enumerator explained the reason for his visit to each householder.[75]

It is evident that the publicity in the South was not particularly effective, which could mean a difference between an accurate and a grossly deficient enumeration. A clear example of undercounting was revealed by the Western Nigerian Free Primary Education Program in 1955. Based on the 1952-1953 census count it was projected that 170,000 would attain the ages of six and seven in 1955. Preparations were made accordingly. However, actual registrations conducted in December, 1954, showed that there were 392,000 children who were within that age group. This represented 230 percent more than the number deducted from the 1952-1953 census.[76]

One point is certainly clear - it was not until the North made the census figures the basis for the allocation of seats under the 1954 constitution that criticisms of the 1953 census became vocal. The more politicians leaned towards regional autarchy and the use of the population figures as the basis for allocation of politically relevant values to the regions, the more the population figures were politicized. Once it had been politicized, it was unrealistic to expect that the next census would be conducted in a calm and dispassionate mood, free from political calculations. It is within this context that we turn to an analysis of the events which led to the conflict over the 1962 Census recount.

The 1962 Census Enumeration

The 1962 census was the first enumeration since independence in 1960. By this time people had come to realize the importance of population figures in the distribution of social services and amenities. The use of the census figures for local council representation had brought home to every community the importance of accurate enumeration.

For the governments, accurate census figures were sorely needed for constituency demarcation for allocation of representatives to the various legislative bodies. It became absolutely clear that realistic economic planning, the allocation of revenues and various facets of public hinged on accurate population statistics.

In the political sphere there was a feeling in the air that the 1962 census would lead to a dramatic change in the power configuration of the regions at the central legislature. The 1952-1953 census had determined the distribution of 312 seats in the central legislature among the regions. The North had 174 seats, the East had 73 seats, 62 seats were assigned to the West, and Lagos was allotted 3 seats. From the district level to the regional level, interest in the new census was very high. There was also a tinge of national pride involved. People felt that this census would not only be the most detailed and most complete census Nigeria had ever taken, but would be "an example for other countries less developed than Nigeria."77 High hopes were obviously entertained about its accuracy and scope. Preparations were made to ensure that the 1962 figures and the statistical data collected would provide a solid foundation for future census enumeration in Nigeria.

All along the Southern politicians had felt that the population of the South was greater than that of the North but that the British had manipulated the figures in favor of the North. The Southern politicians, therefore, believed that the census would bring to an end the Northern Region's domination of the central legislature based on its population. The politicians were confident that now that the Southerners understood the full meaning of the census, opposition to it would cease, and would lead to a material change in the figures. It was also the politicians' belief that improved medical facilities in the South had resulted in less infant mortality and a decrease in the death rate, and that this was far more pronounced in the South than in the North.

There was much enthusiasm for the 1962 census. The requirements and standards for census enumeration laid down were evidently high.[78] But what were the motives behind the enthusiasm? What were the objectives of the census? Traditionally census enumeration carried with it a connotation of liability for those being enumerated. From the days of the early Egyptian kingdoms, and the Babylonian, Persian and Roman empires, cadastral surveys had been carried out to determine what group was liable for what burden on behalf of the polity. Conscript labor, taxation, and military duties were imposed on the basis of the data provided thereby. Even in the seventeenth and eighteenth centuries, when the idea of general enumeration for scientific, administrative and developmental planning purposes came into vogue, that undertone of liability to, accountability to, and control by the polity was not entirely absent from the census idea. Nonetheless, as population census came to be regarded more and more as a fundamental source of information both practical and scientific - about a polity, opposition faded.

In Nigeria population figures were looked upon essentially as a basis for allocation of revenues and representation at the center. Thus, in Nigeria census enumeration became inextricably enmeshed in the struggle for power between the regions. The struggle was complicated by the fact that census enumeration was placed by the 1963 constitution on the concurrent list of legislative powers of the federal and regional governments.[79]

This meant that each of the regions had full responsibility for the enumeration within its own confines, subject, of course, to such joint arrangements as the federal government might devise for the coordination of the enumeration throughout the federation.

Each region, therefore, appointed a regional census officer who was under the regional Ministry of Planning and was responsible for planning and organizing the enumeration throughout the region. To ensure inter-regional comparability of date, consistency of technique and syncronization of timing, a federal census office was established. Under the leadership of the federal Chief Census Officer, several meetings were held with the regional census officers to secure a measure of consistency in organizational format, data collection, and timing. It is significant that these meetings were held, not only at the federal Census Office, but in each region on a rotating basis. The idea was emphasized that each region was master within its own domain and that it had joint responsibility with the center. The power relationship was that between coordinates, not subordinates. Yet the funds for running both the regional and federal census offices were provided by the federal government and part of the publicity was on national radio network. Much was done to give a national cast to the whole census effort.

Nonetheless, each region organized its own training of supervisiors and enumerators. Ministers and party functionaries in each region were involved in the publicity, urging all not to be left out in the enumeration. Pamphlets, tracts, and posters of all sorts were circulated in every vernacular, language, or dialect. The air of suspicion which had pervaded the 1931 and 1952-53 census in the South gave way to enthusiastic support. Instead of avoiding the enumeration, not a few were willing to condone, and abide by double counting, both in the North and the South. The census was not just a population count coupled with a compilation of vital statistics; it was seen as a political contest between the regions. The greater the number of people within a region, the greater the chances for that region to gain more seats and consequently more power and influence in the federal legislature.

In a country where claims to special treatment are based on gross numbers as indicators of need,[80] population figures could not but assume a special political importance which would make accurate enumeration at best problematic. The competition for federal funds, and the reallocation of seats, on the basis of population, had made it impossible to conduct a fair census which is above suspicion. As we noted earlier in this chapter, if the registration of children in the Free Primary Education System of the West, which showed an undercounting of 230 percent, had occurred in the course of a general census, the census officers would have termed it a gross inflation. But since this had only a regional impact, nobody complained that a 230 percent increase within three years was unrealistic. It was not that the number of children had increased at that rate, but there had been serious undercounting in 1952-1953 in the Southwest, which had led to faulty projections.[81] It is with this in mind that we can look, with measure of objectivity, at the crisis over revenue allocation in 1962 and 1963.

Unlike the 1952-1953 census, which was staggered over a period of more than one year from May, 1952 to June, 1953, the 1962 census was conducted in all parts of Nigeria between May 5, and May 21, 1962. The results were processed and analyzed in each region and sent to the Office of the Chief Census Officer in Lagos. When the results reached Lagos and were tabulated, the figures from the East were shown to have increased over 70 percent; those from the North and the West were in the process of being compiled. But the census officer, without waiting for the figures from all the regions to be tabulated and without attempting to verify the figures, stated in his report that:

> The figures recorded throughout the greater part of Eastern Nigeria during the present census are false and have been inflated. The figures for the five divisions of Awka, Brass, Degema, Eket, and Opodo, which have recorded increases of over one hundred and twenty percent, can easily be rejected out of hand.[82]

It is noteworthy that, of the five divisions mentioned, only one belonged to the Ibo, the major ethnic group in the East. If there had been any inflation - and it was rather im-

58

prudent to declare that there had been any inflation without a spot check of the figures - four of these provinces were in ethnic minority area. According to Post and Vickers:

> There had been deliberate inflation by local enumerators in the hope of influencing the distribution of rewards; it is perhaps particularly significant that four of the five highest increases were recorded in divisions inhabited by minority sections, which tended to feel themselves at a disadvantage relative to the Ibo.[83]

Mr. Warren, the Chief Census Officer, had made his report to the minister even before the total results of the census from all the regions had been received. Referring to the West he noted that "...provisional total figures were available for only five (provinces) due in my view to weaknesses in the census organization in the region."[84] The problems of the census in the West were complicated by intra-ethnic conflict in the region. Due to factional disputes between the Action Group members, who were all members of the Yoruba ethnic group, the Western House of Assembly was dissolved and the cabinet suspended. From May 19, to December 31, 1962, a state of emergency was declared and an administrator - a Yoruba - was appointed.[85] The conflict had a detrimental effect on the census. Dr. Aluko observed that:

> Neither the staff nor the finance needed for the checking and efficient processing of the census data could be found. Many of the non-civil service staff recruited by the Census Office were relieved of their posts and replaced by new ones because they were suspected of owing allegiance to the Action Group, which had formed the Regional Government before the emergency.[86]

In the West the conflict was intra-ethnic and intra-regional. In the East there was a pronounced attempt by the ethnic minorities to increase their numbers so as to achieve a stronger bargaining position in the regional power structure. At the federal level the conflict was essentially between the Northern Region and the Eastern Region. It is perhaps noteworthy that, although the census in the Western Region was completed before December and showed over 70 percent increase,[87] the federal Minister of Economic Development, Waziri Ibrahim from the Northern Region, quoted the Chief Census Officer's report dated July, 1962, without mentioning the comparable increase obtained in the East and West.

No mention was made of irregularities in the North. Yet, according to the debates in the Eastern House of Assemlby,[88] counting was still going on in the Northern Region in November, even though the census was supposed to end officially on May 21. The official Northern reply to this allegation was that, in essence, the report was true, but that enumerators were only recounting 20,000 Ibos who lived in the Gboko division of the Northern Region. They had allegedly travelled to their homes in the East to be counted in order to swell the population of the East and decrease that of the North.[89] This is, in fact, a serious problem posed by the regionalization of the interests and loyalties of the citizens. A person whose parents are from the North, East, or West, who was born in another region, remains a member of his parents original region. During this period 'aliens' in the North were not allowed to own land, and they were only employed on contracts. In fact, they remained strangers in parts of their own country. The question was, should they be counted in a region where they were treated like strangers without any right to be represented in the regional legislature? This is but one of the questions posed by the move towards regional autarchy, which had culminated in the 1954 Consitution of Nigeria.

Even the Chief Census Officer of the federation was alleged to be involved in this game of manipulating the census figures. The publication of the census figures by the Chief Census Oficer was unduly delayed - in fact, they were never officially published. In the meantime, the air was rife with rumors that Southern and Northern politicians were trying to tamper with the census figures. Each region accused the other of trying to inflate the census in order to gain more representation at the central level.[90]

The *Daily Times,* a relatively non-partisan paper, wrote an editorial expressing concern that:

> There had been conflicting and distrubing specualtions concerning the national census held in May this year. The specualtions do not inspire confidence. First is the fact that six months after the census was held, the results have not been announced..."[91]

The paper noted that, without any doubt, the whole matter was disappointing. It urged the Prime Minister to "reassure the nation that the figures were not any way being mishandled."[92] The Minister of Economic Development had said in the House of Representatives that they contained inaccuracies and that he would not revise false figures; that if there was no way to arrive at a reasonably accurate figure, the only alternative would be to repeat the process all over.[93] But up until December 5, 1962, when the federal House of Representatives was called into session, no action had been taken to resolve the issue. Secret negotiations had taken place between the federal Minister of Economic Development, the Premiers of the East and the North, and the Administrator of the Western Region. Both East and West agreed initially to a verification of the census figures. The North agreed with the proviso that the verification would be in selected areas and confined only to a simple head count.[94]

Both the East and the West balked at the agreement and the attempt proved abortive. In spite of obvious and publicized mismanagement of the institutional machinery of the census, the regional governments were able to overawe the center and impede the attempt. The North, for obvious reasons, allowed the minister to carry out verification. Of course, the federal minister, being a member of the party in power in the North, had the fully cooperation of the region. The minister, however, did not complete his verification before the meeting of the federal House of Assembly on December 5, 1962. He, therefore, read the report which the Chief Census Officer had prepared in July. He emphasized that the figures from the East had been inflated. The report touched off a lively, and largely acrinomious, debate in the house.

The opposition parties, consisting of the Action Group from the Western Region and the United Middle Belt Congress, a party composed of minor ethnic groups in the North, called for a debate on the report. The National Council of Nigerian Citizens, which formed the ruling coalition at the center with the Northern People's Congress, endorsed the call for a debate. The lines were drawn between all these parties and the Northern People's Congress. The speaker, however, denied the request; thereupon, all members of the parties who had called for the debate walked out of the house except the NCNC members of the coalition cabinet. A full-blown crisis crystalized around the census issue.

The Eastern Region and the Northern Region were the chief protagonists; attacks and counterattacks were traded; insults were hurled freely. As Dr. Aluko observed:

> It looked as if the census controversy would split the nation asunder. The charged situation was relieved when the Prime Minister (himself the parliamentary leader of the NPC), rebuked the Federal Minister of Economic Development for accusing the East of inflating the census figures.[95]

While the politicians were at one anothers' throats, conflicting reports on the census multiplied. The federal Ministry of Information issued a tract entitled, "One Hundred Facts People Must Know."[96] This tract was distributed to the senators. In the tract the 1962 census figures were given as follows:

Northern Nigeria - 22.5 million
Eastern Nigeria - 12.3 million
Western Nigeria - 8.0 million[97]

This tract was strictly a part of the attempt of the Ministry of Information to brief the senators and was not intended as an official publication of the census figures. The 1962 census figures were never officially published. But, no sooner was this tract in the senators' hands, when the *Daily Times* reported that there was a disagreement among the federal cabinet members on the census figures. It stated that the Chief Census Officer has been eased out of his job and that new figures had been submitted to the cabinet as the final figures. The paper quoted the following figures:

> Northern Nigeria - 30 million
> Eastern Nigeria - 12 million
> Western Nigeria - 10 million[98]

It was patently clear that verification of the Northern figures by the federal Minister of Economic Development had led to an increase in that figure of nearly 8 million. This action was not calculated to restore public confidence in the impartiality of the federal decision making process. As James O'Connell observed: "Nothing so much proved the weakness of constitutionalism in the country as the effort which both governments and communities put into inflating their returns."[99] The Minister of Economic Development had said that: "the impression of the manner in which a country conducts its affairs is one of the factors which earn for it the respect or disrespect of the rest of the world."[100] But it is clear from the result of his verification of Northern census figures that whatever his personal opinion, he was not able to transcend the regional barriers. He had, after all, been appointed federal minister because the party in power in his region controlled the federal cabinet. Whatever his personal qualities, he owed his position not to the nation as such, but to his region. And on the scale of precedence, the interest of that region had primacy over any national consideration. His verification showed an increase of 8 million in the census figure of the Northern Region.[101]

The crisis had intensified and the nation waited for a solution from its elites. However, the institutionalization of regional autarchy had prevented the emergency of any interest that was national rather than sectional, federal rather than regional, and it is in this context that we must assess the role of the Prime Minister, who was, after all, a deputy leader of the party in power in the Northern Region. Immediately after the meeting of the House of Representatives on the fifth of December, 1962, the parliamentarians of the National Council of Nigerian Citizens, the junior coalition partner in the federal cabinet, had called upon the Prime Minister to set up a census committee. The committee was to include representatives of all the regional governments in the federation to decide on what principles and procedures should be adopted for verification of the census results. They also urged him to assume full responsibility for the conduct of the census.[102]

The Prime Minister had come to the conclusion that further verification of the census results beyond those attempted earlier would be futile. He, therefore, decided to scrap the whole 1962 census results and order a new census. There was a perceptible sigh of relief throughout the nation. The Daily Times endorsed the decision and expressed the mood of the nation when it commented that:

> We need hardly emphasize the dangers we would have been exposed to, both at home and abroad, were we to insist on parading the discredited figures. We fully endorse the taking over by the Prime Minister of complete control of the new census.[103]

Nevertheless, census taking falls constitutionally within the concurrent jurisdications of the federal and regional governments. Personal leadership qualities notwithstanding, the institutional machinery precludes the Prime Minister's exercise of real and effective control. He set up a census board, composed of representatives of the federal and regional governments, with himself as chairman. However, regional politicians had learned that elections and representation could be won or lost on the census rolls. So intense was the regional antagonism aroused by the census, that it was unrealistic to expect the new census taking to be uneventful. The events surrounding the 1963 census bear this out.

The 1963 Census Enumeration

Under the chairmanship of the Prime Minister, the Central Census Board set out to plan a new census enumeration throughout the Federation of Nigeria. The federal government budgeted the sum of 2.5 million pounds for the conduct of the census. Each region was to plan and execute the census operation within its own territory. The census board arranged for inspectors recruited in one region to be sent to another region to conduct sample surveys and check the returns of the enumerators in that region. It was decided that when the enumerations were completed and forwarded to Lagos, a demographic test would be used to verify the results. The operation was to be carried out from November 5 to November 8, and was to consist of a head count.[104]

The preparations took place in an atmosphere of cooperation and calm; the enumeration started off without incident. But the presence of a team of inspectors from other regions was bound to create incidents and sharpen antagonisms. One of these incidents deserves comment as it reveals one of the causes of friction which was deeply felt, but rarely expressed. In the North, women were, by tradition, confined in purdah - an enclosure where they were secluded from public observation - and were not allowed to vote. During the census of 1963, a team of observers from the Eastern Region insisted on entering the purdah to watch the counting of women. This was interpreted as gross insensitivity to the religious sentiments of the Northerners; nevertheless, the count was completed without major incident. Preliminary results were published in February, 1964. The figures were very similar to those of the 1962 census:

>North - 29,777,968
>West - 10.2 million
>Midwest - 2.5 million
>East - 12,811,837
>Lagos Territory - 657,352

The total population for Nigeria was given as 55,653,821. It is interesting to note that percentagewise the North and the South maintained the same ratio as they had after the 1952 census - the population ratio maintained a curious balance for 11 years. The North contained 53.4 percent of the Nigerian population while the Southern regions taken together accounted for 46.6 percent. Within a decade the total population of Nigeria had increased by 74 percent. The percentage increases of regional populations were as follows:

>Northern Region - 67 percent
>Eastern Region - 65 percent
>Western Region - 100 percent

Of all the regions, only the East returned the same figures that were given in the 1962 census. The other regions showed marked increases in population within one year. Table 1, below illustrates this point.

TABLE 1

COMPARISON OF 1962 AND 1963 CENSUS FIGURES

	1962 Census	1962 Revised Figures	1963 Census Figures
North	22.5 million	31.0 million	28.8 million
East	12.4 million	12.3 million	12.4 million
West	7.8 million	7.8 million	10.3 million

Midwest	2.2 million	2.2 million	2.5 million
Lagos	0.7 million	0.7 million	0.7 million
Totals:	45.6 million	54.0 million	55.7 million

SOURCE:

Walter Schwarz, *Nigeria,* Frederick Praeger, 1968, p. 163. As both the 1962 original and revised figures were not published officially, figures given by various sources differ. We decided to follow Walter Schwarz, because it gives the most complete analysis of the figures so far seen by us.

The reaction by the Southern politicians and Northern minorities was swift and negative.[105] Like the 1962 census, it gave rise to intra-party and inter-regional conflict and controversy. The census board was compelled by the furor over the census to send teams of statisticians to undertake spotchecks of selected areas of each constituency in all the regions. This check, known as the demographic test, uses certain indicators to check the reliability and extent of the irregularities in the census figures. The table below (Table 2) shows the result of this demographic test.

TABLE 2

DEMOGRAPHIC TEST OF THE 1963 CENSUS FIGURES

Regions	Constituencies	Number That Passed The Test	Number That Failed Part of the Test	Number Failed All the Tests
North	175	99	77	49
East	73	53	20	5
West	47	20	27	10
Mid-West	15	8	7	3

Source: *West African Pilot,* February 29, 1964

These tests show that the census figures were inflated in all the regions. There is no evidence to suggest that inflation of the figures was not prevalent throughout the federation even from the onset of the census enumeration in 1962. The fact that Mr. Warren, the Chief Federal Census Officer, first noted in his report that the figures from the Eastern Region were grossly inflated does not of itself prove that inflation of the census figures occurred only in the Eastern Region.[106] In the first place enumeration was still going on in the West and Northern Regions and no verification of the figures had been undertaken even in those areas that showed unusual increase. Moreover, the results from the West were not even completed, as the report clearly indicated. He noted that of the 62 census districts, only five had turned in provisional total figures.[107] There was no attempt here to justify any of the regional figures.

Regionalization of rights, loyalties, and privileges made it difficult to transcend regional particularism. Mackintosh noted the case of one junior official from the North who allowed himself to be counted six times.[108] To him it was a show of loyalty to the region in its competition against other regions. The unrelenting drive toward regional autarchy had warped any objective approach to the census problem. For example, during the 1963 census enumeration, the census board had selected certain areas where a sample count of about one-thirteenth of a district was to be made by a team of two census inspectors - one from the home region and one from another region. These sample areas were to be kept secret because a surprise check was more likely to reveal any trace of inflation. It was alleged that "the areas to be sampled were disclosed to the North long before the census took place." [109]

The census board issued a bulletin stating that:

> We wish also to point out that it is the feeling of one or two members that the timing of the release of information regarding the identity of enumeration areas to be sampled was unfortunate in the sense that it could have afforded a great deal of opportunity for unfair practice to anyone who might be so inclined. We must add, however, that so far, the Board has had no conclusive evidence in this direction even though one or two members have expressed serious misgivings.[110]

The attempt by the Premier of the Eastern Region to denounce the census results and seek their cancellation called forth counterreactions from the Premier of the Northern Region. He announced that the census "had been properly and efficiently conducted and that no better organization could have been made."[111] In the meantime, the Premier of the Eastern Region had summoned a meeting of the top members of his party, the National Council of Nigerian Citizens (NCNC), to discuss the possibility of cancelling the census. On the same day of this meeting in Enugu, the Premier of the Northern Region summoned the leaders of his party, the Northern People's Congress (NPC), to Kaduna. As a result of this meeting the NPC came out with a statement that, "it is the intention of the Government of Northern Nigeria to proceed to work" with the census figures "for the purpose of planning..." and that "as soon as possible a delimitation commission will be appointed"[112] to demarcate constituencies for the purpose of regional representation. The Western Region came out in support of the Northern viewpoint; the newly created Midwest Region reluctantly fell in line, [113] and the 1964 census figures with all their limitations became official.

The preeminence of regional power and loyalty was dramatized by the census crisis. The center was completely immobilized; the regions over-awed the center. Not only where the functionaries at the center, including the Prime Minister, deputies of the political parties in power in the regions, they were subordinates in the party hierarchy. Thus, although the center had concurrent jurisdiction over the census, its functionaries, being subordinates to the regional political leaderships, could not in practice assert their independence of that leadership and exercise any jurisdiction in the interest of the federation as a whole.

It is, therefore, the nature of the institutional arrangement that determined the character, scope, and circumstances of the conflict. Once the institutional machinery had failed to mediate the conflict, other ramifications emerged and exacerbated the conflict. It is under such conditions that individual and ethnic considerations entered into the calculation. The part played by ethnicity in the census conflict and crisis is illustrative. The attacks on the 1952-1953 census were subdued and were directed against the colonial power sturcture. It was alleged that the British had favored the North because the North was more favorably disposed toward the Brithsh. The conflict over the 1962 census had pronounced ethnic overtones. As we noted, four out of five divisions in the Eastern Region which showed unusual increases in population figures were in ethnic minority areas. There are two possible explanations for this: 1) due to pronounced local opposition to the 1953 census, these areas were seriously under counted by the British officials; or 2) as Post and Vickers suggested, the minorities inflated the figures because they 'tended to feel themselves at a disadvantage relative to the Ibos,'"[114] who constituted the largest ethnic group in the region.

Among the Yorubas, in the Western Region, intra-ethnic conflict materially affected the conduct of the 1962 census. The non-civil service census staff who were sympathetic to the Action Group during the 1962 Western Regional crisis were relieved of their posts by the rival Akintola faction.[115] Some of the census staff who retained their posts were unwilling to cooperate with the administrator appointed to the region. After the parliament was dissolved due to intra-ethnic conflict, not only was the enumeration in the Western Region unduly delayed, but there is no doubt that the results were not free from taint. An enumeration conducted under a state of emergency, even when the enumerators and supervisors are cooperative, can hardly be accurate.

At the central legislature the conflict surrounding the 1962 census was complicated by a multitude of conflicting considerations. Although the Northern People' Congress (NPC), which was in power in the North, saw the conflict as a North-South confrontation, ethnic minority parties in the North, such as the United Middle Belt Congress (UMBC), condemned the census in no uncertain terms.[116] In fact, the UMBC party members walked out of the federal legislature with members of the Action Group and the NCNC backbenchers.

The crisis surrounding the 1964 census also developed pronounced Ibo-Hausa overtones. In November, 1963, while preparations were being made for the 1964 elections, the President of the Republic, Dr. Nnamdi Azikiwe, toured the North. During his tour he was inundated with petitions from Southerners, a vast majority of whom were Ibos from the North. The petitions alleged that they were being evicted from their homes because of the conflict over the census between the NCNC and the NPC. Some who owned businesses were said to have been forced out of them and specifically asked by the regional government to surrender their businesses under the "Northernalization policy."[116] As soon as the census results were published, the conflict took on an intensely ethnic and personal cast. Dr. Okpara, an Ibo, the Premier of the Eastern Region, detailed his charges against the North, pointing out specific cases of irregularities uncovered by the Eastern team of observers who were mostly Ibos.

The Prime Minister of the Northern Region replied in kind. He charged the team of Ibo observerss "with wholesale acts of deception and sabotage."[117] In the Northern House of Assembly, some members demanded punitive action against the Ibos for their challenge of the Northern census figures. They urged that the Ibos in regional public service - most of whom were on contracts - be dismissed without delay. It was specifically stated that "certificates allowing Ibos to occupy plots of land should be revoked and that mercantile houses should be given a time limit within which to dismiss all Ibos."[118] Because the NCNC which was controlled by the Ibos had challenged the validity of the Northern census figures, a member of the Northern House of Assembly, Mallam Maude Ahmadu Sidi Gyani, representing Zaria Southwest, disclosed that he was planning to use his position as district head of that area "to draft all native authority policemen under his authority to deal with the Ibos." Various measures were suggested by the members to exclude the Ibos from all business ventures in the North as retribution for their attack on the Northern census figures. Self-interest, rather than any feeling of common nationality, prevented the official implementation of these measures. As mackintosh pointed out:

> Feelings were rising to such heights that some officials became alarmed and pointed out to the Premier that at this stage in the development of the North a mass exodus of Southerners would have a crippling effect. As a result, the Sardauna made a statement in the Northern House of Chiefs urging that no unilateral action should be taken against non-Northerners living in the Region.[120]

But, of course, one the forces of hate and recrimination are let loose, it is hard to call the enraged to sanity and calm. By the following day, after the attacks on the Ibos in the Northern House of Assembly, more than 2,000 Ibos in Kano alone had been expelled from their market stalls. There was spontaneous, seemingly uncoordinated evictions of Ibos from Gusau, Funtua, and Katsina. Rumors spread that this was only the beginning of the complete elimination of Ibos from the North. Faced with this imminent threat, a delegation of Ibos from various parts of the North, especially from Kano, Kaduna, and Zaria, went to the President of the Federation to urge immediate action. The President, himself an Ibo, urged them to seek remedies in the courts. It was obvious that in the face of political action connived at, if not backed by the Northern Emirs and representatives, the courts were powerless to ensure fairness and equity. The chairman of the NCNC Working Committee, Dr. Mbanugo, sent an urgent telegram to the Prime Minister, Sir Abubakar, pressing for immediate intervention. The Prime Minister tersely replied that he had no notice of any eviction and asked the chairman to substantiate his allegation. Of course, the Prime Minister, as Deputy leader of the NPC, could not, even if he wished, force his party leadership to change a course of action which was completely consonant with the party ideology of North for the Northerners.

Thus, contrary to the assumption of many scholars that the mass expulsion of Ibos from the North had been a spontaneous reaction to the military coup d'etat of 1966, there had been an earlier intention, following the census controversy of 1962, if not a plan, to diminish, or even eliminate Ibo presence in the North. The underlying cause is partly economic and partly political. The drive toward regional autarchy and the NPC motto of North for the Northerners could not but lead to a situation in which the political elites would seek to control the economic life of the region. Regional autonomy cannot become a reality unless the means of production and distribution are squarely in the hands of the regional elite. Moreover, the most effective means of eliminating the Eastern Region from the power struggle at the center was by destroying its economic base. Nothing could be calculated to produce this effect better than a mass repartiation of Easterners and the consequent dislocation of their economy. The census controversy served as a pretext.

The census controversy, therefore, brought conflict between the East and the North one step closer to the eventual confrontation which came with the military coup d'etat of 1966. The scenario of that conflict had been visible from the census controversy of 1964. One of the root causes of the confrontation was that, by virtue of sheer numbers, the North was more powerful than all the other regions combined. Any threat to its numerical superiority was viewed as a threat to its very survival and unleashed a retributive reaction. It is only too true, as B.J. Dudley observed, that:

> The domination of the center, which the NPC's monopoly practices ensured, rests on the North's overall representational majority and it was the determined effort of the North to preserve this majority which caused the census crisis of 1964.[121]

Representation at the center is extremely important since the center is the final clearing house for issues that are of particular importance to Nigeria as a whole. However, few scholars have alluded to the significance of the census figures with regard to revenue allocation among the regions. The Hicks-Phillipson Report of 1950 noted that:

> The population of Nigeria and of its component Regions is a subject peculiarly relevant to our enquiry for the reason that the representatives of the Northern Region both in the regional and General Conference demanded that the available non-declared revenue of Nigeria should be divided between the regions in proportion to their populations.[123]

It cannot be doubted that as far back as 1950 the North had developed a financial interest in ensuring that the census reflect a figure which would support its claims for more revenue. As far back as 1950, Hicks, and Phillipson warned that census-taking in Nigeria would not be easy because of the financial and political interest which the North had in population figures.

The politicization of the cnesus complicated the Nigerian experiment in census-taking. It was not without reason that immediately after the Supreme Court threw out the Eastern Governments' motion that the census figures be invalidated, a revenue allocation review board was set up in an election year. The Binns Commission on Fiscal Review was set up in 1964 before the elections and just as the storm over the census was dying down. The following allocation which it recommended is understandab-

66

ble in terms of the 1963 census figures. It recommended that each year the federal government should allocate to the regions 8.75 million pounds which should be divided as follows:

>Northern Region 2.0 million pounds
>
>Western Region 0.60 million pounds
>
>Eastern Region 0.80 million pounds
>
>Midwest Region 0.35 million pounds[124*]

Here it can be seen that the census crisis exacerbated the revenue allocation crisis. These in turn reinforced the crisis over the 1964 election. The combination of these three issues produced the storm that wrecked the foundation of the Nigerian Federation. The census crisis, however, was by far the most important of these concurrent and reinforcing crises, for on it depended the final outcome of the other two.

CHAPTER 5

CONFLICT OVER REVENUE ALLOCATION IN NIGERIA, 1946

Although the conflict over revenue allocation had been one of the principal causes of the collapse of the First Republic in Nigeria, this important issue has received scant attention from scholars of the Nigerian political scene. It is, therefore, the purpose of this section to illustrate how the institutional arrangements for revenue allocation complicated and in large measure inhibited the growth of economic and poltical interdependence among the various regions between 1946 and 1964.

"Budget," accoring to Aaron Wildavsky, lies at the heart of the political process."[1] In Nigeria, in particular, political conflicts are further complicated by the problem of ways and means of attaining the institutional objectives resulting from the various constitutional arrangements. This is not peculiar to Nigeria. On examining the economic basis of the American Constitution, Charles Beard remarked that:

> ...many fathers of the constitution regarded the conflict over the constitution as springing essentially out of conflict of ecomomic interest which had certain geographical or sectional distribution.[2]

Beard's statement applies with greater force and cogency to the conflict over the Nigerian Constitution. The issues in Nigeria were complicated by the difficulties of reconciling the policy of maximum regional autonomy with the delicate flexibility in fiscal matters required to ensure a spirit of interdependence necessary for the success of a federal structure in a pluralistic society such as Nigeria.

There is no doubt that effective regional autonomy is absolutely essential for the survival of a federal structure. It is crucial to the success of a federation that regional rights and identities be safeguarded. But there must also be a clear understanding of the advantages issuing from mutual interdependence and from a healthy balance of the strengths and weaknesses of the participating units particularly in economic and manpower needs. The balancing of these needs is indeed the very underpinning of the sense community and mutual responsiveness critical to the success of any federal experiment.[3]

But the states cannot develop this mutual responsiveness unless the political institutions designed to mediate their political interaction are similar. In fact, K.C. Wheare singled out similarity of political institutions as "one of the strongest of the forces which help states to work together."[4] In Nigeria, on the other hand, the British who had the primary responsibility for deciding the format of the institutional framework of Nigeria decided on differential incorporation of the various units that made up the country. In a dispatch to the British Secretary of States, Sir Arthur Richards, the Governor of Nigeria in 1944, outlined the basis for the constitutional advance of Nigeria as follows:

> "The problem in Nigeria. . .is how to create a political system. . .a system within which the diverse elements may progress at varying speeds amicably and smoothly towards a more closely integrated economic, social and political unity without sacrificing the principles and ideals inherent in their divergent ways of life. . .I propose to devolve upon the regional councils (to be created under the Richard's Constitution of 1947) a large measure of fiscal responsibility. . ."[5]

The idea of each region developing at "varying speeds" without sacrificing "the principles and ideals inherent in their divergent ways of life" forstalled the development of institutions with common values in economic as well as in political fields. In fact, Nigera never really existed as an organic unit interacting and interchanging such benefits and responsibility as would foster a sense of community. As Margery Perham noted, the union of the different regions into one Nigeria in 1914 "was a union of three British administrations rather than three populations. For another thirty years or more there was not British policy from above or African pressure from below to stimulate a real unity."⁶ It was, therefore, idle t expect a closely integrated economy and similarity of political institutions without a conscious effort on the part of the British who controlled the administration of the three regions.

Furthermore, the devolution on each region of a large mearsure of fiscal responsibility to enable it to develop at its own pace accentuated the spirit of competition among the participating units, this policy of resolution stifled the spirit of mutual cooperation and mutual responsiveness necessary for the development of a sense of community among the participating units in a federation.

The very fact that emphasis was on separate development and the devolution of power and resources from the central government to the states and not on contribution of resources and the surrender of certain powers by the states to the federal government removed the element of common enterprise and common sacrifice in pursuit of a common aim. It precluded that common endeavor to "balance goals and capabilities" involved in the estblishment of a viable federation out of a plurality of states.

The result was that each region strove to maximize the resources for it sown separate development; thus, emphasis was on sharing of resources. The eventual outcome of this emphasis on sharing was that the revenue allocation issue became essentially one of financial administration between the regions unencumbered by any thought of interdependence between them or the viability and strength of the federal structure. In fact, Sir, Sydney Phillipson, the British financial secretary in Nigeria, saw this tendency to treat the revenue issue as one of financial administration as the main source of contention. He observed that "much of the debate (over revenue allocation) in Nigeria has been confused and unreal because the issues have been over simplified and the over simplification arises largely from a tendency to regard the problem as one of financial administration.⁸

Certainly, all revenue allocation involves to some extent an element of financial administration. But in a federation the problem is complicated by the requirement that both the regional and federal government must possess enough resources to perform their specific functions. The problem of adjusting the balance between resources and function; between the competing needs of the different regions and the federation as a whole, is indeed a difficult one. The factors impinging on an equitable allocation of scarce revenue for the performance of functions cannot be weighed in the nice balance of the jeweller's scale. Even if this was possible, it is more than likely that the cost of the discharge of these functions would not keep pace with regional financial capabilities. As the Australian Commonwealth Grant Commission said in its first annual report in 1934:

> "It is impossible in a federation nicely to adjust the functions entrusted to the members to their financial resources; some members may have more financial power than actually needed, and another less. Consequently, some adjustment may have to be made in the form of a redistribution of the revenue from the more favoured to the less fortunate member of members of the union."⁹

Adjustment is therefore the key element in the craft of federal financing. Consequently, the level of efficiency and effectiveness of the institutional mechanism for adjusting the allocation in a federation determines to a large extent the nature of conflict or cooperation not only in fiscal matters but also in the social, cultural and political fields. J. R. Hicks, one of the architects of the Nigerian Revenue Allocation System, was certainly correct when he said:

> "The stress and strain within the body politic are naturally much more severe when in addition to the conflict between the parties normal in

democratic community there is also the possibility of sharp conflicts of interest between the states making up the federation: for the proper working of the Federal Institutions (emphasis mine). These observations are apposite to the political circumstances of Nigeria and not the least to the vital constitutional question of the division of revenue."[10]

The constitutional question of the division of revenue in Nigeria has a long and tortuous history dating from the amalgamation of Northern and Southern Nigeria in 1914. Jeremy Raisman, one of the many fiscal commissioners appointed to study the problem, pointed out in 1958 after a careful examination of the issues that the division of revenue between the various parts of Nigeria posed a recurrent problem since the amalgamation of the North with the South in 1914.[11] In reality it was the revenue issue which was the overriding factor in the decision to amalgamate the two sections. This point was underscored by the chief secretary of the Nigerian government when he said in a legislative council debate that

"Northern Nigeria was amalgamated to Southern Nigeria because, quite openly stated, Southern Nigeria was rich"[12]

This history of revenue allocation in Nigeria from 1914 to 1946 is outside the scope of this research.[13] But a statement from the Governor of Nigeria, Sir Bernard Bourdillon suggest that the problem was essentially the problem of lack of clear institutional guidelines. He stressed in 1935 that:

"the whole question of the distribution of income and expenditure between the government and the native administrations is an exceedingly difficult one. At the moment we are proceeding haphazardly with very little in the way of recognized principle to guide us. It rather looks to me as if the time has come for an organized enquiry with the object of laying down at any rate a few principles by which we can be guided in the future.[13a]

Phillipson Commission

Such an enquiry was never conducted until 1946. In that year the British had made a decision to introduce a new constitution (eventually called the Richards Constitution) into Nigeria. As part of the preparation of the ground work for the new constitution Sir Sydney Phillipson, a British colonial official, was appointed in 1946, to formulate the financial procedure required to meet the needs of the institutional provision to be made under the Richards Constitution. His task was to determine: (a) "what items of revenue other than the regional share of direct tax should be declared regional" and (b) "the basis of allocation of the available non-declared revenues to regions."[14] Sir Sydney Phillipson's first task was to define what revenue could be declared regional. Those items of revenue which were not classed as regional would constitute the non-declared revenue.
He laid down the principle that an item of revenue to be declared regional must "be identifiable with the region and locally collected by regional authorities." Furthermore, that the revenue must be one "in respect of which no national or important consideration of policy " is "likely to arise"[15] such as fees and licences. The non-declared revenues were defined as customs duties, company taxes and certain revenues which were clearly without geographical origin (e.g., interest)."[16] The crucial task which faced the Phillipson Commission was how to allocate the available non-declared revenues to the several regions. Two questions were uppermost in Phillipson,s mind. One was whether to allocate the available non-declared revenue to the region on the principle of derivation. Under this principle each region would rec eive a share of the available non-declared revenue in proportion to its contribution to that item of revenue. The other question was whether to apportion the available non-declared

revenue on the principle *of even* progress.[17] This principle, as defined by Phillipson, dictated that the available non-declared revenue be apportioned to the region in proportion to their needs and that the population of each region should be the indicator of the extent of need. The commissioner was not totally unaware of the consequences for the two policies he was contemplating. 'He was fully conscious that the integration, advancement, and harmony of 'Nigeria, as a whole, would be enhanced by a fiscal policy which would facilitate even development and enhance the progress of the various regions.[18] He was equally aware that the principle of derivation would undermine the feeling of interdependence and accentuate the differences in the rates of development of these regions. But the very policy which underlay the proposed Richards Constitution had contemplated "a system within which the diverse elements may progress at varying speeds amicably and smoothly..."[19] The constraint of policy dictated that the principle adopted should be one of uneven development. The main objective of that policy was neither fiscal adequacy nor fiscal autonomy for the regions. It was intended to be practical training in fiscal management.[20] This point was emphasized by Phillipson as follows:

> If, as is obviusly desirable, a sense of financial responsibility is to be inculated into the new regional councils...it is clear that the scale of expenditure on regional purposes in each region ought to be related to the amount which that region contributes to the rvenue as a whole

He further reasoned that:

> All revenues available for regional purposes, whether declared regional or not, will be voted to the regions by the Nigerian Legislative Council; it follows that so long as this holds good, the position of the regions is analogous to that of the "housekeeper" who is provided with an amount in no way fixed by her, for running the house to the best advantage possible within such an amount. This is an important but limited responsibility...[21]

What was, in fact, intended by the proposed Richards Constitution in 1946 was a measure of administrative decentralization under which the regional councils would have only the power to review the annual and supplementary budgets. All revenues available for the discharge of the functions assigned to the regions must be voted to the regions by the Legislative Council of Nigeria.

Taking all the above mentioned factors into consideration, Sir Phillipson proposed that block grants from the available non-declared revenue should be assigned to the various regions on the "principle of derivation" (that is in proportion to their direct contribution to the central revenue of 'Nigeria). Once this basic decision had been reached, the crucial question for the commissioner became one of finding the necesary criteria which would enable him to assess with a measure of accuracy the correct contribution of each region to the central revenue.

After examing the statistics of the trade turnover for the year 1946 supplied by the major companies operating in Nigeria (mostly expatriate firms) he prescribe a formula[22] for computing the relative contribution of the three regions to the non-declared revenues of 'Nigeria. On the basis of this formula he stated that in terms of percentage the relative proportion of revenue contributed by the three regions to the total non-declared revenue of Nigeria as of 1946 stood as follows:

Northern Region - 46%

Western Region - 30%

Eastern Region - 24%

He than compared these figures, derived from his formual, with the percentages of expenditure on regional services which, in the same year (1946), stood as follows:

$$\text{Northern Region - 36\%}$$

$$\text{Western Region - 26\%}$$

$$\text{Eastern Region - 38\%}$$

As a result of this comparison, he observed that the Northern Region was contributing more and spending less, the Western Region a little less, while the Eastern Region was contributing less and spending more. He suggested that little could be done to adjust current service to mirror the relative contribution of each region because it would cause severe disruption of existing services, particularly in the Eastern Region. Consequently, he recommended that his formula should be regarded as the "ideal percentage" and as a guide for the future allocation of the available undeclared revenue of 'Nigeria among the regions.[23]

In the meantime, he recommended that an adjustment should be made in capital grants to ensure that the Northern Region was given a share "less disproportionate to its contribution to the non-declared revenue of Nigeria."[24] His recommendation also urged that a Revenue Board should be creatd to ensure that "the interest of Nigeria as a whole is given due weitht in the allocation of revenues and other public funds for Nigerian and regional expenditure;" 'It would also be the objective of the board "to achieve as early as may be and, in any event, within a period of five years, a condition of things in which it will be possible to allocate to each region for expenditure on regional services and works: (a) the full amount of government share of the tax collected under the Direct Tax Ordinance, 1940 (as subsequently amended), and all other revenues declared rgional; (b) a grant from the other revenues of Nigeria not included in (a) above or from the other public funds of Nigeria in strict proportion to the contribution which the region makes to those other revenues."[25]

These recommendations were embodied in the Statement of Administrative and Financial Procedure and annexed to the Richards Constitution of 1947.

The Phillipson Report has been criticized on several grounds. R.J. May observed that Phillipson could not reconcile the principle of even progress with the principle of derivation, and "came down in favor of the principle of derivation."[26] Dr. Adedeji, on the other hand, noted that "stsrict adherence to the principle of derivation" had bben "relegated from an immediate objective to an ultimate objective over a five year period."[27] It was not so much that Phillipson was unable to reconcile the two principles; rather, he was clearly aware that the unity of Nigeria would be enhanced if a way could be found to cushion the harsh impact of the application of the principle of derivation. His suggestion that the application of the principle of derivation should be spread over a period of five years was intended to soften its impact.

The report also came in for a good deal of criticism on statistical grounds. On these grounds it was certainly vulnerabvle to the charge that the statistics fo a tolorably accurate determination of the contribution of the various regions to the non-declared revenue of Nigeria were either non-existgent of hopelessly inaccurate in this areas where they existed. The following quotation from P.N.C. Okigbo represents the tenor the criticism:

> The first step in the solution of this problem was statistical and concerned the determination of the non-declared revenues. In the then known state of data, this task could not be immediately and satisfactorily fulfilled."[28]

Whatever may be said about the Phillipson Report, it must be admitted that it was the first realistic attempt to create policies and institutions for revenue allocation between the various regions of Nigeria and the central government. Furthermore, the elasticity of his proposal is borne out by the fact that in 1948-49 and 1950-51 it was modified to give room for an element of a principle which took into account the needs of the various regions.[29] While it is true, as Adedeji stated, that Sir Phillipson's most enduring contribution to the development of federal finance in Nigeria was his recommendation, "that revenue allocation should ultimately conform to the principle of derivation,"[30] it must not be forgotten that he was devising an institution for revenue allocation in which the power of the purse would reside in a colonial power center. The degree of decentralization that was envisaged was a far cry from that of a federal structure. It was, indeed, a highly decentralized unitary system in which each component unit was, according to settled British policy, to develop at its own pace.[31]

In fact, the problem with the Phillipson Commission Report was that the pace of political developments in Nigeria rendered the policy on which it was based obsolete and, therefore, made the recommendation impracticable. The mounting criticism of the provisions of the Richards Constitution led eventually to a decision in 1950 that a new constitution should be drawn up to replace it. The debate over the proposed constitution raised anew the problem of revenue allocation between the component regions of Nigeria. The Northern Region based its argument on the findings of the Phillipson Commission and complained that it was contributing more and getting less from the revenue of Nigeria.

Mallan Tafawa Balewa (later Sir Abubakar Tafawa Balewa) stressed the point in the proceedings of the General Conference on the review of the constitution held in Ibadan in 1950. He pointed out that until 1947 the North was not represented in the legislative council which made laws for Nigeria. However, in 1947 when the northerners became members of the legislative council they began to understand the situation and to "ask the *government* (emphasis mine) why this unfair distribution of revenue" and what were the basis for the allocation to the various regions.[32]

The simple fact was that the colonial government in Nigeria had no definite policy for the allocation of revenues to the various regions until the Phillipson Commission Report of 1946. It was equally true that although both the southwest and the southeast were represented in the old legislative council they had no voice in the fiscal policy of the government. Yet it was this very colonial government which publicized the fact that the revenue had been unfairly allocated. In an address to the Colonial Affairs Study Group of the Empire 'Parliamentary Association, Sir Arthur Richards, the Governor of Nigeria, at that time, said:

> "I found that the North, which pays its taxes almost as obediently as people do in England, and which contribute more than any other section of Nigeria to the general revenue, is the part of Nigeria which had the least spent on it by the central government. The eastern provinces, the part of Nigeria which is most vocal and which clamours and calls for more education and for more of everything is the part which contributes less that the other two regions to the general revenue, and it is also the part upon which the government has been spending the most."[33]

There is some truth in the statement that the Eastern Region was under-going a vigorous expansion in the educational field. But much of the credit for this expansion was due to the work of voluntary agencies and enterprising individuals. Whatever might have been the merits of the statment, its adverse impact on the political future of Nigeria cannot be overestimated. Of all the incentives for any form of amalgamation of political units, "widespread expection of joint reward for the participating units through strong economic ties,"[34] is by far the strongest. Once this expectation of joint economic reward is caled into question, the participants begin to reassess their commitment to an association which would benefit others at their expense. This concern is clearly articulated by Mallam Tafawa Balewa in the following statement:

> Now we were told now and again that the overall interest of Nigeria must be considered. That is to say, the Eastern Provinces and the Western Provinces who cannot supply the funds for their own development must use funds from the North to develop their areas."[35]

For this reason the Northern Region demanded that in the future allocation of revenue should be on per capita basis. And sine the estimated population of Nigveria gave the North more than 50 per cent of the population of Nigeria, the North hoped to get more than 50 per cent of the available non-declared revenue. Because of the opposition of the two Southern Regions this Northern proposal, it was decided that an independent commission should be set up to make recommendations on revenue allocation. The recommendation if accepted by the constitutional review conference would become part of the constitution to be adopted in 1950. Dr. J.R. Hicks, Felow of Nuffield College, Oxford, Sir Sydney Phillipson, the Financial Secretary of Nigeria (British) and Mr. D.A. Skelton, Assistant Deputy Minister of Trade and Commerce to the Government of Canada, were appointed Commissioners, Mr. Skelton was drowned while sailing in Lagos (Nigeria) harbor. The Commission became known as the Hick-Phillipson Co0mmission.

The Hicks-Phillipson Commission: 1951

The Hicks- Phillipson Commiszsion on Revenue Allocation was set up as a part of the process of the review of the Richards Constitution initiated in 1950. The particular objective of the commission was to find solutions to the issues raised by the Phillipson Commission of 1946 which provided the institutional basis for revenue allocation under the Richards Constitution. By publicizing the importance and implications of revenue allocation to the development of the regions, Phillipson extended the frontiers of regional political conflict into the area of revenue allocation. The emphasis on the principle of derivation as the basis or revenue allocation gave a fillip to the concept of regional autonomy and destroyed the will to maximize the collective gain of the regions which is an indispensable objective of political integration.[36] By advocation the deveolution of revenue from the cental gov ernment to the regions it made the extraction of as much revenue as possible from the federal government, a cardinal regional policy and ultimate determinant of that policy.

Thus, the prevelant mood in the discussion at the conference for the review of the Richards Constitution, especially on the revenue issue, was one of drift - drift away from the center and drift away from each other. As C.D. Onyeama, one of the delegates to the conference aptly phrased it;

> Every one is thinking about his Region. Nobody seemed to be concerned for a moment about the Centre. The North want this for the North. The West wants the other for the West and we want this for the East - as for the Centre it can go to the devil. Surely, Mr. Chairman, it would certainly lead to great difficulties in the future...I, myself very much deplore the fact that we have been led in the past six years to think in Regional terms...Now we here in this conference say the North can look after itself, the West can look after itself, the East can look after itself. Surely when (regional) economic development becomes the order of the day we are losing that very link which we look upon as the binding force of Nigeria.[37]

Nobody seemed to care about the center because, at this time (1950), the central institutions were solidly in the hands of the colonial officials. In fact, it was obviously in the interest of the colonial authorities to divert the attention of the politically active elite to regional issues. This interest found expression in the policy enunciated by Sir Arthur Richards that the various regins should be allowes to progress at varying speeds "without sacrificing the principles and ideals inherent to their divergent ways of life."[38] As the regions became the only institutional units within which Africans could organize themselves politically, revenue allocation to the regions became a necessary source for the development of institutionla resources to faciliate such organization. It was common knowledge in British colonial circles, that by pointed reference to equity and fairness in revenue allocation, the attention of the regional elite would be diverted from the important task of establishing a strong federal structure to "the wholly unfruitful question"[39] whether one or another region is "receiving less or more than it ought to receive."[40]

These considerations determined the purpose, scope and tenor of the terms of reference of the Hicks-Phillipson Commission appointed in 1950 by the Conference on the Review of the Richard Constitution to make recommendations on the method of revenue allocation under the proposed constitution (the Macpherson Constitution of 1951).

The commission was empowered to submit proposals for achieving, within a period of five years, a more equitable allocation of revenue between the three regions and the center. Because of the complaint of the Northern Region that it had been unfairly treatd in the past on the issue of revenue allocation, the commission was mandated to investigatge whether any region had been unfairly treated in the past and if its investigation proved that *"one Region has been unfairly treated during past years, that Region should be allowed a block grant so as to make up part of what it has lost"*[41] (emphasis mine). The commission was not only empowered to submit proposals for future allocations of revenue, it was definitely mandated to make grants on its own initiative.

The Hicks-Phillipson Commission first addressed itself to the issue of unfairtreatment, specifically to the complaint by the Northern Region that it had been unfairly treated ov er the years. The commissioners commented that those who placed on them "this particular task cannot have fully understood the real nature and extent of the requirement."[42] It was their considered opinion that Northern Nigeria "must have derived considerable incidental benefits from the devellopment of the coastal districts before amalgamation."[43]

Finally, they characterized the task of investigating unfair treatment as "pointless" since "the problem of equity or fairness can scarcely arise as between political entities until such entities have come into existence."[44] One is, however, left with the nagging suspicion that the issue was raised not because it was amenable to rational solution, but to slow the pace of political development by fostering inter-regional suspicin and conflict. It is an acknowledged fact that "countries (regions) whcih start from a position of relative weakness tend to be suspicious of economic integration for fear of becoming victims of exploitation by the powerful neighbors."[45] The Northern Region has the dubious distinction of being the largest in size and population and yet the least developed educationally (in terms of western education). Consequently, it grew suspicious that withdrawal of British authority would mean the domination of its institutions by the more educationally advanced southerners. Hence, it insisted on complete religional autarchy. Therefore, the nature of the institution for revenue allocation devised by the Hicks-Phillipson Commission was really dictated partly by British interests and partly by the interest of the Northern Region.

Before discussing their recommendatins, however, it is necessary to underscore their underlying assumptions. The commission was given a measure of latitude and urged to "handle the subject broadly and according to its judgement of what might be required to ensure a workable and an acceptable scheme of revenue division."[46]

It was, indeed, a comprehensive report which began with a survey of general principles of federation and federal financing.[47] The commissioners believed that the ultimate objective of the experiments in constitution making in Nigeria would be the establishment of a federal system of govenment, no doubt witn the British in control of

75

the central institutions. They, therefore, state that they were considering questions of revenue allocation "as one aspect of the establishment of a federal constitution in which the main component parts will possess the attributes of stats in a federation including legislative powers over certain fields."[48]

The commissioners further noted as highly significant, the fact that "the new regional councils were based firmly and squarely on the already established Native Administration in Nigeria"[49] and that thus "the most characteristic and important political achievement of British administration in Nigeria, the Native Authority system, was incorporated in the new constitutional structure."[50] They concluded that this incorporation of the naitve authorities"has had ceretain financial consequences relevant to our enquiry."[51]

There was understandably a note of pride in trying to preserve, even in a modified form, a system which symbolized the most charactgeristic and important achievement of British administration in Nigeria. But the problem which faced the commission was how to reconcile the principle of financing native adminstration controlled by the indigenous elite with the principle of federal financing in a federation controlled by the colonial elite. They observed that:

> It is almost a commonplace to say that the question of the fair division of revenues between the component parts of a federal stgate constitutes a fundamental difficulty attaching to this particular type of constitution; even purely unitary states do not entirely escape a difficulty of similar nature. Recognizing this we have tried to set the Nigerian problem of allocation, which possesses local features of unusual difficulty against the general principles of federal-state finance.[52]

The problem facing the Hicks-Phillipson Commission was how to devise a suitable institutional formulation that would meet the peculiar local features of Nigeria - the Native Authority system - and still conform to the standards of federal-regional financing. After deploring the fact that their problem of finding a suitable allocation system "would have been very much easier had the main components of the proposed federal state been less unequal in area and population"[53] the commissioners proceeded to lay ground rules for their recommendations.

Four principles dominated the commissioners' consideraton of the revenue allocation problem in Nigeria. These were: (a) the principles of derivation,[54] (b) the principle of indepenent revenue to ensure the autonomy of the regions in a federation, (c) the principle of need, which would enable the federal government to funnel funds to meet the peculiar needs of certain areas which were those of genuine, proven and urgently needed aid; (d) the principle of national interest, designed to enable the government to expend funds on projects which were of national inportance and which would maximize the collected gains of the federation.[55]

Each of these principles was extensively discussed by the commissioners. However, only a few points which will shed some light on the recommendations of the commission will be mentioned in passing. The principle of derivation came in for a good deal of criticism from the commissioners. They noted that the principle of derivation which dictates that each region receive a share of the available non-declared revenue [56] of the federation in proportion to its contribution to the general revenue was more suitable to a customs union in which the joint administration "is nothing more than an agent of the member states;"[57] that the principle placed undue emphasis on the principle of regional self-dependence "and tended to obscure the equally valid and perhaps more important principle of the needs of the people viewed as citizens of a united Nigeria." They argued that the available non-declared revenues of Nigeria "were the revenues left over after due provision had been made for the Nigeria central services and works." The fact that the central government "had the first cut of the cake," was in their opinion, "open to objection" by the regions, but that objection never did, in fact, materialize."[58] It did not materialize because at this stage (1951) the central government was controlled by the colonial authorities. Eventually, when the central government was controlled by Nigerians in 1960, the fact that the federal government controlled the bulk of the general revenue led to a struggle by the different regional parties for the control the federal instututions because of the institutional resources at its disposal.

The most telling criticism which was leveled on the principle of derivation deserves to be quoted in full:

> For the more important sources of revenue, e.g., Import Duties and companies tax, the attempt to determine their regional orgins involved laborious calculations which, in the absence of reliable statistics on many relevant elements of the problem could only be done by the use of broad assumptions and approximations. The results were thus unsatisfactory and open to challenge.[59]

In spite of these structures, the commissioners recommended that part of the revenue allocated to the regions, in particular the "customs duty on the import of tobacco, manufactured and unmanufactured, into Nigeria and the excise duty on tobacco manufactured in Nigeria"[60] should be on the principle of derivation. It is also interesting to note that they took the trouble to recalculate the regional import consumption figures on which Sir Phillipson had based the payment on the bases of derivation. From this recalculation of regional consumption, they noted that the Western Region was cheated in favor of the Northern Region. The comparative figures obtained by both the Phillipson Commision and the Hicks-Phillipson are as follows:

REGIONAL DISTRIBUTION OF IMPORTS

	North	West	East
1946 figures as caluclated by Sir Phillipson	35%	34%	31%
1951 figures as calculated by Hicks-Phillipson	25%	45%	31%

SOURCE:
Report of the Commission on Revenue Allocation, 1951 (Lagos: Government Printing Press).

On the principle of independent revenue, the commissioners argued that in the interest of regional autonomy, financial responsibility and functional efficiency, the regions should have an independent tax base of their own, over which they would have full control. They, therefore, recommended that revenue already declared regional should be exclusively under the control of the regions and that the regions should have the power to fix such rates of tax at their discretion. Furthermore, that tax on petrol should be declared regional. In addition, they urged that an enquiry should be made to see if there were any other taxes which the regions could be empowered to levy.[61]

The commissioners next addressed themselves to the principle of need. They observed that if Nigeria were to become "more than a mere association of independent regions" bargaining for their rights, the question became "one of fair distribution among the people of Nigeria who should have equal claims" irrespective of regional origin. Under these circumstances the concept of need came into play. But they noted that reasonable indicators of need were hard to come by and that such "refinements are not possible in Nigeria."[62] They, therefore, regarded population as a crude indicator of need and it formed the basis of their recommendation for a capitation grant. The commissioners urged that a substantial grant should be given to each region for every adult taxpayer in that region. "The amount per capita should be determined from time to time by the Council of Ministers."[63]

The grant of substantial amounts on the basis of population gave additional significance to the relative population of the different regions and complicated the task of getting an accurate census of the population of the regions.[64] What made this capitation grant a major source of conflict between the regions was not only that the population figures were under a cloud of suspicion but that the rate per capita of the grants had to be determined by the council of ministers. With the population of the Northern Region being more than the total population of the two southern regions, any change in the rate - say from 5 shillings per capita to 7 shillings per capita - would mean a great difference in the amount given to the Northern Region and the amounts given to each of the other two regions. For example, a capitation grant of nine shillings would mean an increase of 252,000 pounds in the revenues hitherto received by the Northern Region from the federal government, and an increase of 45,000 pounds to the Western Region and a decline of 280,000 pounds to the Eastern Region.[65]

Furthermore, any capitation grants made to the regions by the council of ministers were declared to be "obligatory charges on the revenues of Nigeria to be met as due without formal appropriation by vote of the Legislative Council of Nigeria and the provision for these payments shall appear in the Appropriation Ordinances and in the Eastimates of Nigeria as appropriated by this order (Nigerian Revenue Allocation 'Order in Council of 1951) for the purposes therein stated."[66]

The fact that the council of ministers had the exclusive power to determine the per capita rate of the capitation grant and that these grants were obligatory charges on the revenue, shielded from public debate, made that council the chief distributive institution of the central government. The commissioners had specifically warned that unless decisions on revenue allocation were placed outside the political arena for a suitable period it would be impossible for the new federal arrangement to work.[67] Yet, despite this warning, or perhaps because of it, they themselves placed the question of the amount of the most substantial grant to be given to each region squarely in the hands of the council of ministers - the highest political organ in the nation. Thus, the desire of the regional political parties to control the council of ministers was intensified by the fact that the council controlled the allocation of a substantial amount of revenue for regional services.

Taking into consideration the national interest of Nigeria, the commissioners recommended special grants of one hundred percent of the regional expenditure for the police and 50 percent of the expenditure for the Native Authority police. On this basis also, the commissioners made provision for federal grants to cover 100 percent of the regional expenditure on education "excluding grants for special purposes."[68]

The commissioners finally reverted to the issue of past unfairness in revenue allocation. They noted that "a large part of the reason for the appointment of the commission" was belief on the part of the Northern Region that it had been unfairly treated in revenue allocation and "that what should have gone to the North was going to the East."[69] They observed ruefully that the "excessive prominence which was originally given to the results of the original derivation calculation"[70] had blown the issue out of proportion and "has produced much inter-regional misunderstanding and friction and this has had unhappy results both on the political and administrative levels."[71] They pointed out that "investigation of the calculations seems to show that the *Northern belief is largely mistaken. It is probable that the 'ideal percentage' attributed to the North was much too large... On the principle of derivation the North has very little case at all*"[72](emphasis mine).

The commissioners noted further that the North had a better case for special assistance on the grounds of "under-equipment"[73] because its case on the ground of past unfairness "cannot be considered to be established".[74] On the basis of under-equipment, therefore, the commission recommended that the Northern Region be given a grant of not more than 2,000,000 million pounds to be determined by the council of ministers and that this grant should be a charge on the consolidated revenue of Nigeria.

It is extremely difficult to justify a "once-for-all grant" of 2,000,000 million pounds to the North which, in the words of the commissioners, "need not be spent at once, but can be spent at such a time as the resources for spending it usefully become available,"[75] when in the opinion of the commissioners:

An allocation of revenue which will satisfy the reasonable claims of the North and the West is not difficult to discover; but one which will satisfy all claims which the Eastern Region as a result of a series of historical accidents has been allowed to develop is past the wit of man to devise."[76]

When one realizes that infra-structure in education and health in the East which are the results of this series of historical accidents were the work of voluntary agencies built by voluntary contribution on the part of the people of the East, one is left with the lively suspicion that the inability of the British authorities to devise a means for satisfying these existing needs is not unconnected with the complaint by Sir Arthur Richards that the East has been more vocal in the demand for more education and more everything;[76] in short, that agitation against British rule had its most vocal exponents in the East.

It must not be supposed that there were no criticisms levelled against the findings of the commission. However, the colonial authority insisted that any material change in the report would "upset the balance among the regions as well as the balance among the principles laid down by the commission."[77] Therefore, with two modifications the report was accepted by the 1951 Constitutional Review Conference and embodied in the Constitution as the Nigeria (Revenue Allocation) Order in Council of 1951.

Within a year, the implementation of the report encountered serious difficulties. This was caused principally by the fall in the expected revenue from duties on tobacco and by the increase in the salaries of the civil service as a result of salary revisions in 1952 and 1953. Therefore, in 1952-1953 and 1953-1954 the regions were given special grants to supplement their revenue. Furthermore, the combination allocation criteria which the commission had hoped would be a "compromise appropriate for federalism" proved in practice a cause of dissension among the various regions. The West complained on the basis of the recalculation of the derivation figures made by Hicks and Phillipson that other regions were developing at its expense. The North complained that the new funding system gave it little leeway to eliminate the "under-development" problem. The East complained that its essenteal services had been severely handicapped by the Hicks-Phillipson allocation system. None was satisfied with the Hicks-Phillipson compromise. Meanwhile, the difficulties encountered in the implementation of the 1951 constitution added another dimension to revenue problems. A decision was, therefore, made in 1953 to review the 1951 constitution. As part of this review it was decided to appoint another fiscal commission to reexamine the problem of revenue allocation and make recommendations to the Constitution Review Conference of 1953. Sir Louis Chick (British) was, therefore appointed sole commissioner in 1953.

The Chick Commission on Revenue Allocation 1953

As noted above, the appointment of the Chick Commission was part of the decision made at the 1953 conference on the review of the Nigeria Constitution. This conference, held in London in July and August, 1953, was the result of the inter-regional conflict and crisis resulting from the independence motion at the central legislature in 1953;[78] the growing dissatisfaction with the 1951 constitution, and the economic difficulties encountered in the implementation of the Hicks-Phillipson Report. It was partly to remedy the defects of the Hicks-Phillipson allocation recommendations and partly to recommend a method of revenue allocation that would meet the needs of maximum regional autonomy proposed under the consittution that the Chick Commission was apponted.

The terms of the reference of the Chick Commission emphasized the need to provide to both the region and the center the degree of fiscal autonomy which would enable them both to be independent and coordinate in their respective spheres. Chick was instructed to allocate the revenues *"in such a way that the principle of derivation is followed to the fullest degree compatible with meeting the reasonable needs of the center and each of the regions"* (emphasis mine).[79]

The Chick Commission stressed the difficulties raised by the application of the principle of derivation as the sole criterion for revenue allocation between the regions in the Nigerian Federation and the limitations of the principle itself. Sir Louis Chick noted in particular that "import duties constitute the largest single source of revenue".[80] But the exact allocation of this revenue on the basis of regional distribution and consumption "cannot be expected," as the large firms which provide the bulk of the statistics on import and distribution "are not always the last link in the chain of distribution";[81] much of the inter-regional distribution of inported goods in Nigeria is carried out by middlemen. These middlemen are mainly petty traders who in most cases do not keep any reliable statistics of their transactions.

The commission pointed out that a large proportion of imports, especially textiles, building materials, bicycles, footwear and manufactured goods made from iron and steel "was imported by small firms"[82] whose "methods of trading and lack, in some cases, of adequate records would preclude the submission of reliable returns."[83] The commission further emphasized that "the principle of derivation cannot be applied to all items of the center's present revenue" such as "interest on surplus funds, loans to statutory corporations"[84] and earnings of government departments. In sum, the required statistics for a fair and accurate allocation on the basis of derivation were totally inadequate.

The commissioner (Louis Chick) expressed some concern over the fact that his term of reference were unduly restrictive. He pointed out that the "consequence of applying the principle of derivation to the extent required by my term of reference "was that the regional governments' share of federal revenue would be larger under the extant estimate but that in the long run the regions would "be exchanging assured revenue for variable revenue".[85] This uncertainty, he said, "would naturally dictate a more cautious attitude to long range planning as it would be particularly unsafe to assume that the revenue from export duties will continue at its present level".[86]

Following his term of reference, Sir Louis Chick (the commissioner) recommended that 50 percent of all proceeds of duties on imports, other than motor spirits and tobacco, be shared among the regions in the following fixed proportions: 40 percent to the Western Region, 30 percent each to the Eastern and Northern Regions; second, that 50 percent of the import duty on tobacco, 50 percent of all excise duties, 100 percent of the import duty on motor spirits, and 50 percent of all export duties, be assigned to the regions in proportion to regional consumption or regional origin of the items; third, that the federal government continue to levy and collect all personal income tax and mining rent and royalties. However, the full amount of the proceeds from these two sources should be returned to the region in which the tax payer (African) lived or in which the mine was located.

"The allocation," the commissioner (Chick) noted, "are not beyond criticism, but I believe that, taken as a whole they are a fair application of the principle" of derivation.[45] He concluded that "the reasonable needs" of the federal government, the Northern Government and the Western Government "have been met."[87] In particular, he noted that the Western Region had revenue surplus of 80 percent of the expenditure estimated (1953-1954).

With regard to the Eastern Region, he emphasized that under the proposed system "the reasonable needs of the Eastern Regional Government have not, however, been met and something must be done to supplement the revenues it will receive under the recommendations I have made".[89] He, therefore, recommended that the region be given a special grant of 5000,000 pounds in the first year of the operation (1954) of the revised constitution and 250,000 pounds in the second year ')1955).[90] The commissioner (Chick) was aware that this was only a stop-gap measure and that it would "reduce the deficit shown by the estimates" to around 180,000 pounds. However, he urged that the deficit be made up by the imposition of produce sales tax. He observed that "the proposal for this tax originated in the Eastern Region but it could not be imposed because of the political crisis (1953)".[91]

The very fact that one region had a revenue surplus of 80 percent while another was unable to balance its budget for essential services could not but leave the impression that the benefits of the federal union were not equitably distributed. This impression was reinforced by the fact that out of the centrally collected revenue for the same financial year, 1953-1954, the central government retained "69.47 percent and the three regions were allocated 30.53 percent to be shared on the basis of derivation".[9] As Sir Louis Chick observed: "only the revenue collected by the federal government in excess of its own needs"[93] was allocated to the regions on the principle of derivation. Criteria to determine the needs of the center were not spelled out. What Commissioner Chick termed the "reasonable needs" of the federal government were in the realm of speculation. As he said:

> Further economic development of Nigeria will depend in a large measure upon financial resources of the federal government. If it is to have the necessary resources, its 'reasonable needs' must be viewed generously and its present reserve must not be distributed lavishly to the regions."[94]

While the reasonable needs of the federal government were viewed generously, the reasonable needs of the regions were not taken into consideration. Only the principle of derivation was taken into account in determining regional shares of the centrally collected revenues. It must, however, acknowledged that the Chick Commission gave the Eastern Region 5000,000 pounds in the first year of the operation of the revised constitution (1954) and 250,000 pounds in the second year on the basis of need. But these grants were too little and too late to ease the serious financial burden of the Eastern Region.

It is not surprising that the Eastern Region criticized the Report of the Commisssion in no uncertain terms. It complained bitterly that the commission was empanelled at a time when the world market in palm oil - its principal product - had reached an all time low. It attributed the primacy of the derivation principle to the intransigent insistence of the leaders of the North and the West, who had cast the Eastern Region in the role of a "beggar."

One of the greatest drawbacks of the Chick Commission was that it operated as a stop-gap measure. It was set up in 1953 and its recommendations were intended to last until 1956 when the constitution was scheduled to be amended. Yet of all the commissions on revenue allocation that had been established up to that point, it was given the narrowest mandate. Noting that a review would be made in 1956, Chick exhorted as follows: "I respectfully suggest, however, that the terms of reference of the Commission appointed to make the review should be framed rather more broadly than my terms of reference on the revenue allocation."[95]

Yet, in spite of the fact that the Chick Commission had the narrowest terms of reference, it presided over the actual allocation of the largest amount hitherto distributed by a revenue allocation commission in Nigeria. It was part of its duty to redistribute the uncommitted reserves of Nigeria, amounting to 40.12 million pounds in March, 1954, and marketing board reserves amounting to 75.5 million pounds in 1954.[96] If there is any place where Sir Loluis Chick took a palpable view of his commission it was in the distribution of the uncommitted funds. By his own admission, "there is no formula that can be applied. Conflicting considerations must be weighed and judgments differ."[97] Here his own personal judgment was bound to carry a lot of weight, and, in fact, it did. His argument is therefore of particular importance assessing the merit of his allocation of the uncommitted reserves. He noted that:

> The redistribution of functions will indeed make it necessary for the Regional Governments to incur considerable capital expenditure on additional buildings and housing and they will also have to provide more working capital for stocks and stores: by far the strongest reason for a transfer of part of the uncommitted central fund is to be

found, I think, in the proposed change in the system of revenue allocation. One of the effects of this change will be to shift part of the burden of a fall in the major sources of revenue - import and export duties - from the Federal Government to the Regional Government; they should therefore, be given part of the reserve built up by the Federal Government to meet this contingency.[98]

Yet in allocating part of the uncommitted fund to the Eastern Region, which at that time was experiencing crippling economic problems because of the fall in the price of palm oil, he did not take the above rationale into consideration. His argument was that the Eastern Region would have "the samllest margin of revenue over expenditure and is the least able to finance additional capital ecpenditure."[99] Therefore, he decided to allocate 2 million pounds to the region. With respect to the Western Region he noted that the "Western Regional Government has the largest variable revenue but will be better able than either of the other regional governments to absorb a fall in revenue."[100] For an unexplained reason he allocated the same 2 million pounds to that region. Referring to the Northern Region he said:

> Nor do I consider the grant of 2 million pounds made to the Northern Regional Government under Section 15 of the Nigerian (Revenue Allocation) Order in Council to Assist it to make up for deficiencies in equipment to be relevant to the distribution of the amount in question. The relevant considerations seem to be these: the Northern Regional Government has the highest level of expenditure on it than either of the other two Regional Governments, and it will have to incur more capital expenditure and provide more additional working capital in consequence of the reallocation of functions than they...The Eastern Regional Government will have the smallest margin of revenue over expenditure and is the least able to finance addition capital expenditure. The Western Regional government has the largest variable revenue but will be better able either of the other Regional Govenments to absorb a fall in revenue.[101]

He, therefore, allocated 3 million pounds to the Northern Region. Neither the pattern of allocation nor the rationale behind it can pass the test of logic. The arguments are circular and contradictory. The allocations do not bear even a remote connection with the arguments that dictated them. The allocation to the Western and Eastern Regions of 2 million pounds each is supported by arguments that are singularly unsound. Furthermore, only 7 million pounds[102] out of 40 million pounds were redistributed to the regions. The federal government had a lion's share. Yet, according to this expressed rationale, part of the burden of the fall in the major sources of revenue- import and export duties would be shifted from the federal government to the regions.[103]

But the most far-reaching and by far the most lasting effect of work of the Chick Commission was the regionalizing of the Marketing Boards. As Adebayo Adedeji noted:

> 'of greater fiscal significance than the allocation of tac revenue on the derivation principle was the decision of the 1953 Constitutional Conference to regionalise the marketing boards and divide their reserves between the regions...In regard to interregional fiscal relationships, the regional control of the finances of the marketing board accentuated regional desparity in financial resources.[104]

A short review of the history of the marketing boards is necessary to understand full implications of the 1953 Constitutional Conference to regionalize the board and to entrust the task of regionalizing the market boards to Commissioner Chick. The marketing boards in Nigeria grew out of the intensification of the efforts in Nigeria to help Britain in its attempt to win the SecondWorld War. The aim was the stimulation and systematization of the production and marketing of primary products such as cocoa, oil palm, ground nuts, benniseed and cotton. Four marketing boards were established and after the war they were incorporated as statutory corporations.

In 1947 the Cocoa Marketing Board was incorporated. Two years later(1949) the other three marketing boards-Ground Nut Marketing Board, Oil Palm Produce Marketing Board, and Cotton Marketing Board-were established. The production of benniseed was not on such a scale as to warrant the establishment of a board.

All four boards came under the umbrella of the Nigerian Produce Marketing Company, Limited, a company which was registered in London. The four marketing boards were sole shareholders. This company was responsible for marketing 98 percent of Nigeria's exportable agricultural products.[105] In the colonial parlance the main aim of the Nigerian Produce Marketing Company, Ltd., was to "obtain the best possible over overseas prices"[106] for Nigerian agricultural exports. In reality it gave to the oclonial power a firm grip on the trade in primary products from the colonies. It ensured for the colonial authorities full control over purchasing power and enabled them to regulate inflation within the metrope. It was used as an instrument for the selective encouragement and discouragement of particular lines of production.[107]

In Nigeria the four statutory produce marketing boards were grouped together under the directorate of a single chairman,"certain common officials and a common executive organization (The Department of Marketing and Exports)"[108] The major task of these boards in Nigeria was the stabilization of the producer prices for agricultural produce. The amount the board paid to the producers of the primary products was decided on the basis of what the boards considered as adequate for the maintenance of the industry. This meant that the prices paid to producers were in most cases lower than world market prices of these products. The difference between the world market prices and the prices paid to producers was accumulated by the boards, after due allowances for expenses, as price stabilization funds. The funds thus accumulated were used to support the producer prices against sudden slump in world prices. In addition, the funds were used to support agricultural research and to promote economic development.[109]

Although the major products are produced in different regions-cocoa in the Western Region, cotton and ground nuts in the Northern Region and oil palm produce in the Eastern Region-the Stabilization Reserve Fund for these various products was held in one account which was controlled by the central government through the Statutory Corporations. When, in 1953, the Constitutional Conference on the Review of the Nigerian Constitution decided to regionalize the Marketing Boards, the total assets set aside for distribution on the basis of derivation were 75.5 million pounds.

It must be observed that the derivation formula worked out by Sir Louis Chick in 1953 was based on the current prices of such items as cocoa, cotton, ground nuts, and oil palm produce. At this time, the price of cocoa was at an all-time high,[110] while the price of palm oil was at its nadir. No account was taken of the fluctuations in the prices of these items over the years(1947-1953) in which the marketing boards' reserve was built up.

On th basis of derivation, Sir Louis Chick divided the accumulated assets of the marketing boards between the regions as follows.[111]

Northern Region - 24.8 million pounds

Western Region - 34.4 million pounds

Eastern Region - 15.1 million pounds

Each of the regions was required by constitutional arrangement (1953) to set aside a certain amount as a first line defense against the onset of economic depression "to be kept in liquid form for use in price stabilization".[112] This measure was recommended by the World Bank Mission to Nigeria in 1954, after the regionalization of the marketing boards. The following is a detailed account of the recommendation by the Chick Commission and the utilization of the fund by the regions as recommended by the World Bank Mission to Nigeria.

Region	Total Allocation by Chick Commission	Recommended Utilization by the 1954 World Bank Mission	
		First Line Reserves	Second Line Working Cap'l.
Northern Region	24.8 million	4.6 million	20.2 million
Western Region	34.4 million	7.6 million	26.8 million
Eastern Region	15.1 million	12.5 million	2.6 million

NOTE: *in millions of pounds,* not dollars.
Report by the Resumed Conference on the Nigerian Constitution, 1954.)

The large amount of 12.5 million pounds which the Eastern Region had to put aside as first line of defense was necessitated by the serious slump of the world market price of palm produce. Because of this there was scarcely any money left to undertake development projects. The North had 20.2 million pounds on the second line of defense against a slump in market prices. This amount was therefore available for development projects. The West which received the largest share of the reserve had over 26 million pounds available for economic expansion projects. It can therefore be seen that reallocation of the marketing boards' reserve created a wide disparity in inter-regional financial resources and development capabilities.

Furthermore, the function of the boards which was to encourage economic development now fell to the regional governments which controlled the financial resources of the boards. The party in power in each region could now make grants out of the marketing boards second line reserves to farmers for the development of agriculture. These grants went mostly to party supporters who kicked back part of the amount they received to the party funds.[112] In addition, the composition of the marketing boards was now determined by the regional governments. Appointment of the members of the marketing boards was now made by the governor of the region on the recommendation of the party in power at the regional levels. The people, thus, recommended for appointment were party supporters. Therefore, regional control of the marketing boards placed in the hands of the parties in power at the regional level was a powerful instrument for dispensing patronage for building up of institutional support. The figures below show that the total grants made by the Northern Regional Government from the marketing board funds to farmers between 1955-1959 was 7 million pounds. Farmers in the Western Region received a total 22.75 million pounds in grants from the marketing boards. In the East the total grants to farmers from the same period-1955 to 1959- was .044 million pounds- less than half a million pounds.

MARKETING GRANTS TO FARMERS 1955-1959 (in millions of Pounds)

Year	North	East	West
1955-1956	-	.011 million	0.50 million
1956-1957	2.50 million	.010 million	20.75 million
1957-1958	2.50 million	.011 million	0.75 million
1958-1959	2.00 million	.012 million	0.75 million
TOTALS:	7.00 million	.044 million	22.75 million

It must be emphasized that the Eastern Region is not inherently poorer than the other regions. As Hicks and Phillipson pointed out as early as 1951, "the natural resources of the three regions are not so markedly different that one is certain to be the richer and another the poorer, in perpetuity."[114] But long range planning was totally absent from the Nigerian experiment in federalism. The accent was on disengagement. The mood especially in 1953 when the commission was established was on increasing contraction of the various links that held the regions together.[115] The emphasis was on regional autonomy. By emphasizing the principle of derivation the regional representatives at the 1953 conference on the review of the Nigerian Constitution opted for a revenue allocation which is only appropriate for a customs union.[116]

Inter-regional conflict and rivalry thus determined both the terms of reference of the Chick Commission of 1953 and left an indelible mark on its recommendations. As Dr. Okigbo aptly observed:

> A general criticism of Sir Louis chick's work is that it was written under a very strait jacket. This is a criticism, not of the validity of his conclusions, but of the terms of reference under which work was undertaken."[117]

Any criticism of the findings of the Chick Commission is in large measure a criticism of the deliberations of the 1953 conference on the review of the Nigerian Constitution which James S. Coleman called "the most fateful constitutional deliberation in modern Nigerian history."[118] The Chick Commission extended into the revenue field the separatist tendency already evident in the constitutional arrangements. It snapped that delicate chain between capabilities and needs, between regional inter-dependence and regional independence in fiscal matters- the very essence of a federal system. It canalized the fiscal groove- the policy which emphasizes North for the Northerner, East for the Easterners and West for the Westerners. The focus was regional.

It is, therefore, not surprising that the report of the Chick Commission was accepted by the delegates to the conference on the review of the Nigerian Constitution, when that conference resumed in Lagos, Nigeria, in 1954.

The Raisman Fiscal Commission, 1958

The disenchantment with the working of the Chick Commission recommendations made a review of those recommendations inevitable. The proposed review of the Nigerian Constitution, which was scheduled for 1957, provided a convenient rationale for a fiscal review. Consequently, Jeremy Raisman and R.C. Tress were appointed by the colonial secretary to undertake a review of the Nigerian revenue allocation system. As Jeremy Raisman was appointed chairman of the commission, the report is popularly known in Nigeria as the Raisman Report.

To understand the recommendations of this commission it is necessary to review in brief the developments which influenced the report. In the first place, Sir Louis Chick had warned the regional governments that as a result of following the principle of derivation to the fullest degree possible, they would be receiving a greater share of federal revenue than they were receiving under capitation grants, but they would be "less insulated from the fluctuations in Nigerian prosperity,"[119] resulting from the vagaries of foreign trade. He also cautioned against the assumption that revenue from exports would continue at its extant high level, and consequently, he advised embarking on commitments that required a more stable economic base. Scarcely had the Chick Commission recommendations been implemented when world market prices of primary produce showed visible signs of decline. This decline was particularly severe in the cocoa industry which was the principal product of the Western Region.[120]

Another event which complicated the scene was the discovery of petroleum in commercial quantities, especially in the Eastern Region. Test drills also revealed that petroleum existed in the mid-western part of Western Nigeria in commercial quantities.

These developments presented the prospect that the vexed question of how to make Nigerian revenue increase at a rate commensurate with its rate of development was

85

within the realm of possibility. Cautious and conservative appraisals not withstanding, the issue became "how to get away from a system under which the distribution of large sums of money rests on calcutions that can never be entirely accurate and which lend themselves to controversy."[121]

The Raisman Commission was, therefore, given a broader term of reference. The commission was asked to take into consideration the intergovernmental allocation of functions as agreed at the 1957 constitutional conference, and to devise a revenue allocation system which would not only give also make allowance for a reasonable degree of expansion. The terms of reference specifically stipulated the overall interest of the federation as a whole must taken into account.

The commission (Raisman) took a critical view of the principle of derivation. However, it concluded that changes in the current system of allocation "ought not to be made without most careful consideration of their full budgetary implications".[122] The Raisman Commission stressed that any change in the existing allocation under the principle of derivation must of necessity "be at the expense of more than one region" and would inevitably entail "budgetary alterations for all."[123]

The Commission then made an effort to combine the principle of derivation with the principle of need. On the basis of the principle of derivation the commission proposed that proceeds from import duties on diesel oil, motor spirits, tobacco products, excise duties on tobacco as well as export duties on produce, hides and skins and half of the revenues on mining rents and royalties should be allocated to the regional governments on the principle of derivation. The commission checked the figures on the basis of which the regional percentages (1953) on the principle of derivation were calculated, and found that on the basis of more recent data than those used in 1953, the Northern Region lost about 500,000 pounds per year out of the revenue due to it on the basis of the principle of derivation because of inaccurate data.

On the basis of need the commission examined the existing taxes to ensure both complete freedom of trade within the federation and the "desirability of securing that the maximum possible proportion of the income of the regional governments should be within the exclusive power of the those governments to levy and collect."[124] The findings of the commission revealed that "the scope for the enlargement of regional jurisdiction" in the field of taxation seemed "disappointingly small."[125] However, the Raisman Commission noted that to the extent that the tax measures "do not suffice to provide the regional governments with adequate revenues" other "systems of grants from federal revenues"[126] must be employed. The commission then recommended the creation of a Distribution Pool of revenue made up of 30 percent of the revenues from import duties collected by the federal government and 30 percent of the revenue from ining rents and royalties, and that the fund in the distributable pool should be apportioned among the various regions on the basis of a formula developed by the commission.

As the revenue from mining rents and royalties constitutes the principal item in the concept of the distributable pool, it is necessary to give a brief history of the revenue from mining rents and royalties so that the dimensions of conflict and crisis arising from it can be readily appreciated. Constitutionally the colonial government of Nigeria had full responsibility for all matters relating to mines, minerals and geological surveys. Until the discovery of mineral oil in commercial quantities, mineral revenues in Nigeria came mainly from coal in the Eastern Region, tin and columbite in the Northern Region. Coal was mainly consumed locally and, therefore, did not yield any appreciable revenue; columbite and tin were extracted from the Northern Region for export. Although the central government levied and collected all the mining rents and royalties, the revenue accruing therefrom was returned in full to the region of origin.

In 1950, the British authorities in Nigeria bought the mineral rights of the United African Company (British) in what Hicks and Phillipson styled "the celebrated transaction by which 1,000,000 pounds had been paid to the United African Company in purchase of the company's mineral rights in Northern Nigeria."[127] In spite of this vast outlay of funds from the central government, both the Hicks-Phillipson Report[128] and the Chick Report[129] recommended that all revenues from mining rents and royalties be returned to the region of origin. The Raisman Report also suggested that the same procedure would have been recommended for the oil. They commented "the allocation of the proceeds of mining royalties has presented us with a most perplexing problem. Although the revenue from columbite royalties rose rapidly at the time of the American stockpiling in 1953-1955, royalties on tin and columbite and coal normally yielded fairly constant annual sums. If these were the only minerals concerned there might be no difficulty in recommending the present system, namely that all "mineral royalties should be returned in full to the regions in which they originate. The problem is oil."[130]

The commission noted that it would be improper to distinguish for purposes of revenue allocation between oil and other mineral royalties. It, therefore, proposed that 50% of the mining rents and royalties should go to the region of origin; 20% of the revenue should be retained by the federal government which would continue to exercise the duty of collecting all revenues from mining rents and royalties. The remaining 30% should become part of a Distributable Pool in which all regions including the region of origin would have a share.

This Distributable Pool made up of 30% of the revenue from customs duties and 30% fo the revenue from mineral rents and royalties should then be divided among the regions in the following proportion - 40% to the Northern Region, 24% to the Western Region and 31'% to the Eastern Region.[131]

Several factors influenced this decision. One was the fact that political rivalries between the regional political parties had led to rapid expansion in regional social services. The regionalization of the civil service, education and health as well as the burden of financing these services which was placed on the regions by the 1954 constitution with its emphasis on the principle of derivation in revenue allocation had placed unbearable strain on regional finances. It was obvious from the recommendations made to the commissioner by the regions and the independent assessment by the commission that a serious and drastic curtailment of regional services was imminent at a time when the revenue of the federal government and regions, taken as a whole, did not justify such an action.[132] The commission (Raisman) acknowledged that, after taking into account "the differing degrees to which the several regions may still have taxable capacity, unexploited particularly since a major part of our exercise has been directed to placing greater fiscal autonomy in their hands. A proper interpretation of this part of our task, in fact, is to see that continuity is preserved and that each region has at least the wherewithal to maintain its existing scale of activities."[133]

In addition to the absolute necessity of maintaining existing services the commission considered the fact that the regional governments as autonomous units had certain minimum responsibilities "which any government has to meet by virtue of its status as a government with legislatures, ministers, and adequate administrative machinery."[134] To these two obviously important considerations the commission (Raisman) added the concept of need with population as a br d indicator of the scale of need; and the concept of balanced development of the federation as a whole.

There is, however, no doubt that the initial reception given the Report of the Raisman Commission was, indeed, favorable, if not exhilarating. According to Dr. Ema Awa, "Nigerians in general applauded the findings of the commission. Whatever criticisms were voiced were confined to matters of details."[135] Dr. Adedeji, who analyzed the report mainly from the purely financial aspect, noted that the Raisman Commission Report was "closer to the Hicks-Phillipson scheme than to the Chick plan." He admitted that when the "political, social and economic changes which had taken place between 1951, when the Hicks-Phillipson Commission sat, and 1958, when the Raisman Commission reported" are considered, the success of the Raisman Commission in restoring "the principles of need and national interest through the Distriubtable Pool was no mean achievement."[136]

One cannot escape the impression that in the heat of regional rivalry for funds, only cursory attention was given to the long-term effect of the proposals. The tentative projections of the Raisman Commission and the obvious gains of the moment were taken as a clear indication of sound regional financial autarchy. Few projections of the impact of the oil revenue prospects and potentials were made. The competitive struggle for fiscal autonomy and political preeminence by each region over the other stifled the need for a calm and critical assessment of the long-term implications of the burgeoning oil boom on the nations as a whole.

In the euphoria created by the increasing oil revenue, each region set forth its own plan of economic development, uncoordinated and unrestrained by any truly national agency. It was, indeed, one of the cardinal mistakes of the Raisman Commission that it failed to set up an institutional framework with clearly defined responsibility designed to monitor and coordinate regional developments in the interest of the nation as a whole. Dr. Adedeji characterized this omission as a "rather cavalier way of dealing with such an important matter."[137]

It must, however, be stated in defense of the commission that their findings were recommendations and, therefore, could be amended before being incorporated into the consitution. In all candor, they had expressed the concern that the regions "have not been subjects to the restraining influence which a calculation of the available revenue resources imposes on every government in framing annual budgets."[138] Ther are in our view two indispensable prerequisites to sound revenue allocation in a federal system. One of them is a clear and unambiguous indentification of the aims and objectives of the federation especially in the economic fields; the other is the establishment of a suitable institutional framework to handle the complex problem of harmonizing immediate and politically expedient objectives with the long term interests of the nation as a whole. Decisions regarding these two objectives are intensely political and must rest on the framers of the Nigerian Constitution. The major responsibility therefore, lies with the framers of the Nigerian Constitution for accepting the finding with palpable neglect of their duty to subject the recommendations to searching scrutiny and failure to establish an ongoing mechanism for continuous assessment and review of the fiscal provisions.

The basic problem was in the aims and objectives of the component regions and the muffled but scarcely disguised interest of the British colonial power to protect its interest through the device of playing one powergul region against the other in a weak federation. Thus, a myopic view of the relationship between the various regions in a federation dictated the nature and format of the fiscal insititutions in Nigeria on the eve of independence (1959).[139]

It is important to note that the Raisman Commission was the last fiscal commission before independence. The only reference in the Independence Constitution for fiscal review in that constitution was Article 164 sections 140 and 141 which provide for a periodic review of revenues allocation system dealing only with *mining rents and royalties* (Emphasis mine).

Whatever might have been the faults of the Raisman Commission's proposal, it must be acknowledged that it lasted longer than any other fiscal commission in Nigeria. There were three before it[140] each had a short and controversial period of operation. The Raisman Commission proposal lasted from 1959 to 1964 with two minor revisions caused by political changes. The first was in 1961 when the Southern Cameroons - a mandated territory-opted out of Nigerian to become part of th Cameroon Republic. As the three regions in Nigeria could not agree on the methods of distriubting the five percent of the Distributable Pool that was assigned to Southern Cameroon,[141] that part of the fund was left in the federal reserves. The remaining 95% was than apportioned as follows:

Northern Region	Western Region	Eastern Region
40/95	24/95	31/95

Another occasion on which a revision was made in the Raisman Proposals was in 1963 when the Mid-Western Region was carved out of the Western Region. The share of the West in the Distributable Pool was split between the Western Region and the Mid-Western Region in the ratio of three to one. Apart from these changes, the Raisman recommendations remained in effect until 1964 when the Binns Fiscal Review Commission was appointed. As the Binns Fiscal Recommendations did not come into operation until after the military coup d'etat of 1966, we shall confine our remarks to the conflict which surrounded its appointment.

Nigerian Revenue Allocation Experience Since Independence, 1960 -
The Binns Fiscal Commission of 1964

The appointment of the Binns Fiscal Commission in 1964 will serve as a convenient starting point for a discussion on the post-independence experience of Nigeria in revenue allocation. As we noted above, the Independence Constitution of 1960 (amended in 1963), provided for a periodic review of sections 140 and 141 dealing with the Distributable Pool and specifically with mining rents and royalties. In accordance with this provision, Mr. J.D. Binns,[142] an Australian, was appointed the sole commissioner in 1964 and charged with the relevant review. He was specificaly instructed to take into account "the experience of the various governments of the federation in the working of the revenue allocation"[143] then in force.

In many ways the method of fiscal adjustment in Nigeria after independence differs from that of other federations.[144] In the first place the review is by constitutional provision limited to mining rents and royalties. It precludes a reassessment of the whole area of taxation. As Okigbo noted:

> "The disparity between direct and indirect taxation in the regional revenue is striking. In the East, the division approached 50% for either category. In the West and the North, the regional governments relied, to the extent of 79 and 75 percent, respecitvely on indirect revenues. The inference is clear: more can be done in these two regions to expand income tax receipts. Second, the disparity does not necessarily reflect a disparity in the distribution of personal income among regions, nor is it a reflection of the relative efficiency of regional fiscal administration."

The crucial problem in Nigeria was that the federal government had surrendered the whole field of direct and income taxes to the regional governments. Therefore, it had no power to ensure that the tax burden was distributed equitably throughout the federation. Moreover, the consititution did not require either the citizens, or the regions as corporate entities, to bear any part of the burden of federal financing except indirectly through the payment of import duties. Fiscal adjustment in Nigeria simply meant a method of getting more federal funds to enhance regional autarchy. The atmosphere was simply one of regional struggle over the sharing of spoils from the federal government.

In other federations[146] the objective of revenue allocation involves a redistribution of the financial burdens between the federal government and the participating units to ensure that the regional and collective needs of the units are more effectively met. C.J. May aptly summarized the main purpose of fiscal adjustment in federations as follows:

> "The function of fiscal transfers therefore is to allocate revenue given the distribution of governmental functions, so as to achieve the greatest satisfaction of all governments. This implies a redistribution of income between units such that the benefits to small and poor units are sufficient to maintain their interest in the federation, while the sacrifice of revenue by large and rich units is not considered by them to be greater than the benefits accruing from federation."[147]

In Nigeria not only were the itmes of revenue to be adjusted, circumscribed and limited, the federal government - that is, the Council of Ministers - a purely political body, was empowered to determine the need for such a review and to appoint a commission after consultation with the regional governments. The vagueness of the term 'consultation' was bound to be a source of conflict. If consultation implied that the federal government had the ultimate responsibility to review and recast the allocation of revenues which were guaranteed to the regions by the constitution, then the whole constitutional device to ensure regional autonomy could be compromised by the redistriubtion of revenue by the federal government.

Since the federal government had the responsibility for appointing a commission, it follows that any region which controlled the center could contrive to have the federal government appoint a commission, if and when it felt that the consitutionally sanctioned distribution was working against its own interests. In Nigeria where the federal government was controlled by the region which was at the same time the least economically developed, the temptation for that region to use its political power at the center to benefit itself was, indeed, very great. It is not known which region actually engineered the setting up of the Binns Commission. However, we have it on the authority of J.P. Mackintosh that it was "largely due to Northern pressure[148] that a commission was set. Dr. Adedeji on the other hand considered the East as the motive force behind the appointment of the commission. Both, however, agreed that pressure of one type or the other was exerted by all the regions; that the federal government "was indifferent about a review."[149]

Whatever the source of pressure might have been, when the commission was set up in 1964, all the regions - the North, the East and the West - were vocal in their complaints against the provisions of the Raisman Commission. The North protested that it was unable to close the gap between its services and investment expenditures. Comparing itself with the other regions, it pointed out that the revenue of other regions, especially the East, "has been more bouyant than its own."[150] The West complained that its finances had been adversely affected by the Raisman Commission's recommendations - that the commission had deliberately slowed its rate of growth. It stressed that "what was intended as a temporary check had turned out to be a perpetual victimization and penalization."[151] The East characterized the concept of a distributable pool as extremely unreasonable, unfair and inequitable. In what constituted a reversal of long-held policy it called for a full return to the principle of derivation. The fact that the region was at this time the richest because of the revenue from oil must have had something to do with this new posture. However, there was no doubt that continuous frustration over revenue allocation from 1946 to 1959, had some effect on this change of policy.

Although the actual discussions before the commission were carried on behind closed doors, the ominous rumblings were loud enough to escape through the panelling. It was clearly discernible from the tone of the debates that the regional representatives had taken extreme and rather intransigent stances. According to J.P. Macintosh, "though they (the argument) were not made public the tone of the dispute caused serious concern among the civil servants in all five governments."[153] Even the newly created Midwest government was bitter over the fact that it was left to bear the burden of developing the infra-structure of a new region without special help from the federal government.

Whatever led to the appointment of a new commission, it was obvious that the appointment of the Binns Commission in 1964 was ill-timed and ill-advised. Apart from the fact that 1964 was an election year, many issues of momentous importance had reached crisis proportion in that year. The Mid-West election of 1963 had led to an open clash between the NCNC and the NPC and by 1964 their fragile coalition in the central cabinet was completely immobilized and faction ridden. Added to that, the conflict over the census figures in 1963 had escalated from a shouting match into a legal case. Although the Supreme Court refused to entertain the suit by the Eastern regional government, it was obvious that its refusla merely turned the conflict into a crisis. As it were, these issues reinforced each other and burst the bonds of restraint. The atmosphere was rife with recriminations. Charges and counter-charges, usual in an election year, were intensified and reinforced by a continuous chain of conflict and crises. The embers of the fire kindled by these conflicts were, indeed, smoldering and scarcely needed any fuel to flare up. The conflict over the Binns Fiscal Report[154] added another dimension to the escalating conflicts and crisis and helped to open the path to the Civil War of 1967. For one thing, the decisions of the commissioner were in the words of C.J. May, "not popular in the Southern regions where there were already complaints that the North had used its political dominance of the central government in order to bias federal expenditure in favor of the Northern Region."[155]

As a general conclusion, the problem of revenue allocation in Nigeria, resulted from a general lack of the will to create suitable institutional structures that were flexible enought to handle the problems of building a federation by a devolutionary method. No concerted attempt was made to define the long-term objectives of the federation in the economic sector. Every approach to revenue allocation in Nigeria has been halting, haphazard and hastily contrived.

Although it was recognized as early as 1946 by Phillipson that the "Nigerian problem of allocation...possesses local features of unusual difficulty"[156] no attempt was made to set up a permanent body of experts with specific responsibility to survey the resources and needs of the regions and the federation; to keep a close watch on the recommendations for revenue allocation and suggest alternative ways for a more acceptable allocation.

As Green and Krishna noted, " the progress of economic integration is very much conditioned by the clarity with which gains - immediate and long-term are demonstrated."[157] The repeated pronouncements of various commissions that one region has been benefited at the expense of the others "diverted the attention of the regions to the wholly unfruitful question of whether this region or that is receiving less or more than it ought to have."[158] The propensity of the various commissions to give compensation for actual or fancied past unfairness heightened the feeling on the part of the regions that the federal union involved sacrifice on their part in favor of others. No realistic attempt was made to project the common advantages.

Finally, according to R.J. May, "if, on the other hand, large units are poor it may prove difficult to redistribute revenue from the smaller rich units sufficient to satisfy the large units while not taking so much from the small units as to remove their interest in federation."[159] The North is the largest in terms of population and area and yet it is the least economically developed. Its claims for special consideration backed by its political predominance at the center made it impossible to achieve a satisfactory allocation of the revenue; matters of revenue allocation are a very touchy issue and the inability to achieve equitable revenue allocation is one of the greatest obstacles to the viability of a federation.

CHAPTER VI

THE ELECTION CRISIS OF 1964

In the previous chapter we were concerned with conflict over revenue allocation and how the policy of maximum regional autonomy complicated the problem of equitable allocation of revenue among the regions. This chapter addresses itself to the nature and dimensions of the conflicts surrounding the federal election of 1964 and the crippling effect of the institutionalization of regional separation on the electoral process. There is no doubt that the transfer of political power in free and fair elections is the hallmark of a legitimate political institution. It is pertinent here that Jean Blondel has said:

> unless some arrangement exists by which governments can be created and ended in a peaceful fashion, the overthrow of these governments will be attmepted.[1]

This prediction is borne out in its entirety in Nigeria where the electoral system designed to ensure peaceful transfer of power at the central level was paralyzed by the struggle for power by regionally based political parties. These parties, with one exception, emerged out of the imperial policy of creating a federal structure through the process of devolving political power on regional groups. As a result, the development of their institutional support and the nature of their interaction at the federal level became inextricably tied to the maximization of regional autonomy.

Dahl has observed that "several kinds of instsitutional arrangements seems to have a bearing on patterns of opposition."[2] In Nigeria, the 1951 constitutional arrangement which provided for indirect election of the three regional houses determined both the patterns of opposition and the character of the major political parties in Nigeria. Therefore, a clear understanding of the issues involved in the 1964 election crisis requires a brief analysis of the origin and development of each of the major parties in Nigeria.

Nigerian politics from 1951 to 1966 was dominated by three major political parties. Each of these parties controlled the government of one of the three regional governments that made up the Federation of Nigeria from 1951 to 1962.[3] The National Council of Nigeria and the Cameroons, which was the first to emerge (1944), controlled the Eastern Regional government and also formed the opposition party in the Western Region until 1962.[4] The Action Group, the second political party to develop, controlled the regional government in the Western Region and formed the opposition party in the Eastern Region after 1956. The Northern Peoples Congress (NPC), the last of the major parties to emerge (1951) controlled the Northern Regional government. A brief history of each of these parties is given below.

The National Council of Nigeria and the Cameroons[5] was formed in 1944 as a result of the efforts of the Nigerian Union of Students. In 1944, the students at Kings College - a government secondary school - went on strike as a protest against the use of their dormitories by soldiers. Some of them were expelled, some were drafted into the army. As a result, the students called a meeting at Grover Memorial Hall in August (1944) and urged the two leading nationalists, Herbert Macaulay, President (a Yoruba), and Nnamdi Azikiwe, General Secretary (an Ibo), to form a national front to oppose British imperialism. As a result the Nigerian National Council was formed; it subsequently changed its name to the National Council of Nigeria and Cameroons (NCNC, 1945). At its origin the NCNC was, therefore, multi-ethnic in composition and pan-Nigerian in outlook. At the initial stage its membership was indirect and associational.[6] It consisted of an aggregation of existing political interest groups - literary clubs, labor unions, ethnic associations and professional associations. Two events which occured in 1945 led to the broadening of its political base to include individual membership though it never lost its associational base. One of the events was the general strike of Nigerian workers which occurred in 1945 and the other was the publication in 1945 of the proposals for the Richards Consitituton which came into force in 1947.

The part played by the NCNC in these two incidents established its reputation as a national party devoted to the interests of the common man and for self-government for Nigeria within the British Empire. As a result of NCNC support and assistance to the strikers, eighty trade unions as well as many individual members joined the party. From 1945, when the proposal for the Richards Constitution was published, the NCNC and the Azikiwe (Zik) group of newspapers attacked the proposals vehemently.[7] When the Richards Constitution became operative in 1947, the NCNC undertook a countrywide tour to protest what was termed its "obnoxious ordinances."[8] It was during this tour that Herbert Macaulay, the President of the NCNC, died and Nnamdi Azikiwe became the President of NCNC.

From 1947, when Azikiwe became the national president of the NCNC, the party became increasingly associated with the Ibos. It gradually lost its national appeal. In 1954 when Azikiwe became the Premier of the Eastern Region the party assumed a regional character with its base in the Eastern Region. However, it remained as an opposition party in the Western Region and was in alliance with the Northern Elements Progressive Union, a minor party in opposition in the Northern Region.

Opposition to the leadership of the NCNC by Dr. Azikiwe, especially in the Western Region, led to the formation of the Action Group in that region. The opposition came to a head as a result of the arrangements made under the 1951 constitution. According to Richard L. Sklar:

> The constitution of 1951 provided for indirect election to the three regional houses of assembly each of which was empowered to choose from among its membership a stipulated number to the central House of Representative. Lagos (capital of Nigeria) was placed under the jurisdiction of the Western Region enabling Azikiwe's opponents to offset his strength in Lagos by mobilizing support among the Yoruba peasantry in rural areas of that region..."[9]

The result of this mobilization was the formation of a cultural organization known as the Egbe Omo Oduduwa (Society of the Descendants of Oduduwa the mythical founder of the Yoruba nation) by Chief Obafemi Awolowo. Out of this cultural organization the Action Group emerged as a political party under the leadership of Awolowo to contest the election to the Western House of Assembly.

Thus, the emergence of the Action Group as a party was the direct result of the establishement of the regional political insitituion under the imperial policy of devolutionary federalism in Nigeria.[10] Although the Action Group started as an ethnically based party, in order to gain political power in the Western Region, which was its organizational purpose, it had to transcend its ethnic base. Two reasons were responsible for this. At this time (1951), the Western Region was multi-ethnic in composition. Secondly, the NCNC had a strong following among the Yorubas in spite of the ethnic appeal of the Action Group. Therefore, in order to gain political control in the Western Region it was forced to transcend its ethnic base and recruit the Edos, the Ibos[11] and other minorities in the Western Region. The necessity for the Action Group to transcend its regional base in order to remain a viable political party in Nigeria was one of its persistent problems and contributed significantly to the Western Regional crisis of 1962.[12]

Equally significant in the formation of the Northern Peoples Congress (NPC) in Northern Nigeria was the constitutional arrangement under the 1951 consitituton. Although the Northern Peoples Congress (NPC) was organized as a political party in 1949, it remained a party on paper until the exigencies of the regional election of 1951 called it into life.[13] As Coleman observed:

> Immediately before the first elections to the new Northern House of Assembly, held in the later part of 1951, the Northern Peoples' Congress was revived and delcared to be a 'Progressive Political Party

as from October 1st, 1951. Partly because its membership was drawn from the ranks fo the higher officials in the native administration (emirate), and partly because the indirect system of election permitted the emirs (kings) to exercise substantial influence over the electoral colleges, the NPC won a safe majority in the first Northern House of Assembly."[14]

It must be ovserved that a majority of the members elected to the Northern House of Assembly were officials; the rest were wealthy businessmen who identified with the traditional power elites. Thus, in the Northern Region both the regional assembly and the regional party (NPC) were dominated by the traditional elites. To ensure that the regional government had close control over the party organization, the central secretariat of the party was transferred to Kaduna, the seat of the Northern Regional government. At the Jos conference held in 1954, the Sardauna of Sokoto, the Premier of the Northern Region became the President of the NPC and the symbiosis between the party and the regional government was complete. The fact that the majority of the party leaders were paid officials of the Native Authority System made opposition to the NPC synonymous with opposition to the whole indigenous political structure of the North. As Dudley pointed out;

> The party is, in fact, the Native Authority and whatever are its deficiencies, the Native Authority (local government) is nevertheless the central institutional reference point of social action for most, if not all, Northerners."[15]

Thus, the interest of the party (NPC) and the interest of the whole institutional structure of the Northern Region became indistinguishable. Although the Northern Region is multiethnic the organizational scope of the party was regional rather than ethnic. As we have noted previously the motto of the party is "one North: one people" irrespective of religion, rank or tribe. Although the party motto emphasized religious toleration, the idea of one North indivisible is based on the Islamic concept of a community of believers and the party represents the consensus of that community and to oppose the party is to rebel from the community of Islam.[16] Thus, religious ideology added a dimension to the intolerance of opposition.

Butwhatwhich reinforces the loyalty and devotion of the three parties to the regional institutions is, in fact, the very threat of opposition - real and potential - within each reagon. None of the three regions which made up the Nigerian Federation at independence was ethnically homogeneous.[17] The Northern Region, in fact, contains five of the ten largest linguistic groups in Nigeria (Hausa, Fulani, Kanuri, Tiv and Nupe)[18] besides a large group of about 200 small ethnic groups in the so-called "pagan tribes."[19] The East contains numerous ethnic groups around the Calabor-Ogoja and Rivers area. We have already referred to the presence of a large number of minorities in the Midwestern section of the Western Region. Thus, the presence of minority groups in each of these regions forced the parties to preoccupy themselves with the consolidation of their power within the regions. Part of the struggle by these parties at the central level was not unconnected with their desire to get as much of the federal resources as possible to develop their regions and thus consolidate their hold on the regional power structures.

Furthermore, part of the cause of the inability of these parties to transcend their regional base stems from the fact that the social services and development projects through which the parties dispensed patronage were by constitutional arrangement placed under regional authority. Therefore, institutional support for these parties and the source of party patronage were regionally based. Consequently, any party leader who left the region and gained election to the central legislature lost control over the institutional resources of the party and with this control over the dispensation of party patronage. This has been a constant source of conflict and crisis in the two Southern Regional parties (the NCNC and the Action Group). In 1953 the fact that the leadership of the party executive (NCNC) and the Eastern Region parliamentary cabinet were in different hands led to conflict between the executive and the cabinet leadership which precipitated the Eastern Regional crisis of 1953.[20] The same conflict between the party executive led by Chief Awolowo at the center and the Action Group parliamentary cabinet in the Western Region led to the Western Regional crisis of 1962.[21] This similarity was pointed out by Richard L. Sklar as follows;

> The Action Group's plight in 1962 was reminiscent of previous crises in the development of the NCNC. It will be recalled that in 1953 the NCNC was rent by the refusal of its eastern parliamentary leadership to accept central party direction. Nine years later, a clash between Awolowo and his successor as Premier of the West, Akintola, cast a shadow over the Action Group's future as a major political party."[22]

In the whole of the British commonwealth, leadership of the party executive is by convention generally associated with leadership of the party parliamentary cabinet. But in Nigeria, because political power was centered in the regions, any party leader who chose to go to the center must reconcile himself to a subordinate role in the control of the institutional resources of the party or face a revolt from the regional cabinet.

We have so far belaboured the regional nature of these parties and their effect on political interaction with Nigeria. But a word must of necessity be said about the nature and classification of these regional parties. An examination of the written sources on the nature and classification of these parties shows a monumental proliferation of terminology bordering on confusion. The first and perhaps most consistent attempt to analyze the Nigerian political parties is Thomas Hodgkin's *Nationalism in Colonial Africa,* first published in 1956. Following in the footsteps of M. Duverger's classification of archaic and prehistoric parties, Hodgkin developed a concept of proto-type parties and real political parties - political parties proper; he classifies Nigerian parties under two types - mass political parties and patron parties. Mass parties base their membership on individuals while patron parties depend on distinguished personalities in the community.[23] In a chapter entitled "Parties and Congress" he puts the NCNC in the mass party category and the NPC in the distinguished personality class. He noted that, "The Action Group in Western Nigeria is something of a hybrid,"[24] possessing both the characteristics of the mass-type and the 'party of personality' type. Hodgkin's later distinction in his book, *African Political Parties,* between mass and elite parties is hardly an improvement since the difference between "elite" parties and 'parties of personality' appears artificial and contrived he implied that "elite" and patron (personality type) are identical.[25] Other classifications of Nigerian political parties are to be found in Ruth Schacter-Morgenthau's *Single Party Systems in West Africa*[26] and K.W. Post's, *The Nigerian Federal Elections of 1959.*[27] Both of these classifications follow Duverger's distinction between 'mass' and 'cadre' parties.

A different school of thought is represented by Richard L. Sklar. In his book entitled *Nigerian Political Parties,* he adopted a typology derived from Sigmund Newman's classification of parties into "parties of social integration" and "parties of individual representation."[28] In discussing Newmann's concept of parties of social integration, Sklar introduced a distinction between "parties of total integration" and the more general type of parties of social integration. However, in an article co-authored with C.S. Witaker, Jr., Richard L. Sklar took issue with the various classifications of Nigeria's political parties especially those which suggest that Nigerian political parties are based on communal participation[29] and asserts that:

> It is a common observation that political parties in Nigeria and elsewhere in Africa rely strongly upon communal participation that is, political alignment on the basis of ethnic or religious affinity. If defined to mean only religious and ethnic ties, however, the concept of communalism provides inadequate insights into Nigerian party politics. Maurice Duverger's analysis of the quality or nature of participation, based on Ferninand Tonnies' classic distinction between gemeinshaft (community) and Gesellschaft (society) is more suggestive.[30]

We must emphasize in conclusion that neat distinctions of the various types of parties in Nigeria are misleading and confusing rather than enlightening. All that can be said with certainty is that like all political parties, Nigerian political parties were interested in controlling power and patronage both at the regional and federal level, that they performed integrative functions at different levels and to different degrees. As Dudley aptly remarked in terms of membership and especially in terms of finance:

> There could be hardly any difference, say, between the NPC, NCNC and AG of Nigeria. All of these now have to rely on government funds shovelled into the party through private contracts, loans, development projects, etc."[31]

The dilemma of Nigerian political parties lies in the fact hat the institutional arrangements established by the Nigerian Constitution placed all the sources of party funding, institutional support and patronage within the regional institutions. But in order to get the necessary funds allocated to the regions and influence the establishment of the various development projects within the regions, the parties must have effective power at the central legislature. Thus, the control of the regional legislature was absolutely necessary for the viability of any political party in Nigeria, while effective voice at the center was necessary to ensure that the region got what was termed its "fair share" of the resources of the federation.

However, none of the political parties (except perhaps the NPC) could win a controlling majority at the central level without forming trans-regional coalitions.[32] The NPC, in fact, was not able to win all the seats in the North without overt repression of dissident minority parties in the North. Therefore, any political party in Nigeria that wished to control the central legislature in a free and fair election must either be in control of institutional resources of at least two of the three large regional governments (North, East or West) or build trans-regional coalitions which would give it a chance of winning a majority of seats without coercing dissident minorities[33] within its regional base. It must also assure unity within its own rank and file to insure that an internal faction does not develop. With this brief analysis we turn to the conflict and crisis over the 1964 elections.

The Nigerian Constitution provides that election to the Federal House shall be held every five years. As the last federal election was in 1959, the next federal election was constitutionally scheduled for 1964. The events surrounding the 1964 election proved beyond all doubt that the main preoccupation of political parties in Nigeria was to win control of the federal legislature. Party ideologies scarcely entered into their calculations; party platform was an unnecessary impediment. All that mattered was winning regardless of cost. It is with these factors in mind that we can understand the complicated patterns of alliance that preceded the election campaign for the Federal Election of 1964.

First, however, it is necessary to give a brief historical account of the organization of the parties before the 1964 election. Before the 1964 election, the federal government was under the control of a coalition cabinet formed by the National Council of Nigerian Citizens and the Northern Peoples Congress parties. The senior partner in the coalition was the NPC. The Action Group party formed the opposition in the Federal Parliament. Each of these three major parties was also the political power in control of one of the three regional assemblies in the Federation of Nigeria.[34]

In 1962, however, internal strife destroyed the Action Group-controlled government of the Western Region.[35] Consequently, a splinter group of the Action Group formed a new party known as the United People's Party (UPP). This party, led by the former deputy leader of the Action Group, Chief Akintola, formed a coalition government in the Western Region with the National Council of Nigerian Citizens, which was until then the opposition party in the Western Region.

Meanwhile, events in the Midwestern section of the Western Region complicated the party struggles in the Western Region. For some time the people of the Midwest consisting of a number of ethnic groups including the Binis, the Ibos, the Itshakiris, the Urhobos and a number of other minorities had been agitating for seperation from the

Western Region to form their own state - The Midwest. They were supported in thier drive for a seperate state by the NCNC. In 1962, they took advantage of the conflict in the Action Group party and secured the passage of a resolution in the Western House for the creation of a Midwest Region.[36]

In August, 1962, the Midwest Region was created. In accordance with the constitutional provision, an interim administrator was appointed to govern the region for a period of six months. Dr. Dennis Osadebay, a staunch member of the NCNC, was appointed administrator. Election to the new Midwestern Regional Assembly was scheduled for February 3, 1963. Towards the close of the interim period the election to the regional assembly gave rise to a flurry of political realignments aimed at securing the control of the new regional assembly.

In September, 1962, a month after the creation of the Midwest Region, an apostle of the Church of the Lord in Benin formed a polotical party with the blessing of the Sardauna of Sokoto,[37] the premier of the Northern Region and the leader of the NPC. This new party was known as the Midwest peoples Congress (NPC). The mainstay of the party were the local members of UPP, the party in alliance with the NCNC in the Western Region, and sympathizers of the NPC, another party in alliance with the NCNC at the federal level. It is, indeed, surprising that although these developments were common knowledge, the alliance between the NCNC and the NPC was in no way disturbed. The NCNC, on the other hand, initiated a coalition with the Action Group in the Midwest. In a statement issued after a meeting with the leader of the Action Group, Chief Osadebay noted that the Action Group and NCNC were two of the most progressive parties in Nigeria and it was high time the two parties got together and waged a struggle against "the conservatives of the North."[38]

Of course, Chief Osadebay tactfully ignored the fact that the NCNC was still in a coalition with the NPC, "the conservatives of the North." Obviously, in the highly unpredictable political weather of Nigeria, party ideology counted for naught where power considerations were at stake. Even the NPC, with its slogan of the North for the Northerners and its pronounced Muslim orientation, gleefully acknowledged that it was in alliance with a party led by a Christian apostle of the Church of the Lord because it needed to transcend its regional barriers in order to get control of the national government. In fact, the General Secretary of the party acknowledged that the NPC was making an inroad into the South and declared that this "operation South is but one of the straws in the wind of the last few weeks which indicate that the creation of the Midwest is acting as a catalyst to a chemical change in the state of Nigerian parties."[39]

The struggle for control of the Midwest Assembly created open conflict between the two parties who were coalition partners in the center. It was openly rumored that the Midwest People's Congress was another name for NPC. Of course, the initials are almost the same. Probably for this reason the Midwest People's Congress changed its name to Midwest Democratic Front (MDF). But a mere change of name was not enough to eliminate the charge, nor did the NPC deny that it was supporting the MDF. These inroads into an acknowledged NCNC stronghold could not but alarm the leaders of the NCNC. Dr. Okpara, the leader of the NCNC government of the Eastern Region, made a public statement inferring that the NCNC and the NPC had made arrangements on the twenty-third of November to provide a joint government for the New Midwest state.[40] The contents of the arrangement were not disclosed.

It must be remembered that barely a month before this purported agreement, the MDF had defeated the NCNC in a by-election to the Federal House in Urhobo West. It was, therefore, unrealistic to expect the NPC to abandon a new ally (MDF) in support of an old ally (NCNC) which posed a potential challenge to its control. Dr. Okpara was obviously outraged by the maneuvers of the NPC and characterized the action of the NPC as a stab in the back.[41] The recriminations of the parties over the Midwest affair were insistent, bitter and strident.

Underlying the bitterness was the fact that the Midwest, in spite of its small population (2,533,337 - 1963 census), was in many respects an invaluable political, as well as economic, asset to any party in power in the new region. For one thing, oil had by this time been found in commercial quantities in the region, and it was obvious that the politics of oil had started to cast its lengthening, and by no means innocuous, shadow over the Nigerian political landscape. Also, with the federal election only months away, minority and dissident elements in all parts of Nigeria were becoming increasingly restive. As far back as July, 1962, Dr. J.O.J. Okezie, the Ibo leader of a minority party known as the Republican Party, rationalized his alliance with the Northern People's Congress (NPC) by maintaining that "judging from the current political trend in Nigeria the NPC was the party most likely to win the necessary majority in the next federal election to form a government"[42] and that it was to prevent this that his party was arranging an alliance with the NPC. What perhaps escaped him was that by allying his party with the NPC he would help bring about an NPC majority in the next election.

Although the NPC controlled the Northern Region which controlled more than half the seats in the Federal House needed to form the government at the central level it was not certain of winning all the seats in the North. In January 1964, the confortable security which the North had felt in its numerical superiority was rudely shaken by a new development. A new coalition known as the 'Northern Progressive Front was formed. The membership of this new front was multiethnic and embraced a majority of the numerous minorities in the North. It consisted of the Nigerian (formerly Northern) Elements Progressive Union, the United Middle Belt Congress, the Zamfara Commoner's Party from the Sokoto Caliphate, and the Kano People's Party.[43] It was obvious that the apparently placid political sky of the North had suddenly become stormy, and it was by no means a tempest in a teacup.

Several factors led to this ferment of political dissidence in the North. From the beginning of party politics in Nigeria, the politics of the North had been regionally oriented but there were a number of minority parties with a pan-Nigerian outlook. In 1948, when the Northern People's Congress (NPC) was formed, it was conceived as a forum for Northern intellectuals. At first it consisted of bureaucrats like the Sarduana of Sokoto, Alhaji Ahmadu Bello, Mallam Abubakar Tafawa Balewa (later Sir Abubakar), and radical intellectuals like Mallam Aminu Kano. When the orginazation was transformed into a political party in 1951, the radical intellectuals like Aminu Kano were edged out by the bureaucrats. The NPC, thus reconstituted, became the effective political power in the North. By 1958, 62 percent of the membership of the NPC National Executives were native administrative bureaucrats[44] and 27 percent were wealthy Northern entrepreneurs. These latter were mainly nonaristocratic and non-Fulani in origin. Thus, the NPC could rightly be said to be made up of aristocrats of birth and wealth. It was essentially regional in outlook and policy.

The radical intellectuals, under the leadership of Mallam Aminu Kano, formed the Northern Elements Progressive Union (NEPU). From the start NEPU was populist in orientation and pan-Nigerian in outlook. However, it did include a number of independent traders and a few wealthy businessmen. The bulk of its support, nevertheless, came mainly from small traders, shopkeepers and craftsmen, and some intellectuals.[45] In pursuit of its pan-Nigerian ideology it became affiliated with a Southern based party, the NCNC, which was also pan-Nigerian in outlook and espoused a populist cause.

The North was not plagued by ideological and class conflicts above; ethnic cleavages emerged in the North at the same time as they did in the South. This can certainly be attributed in large measure to the increased autonomy given to the regions by the 1954 constitution. As long as the center was under the exclusive control of British officials, regional attention was focused on the allocation of valued resources. As soon as the regions acquired considerable autonomy in the allocation of regional resources, ethnic parties made their appearance in the regions.

The first ethnic group to organize a separate political party in the North was the Kanuris (1948). Under the leadership of Ibrahim Iman, the Kanuris of Bornu organized the Bornu Youth Movement. "Its main platform was the creation of a separate Northeast state which would embrace Bornu, Adamawa, Bauchi and the Plateau Provinces."[46] The Kanuris regarded both the NPC and the NEPU as political parties dominated by the Hausa-Fulani ethnic groups. However, since their demand for a separate Kanuri state was in consonance with the NCNC-NEPU concept of Nigeria as a federation of states, they formed an alliance with that coalition.

In 1958, the Bornu Youth Movement broke the NCNC-NEPU alliance and joined the Action Group. The Action Group, a Yoruba ethnic party, was committed to the creation of states so as to destroy the numerical strength of the North and Northern dominance of the central government institutions. Unlike the NCNC, which had thoroughly compromised its stand on the creation of the states in the North by forming a coalition at the center with NPC, the Action Group was both willing and wealthy enough to support dissident groups in the North.

The threat the Action Group posed to the supremacy of the NPC in the North was not limited to its alliance with the Bornu Youth Movement; it was also apparent in both the Ilorin area and the Tiv district. In the Ilorin Emirate, where 90 percent of 400,000 inhabitants are Yoruba,[47] a vast majority of them had formed a political party known as the Ilorin Talaka Parapo (Commoner's Party). This party was solidly in support of the Action Group's ambitions in the North. It was also dedicated to the merger of Llorin with their kith and kin in Western Nigeria.

The greatest threat to the NPC by the Action group, by far, came from Tivland. The Tiv constitute the largest bloc of ethnic minorities in the pagan belts of Northern Nigeria. they numbered about 800,000(1952 census). But their importance stemmed not from their numbers alone, but mainly from their natural inclination to resort to violent resistance. We have noted the riots which occurred in 1960 in the Tiv district of Northern Nigeria.[48]

In 1961, in accordance with the constitutional provision, regional elections were scheduled in the Northern and Eastern Regions. The prospect of a new election led to renewed riot activties on the part of the United Middle Belt Party in the Tiv district in 1961. The NPC promptly arrested six members of the UMBC on theground that they had instigated the riots. Among these arrested was J.S. Tarka, the leader of the UMBC in the Tiv division. In spite of the arrest of the leaders, the people intensified the rioting. According to John P. Mackintosh, "it was not the work of a few travelling groups of professional strong arm men, but rather the uprising of a whole people into a collective paroxysm of anger...those

The paroxsm of anger was directed against the NPC for alleged oppressive measures against the Tiv people. There was even an open threat to decimate all the supporters of the NPC or to drive them back to Hausaland because they supported the alleged oppression of the Tiv people by the Hausas.

In April, 1961, when the election to the Northern House was held, the Tiv people turned out in large numbers to vote for the UMBC candidate. J. S. Tarka, The leader of the UMBC, was voted into the Northern House of Assembly while he was still in prison with the largest majority scored in the Northern Regions in that election - over 30,000.[49]a Tarka was subsequently released and subjected to a trial for his alleged complicity in the riots. He was declared innocent of the charges and acquitted. To quote James O'Connel:

> The turning point in Nigerian post independence politics came in 1961. In May 1961, the NPC virtually wiped out the opposition in the Northern regional election. Only the Tiv, who had been in sporadic revolt since 1960 remained recalcitrant.[50]

This recalcitrancy led to increasing victimization and repressive measures by the NPC government of the Northern Region. The NPC appointed chief was induced to use coercive measures to force the people to join the NPC.[51] The Tiv Native Authority controlled by UMBC elected members were paralyzed by the incorporation of traditional members into the council by the NPC. These nominated members were specifically instructed to vote for the government or lose their paid posts as district and village heads. Various tactics were used to coerce the Tiv into submission.

Nonetheless, while the NPC was trying with a measure of success to destroy the last stronghold of the opposition, the Tiv district, events in other parts of Northern

Nigeria, led to the revival of opposition parties in the North. In 1963, the Emir(King) of Kano in Northern Nigeria was deposed by the NPC government. Resentment over the deposition of the Emir led to the formation of the Kano People's Party supported by a powerful Muslim organization known as the Tijaniyya Brotherhood of which the deposed Emir was the leader. This event coupled with the continued resistance of the Tive people led to the formation of a coalition of the opposition parties in October, 1963. This new coalition, known as the Northern People's Front, was a party formed by dissident Hausa-Fulani intellectuals and commoners, the Burnu Youth Movement, the Kano People's Party, the Nigerian Tin Mines Workers' Union, and the Northern Federation of Labor. They pledged to present a common slate of candidates for all elections in Northern Nigeria to work for the creation of more states and for the lasting unity and stability of the country. They also agreed to work with other parties in Nigeria which had similar objectives. The most significant aspect of the creation of the front was the resolve of the front to wage a determined struggle against exploitation, oppression and suppression by the NPC and to fight for the toiling masses of the North and the Federal Republic of Nigeria.[52]

The organization in the North of a coalition opposed to the NPC raised hopes in the Southern political circles that the stranglehold of the Northern People's Congress on the politics of the North could be broken. This hope (largely misplaced) led to a flurry of alignments and realignments in the Southern political parties.

In December, 1963, the two greatest rivals of the Northern Peoples Congress -the NCNC and the rump Action Group began to negotiate for a possible coalition of the three parties. Reference has already been made in this chapter to how the new Premier of the Midwest had broached the idea of coalition between the NCNC and the Action Group to fight against the political preponderance of the NPC at the center. In fact, arrangements for the merger were concluded at the beginning of December, 1963. This arrangement was highly unpopular with a number of NCNC party leaders in the midwest and the Western Region. Chief Okotie-Ebo, the NCNC Federal Minister of Finance from the Midwest, termed it a "marriage of convenience."[53]

In the Western Region the reaction to the merger was swift and negative. The Western Regional Working Committee of the NCNC took exception to the NCNC-Action Group merger. They termed the merger an embarrassment to the NCNC members of the Western Region. It must be remembered that at this time the NCNC was still in a coalition with Akintola's UPP, an arch-enemy of the Action Group.

The immediate result of the alliance with the Action Group was the breakup of the UPP-NCNC coalition in the West and the formation of a new party known as the Nigerian National Democratic Party(NNDP). The members of the NCNC in the West resigned their membership and joined the new party in droves. Mr. Akintola, the leader of the new party (NNDP), based his appeal for membership on alleged Ibo domination and asserted that his aim was to restore "the lost glory of the Yorubas."[54] Mr. Akintola had been a principal figure in the 1962 Western Regional crisis which destroyed the Action Group. After destroying the Action Group, a party which had done so much to enhance Yoruba glory, he could hardly be a creditable apostle of Yoruba nationalism. The members of the NCNC in the West who joined the NNDP justified their action on more practical grounds. They maintained that the central working committee of the NCNC was essentially "interested in shattering the governing NCNC-UPP coalition" and with this in mind had proposed an unpopular and impractical alliance in the Western Region with the Action Group.[55]

This alliance between the NCNC and the Action Group, in spite of opposition from high ranking members of both, was formalized on June 3, 1964, and became known as the United Progressive Grand Alliance. The alliance immediately attracted the support of the Northern Peoples Front noted above. The NPF, in turn, joined the United Progressive Grand Alliance(UPGA). As the UPGA was extending its alliance the disaffected members of the NCNC and the Action Group in the West joined Chief Akintola's Nigerian National Democratic Party (NNDP).

As soon as the Nigerian National Democratic Party (NNDP) had consolidated its hold on the Western Region, it initiated negotiations with the NPC for an alliance. The NPC, which had watched the NCNC coalition- building experiment with grave apprehension, was only too pleased to enter into the alliance. Once this arrangement was complete, the NPC took decisive steps in building a coalition that would rival the NC-NC-dominated United Progressive Grant Alliance. It, thus, established an alliance with the dynamic party led by Dr. Chike Obi, an Ibo; The Republican Party led by Dr. Okezie, another Ibo; and the Niger Delta Congress (NDS), a minority party in the Eastern Region of Nigeria. These alliances, together with those already concluded with the NNDP and the Midwest Democratic Front, gave the NPC a pan-Nigerian outlook. On August 20, 1964, the alliance became known as the Nigerian National Alliance (NNA)

Thus, on the eve of the 1964 election, two coalition parties prepared to face each other for the election to the Federal House of the Assembly. Both coalitions were multi-regional and multi-ethnic in composition. This development was viewed by the NPC and the NCNC as positive, forward looking, and healthy manifestation of the democratic process. As the manifesto of the NNA phrased it:

> The coming together in one organization of the North and South, Ibo and Yoruba, Efik and Hausa and all other ethnic groups is the greatest blessing that ever happened to our people. It will underlie our strength and what is more it will ensure that all our people, the strong and the weak, will get a fair deal.[56]

The expectations of the UPGA were even more heartening. They stated in their manifesto that:

> As an article of faith UPGA will continue to support the idea of national parties and oppose regional parties. It is not difficult to see that one Nigerian nationality can hardly emerge on the basis of regional parties. All forms of extreme regionalism must therefore be openly discouraged and opposed. If a young man from Ibadan feel like a stranger in Sapelle and a man from Benin feel like a foreigner in Enugu and a man from Calabar feel like a foreigner at Maiduguri, then we still have a long way to go before we can really claim to be one country.[57]

The formation of opposing coalitions at the federal level by these two parties (the NCNC and the NPC) that were in a coalition in the federal legislature since 1959 can be seen as a clear realization that none of the regional parties could win a controlling majority in the forthcoming 1964 federal elections. There is nothing either strange or extraordinary about this development. According to Robert A Dahl:

> An opposition will try to convert additional voters and gain additional seats in parliamentary elections but it will assume that it cannot win a parliamentary majority; hence, it will concentrate heavily on entering and gaining as much as it can by entering into coalition bargaining.[58]

The fact that the two principal parties (NCNC and NPC) which were engaged in forming opposing coalitions were, at that very time, coalition partners in the central legislature does not of itself constitute an anomaly. In fact, it is erroneous to describe it as "double dealing and dirty politics,"[59] as T.O.S. Benson, the dissident vice-president of the NCNC, characterized it. It is perfectly in accord with opposition politics in a democracy.

Yet, in spite of these apparently democratic tendencies and the trans-ethnic and trans-regional nature of the coalitions engaged in the electioneering competition, the 1964 federal election was bogged down in a crisis. The inability of the major parties to resolve this crisis led to a military coup d'etat which led to the end of democratic government in Nigeria. What happened then? it is a major premise of our analysis that commitment to regional seperation enshrined in the Constitution of 1954 became an effective barrier against the counter-influence of trans-regional and trans-ethnic coalitions. According to Bernard Berelson and Gary A. Steiner, "Once a person commits himself to a position, that commitment itself becomes a barrier against change, however immediately counter-influences are brought to bear."[60] This barrier becomes all the more impregnable when it has received the blessing of entrenched constitutional provisions as was the case in Nigeria under the First Republic.

The Nigerian politicians were aware of the destructive influences of entrenched regionalism. The manifesto of UPGA openly charged that:

> Regional politicians have erected iron barriers between one region and another. As a result, they have succeeded in drastically curtailing the constitutional rights of the people. Individual citizens are no longer able to move freely, to engage in gainful occupation, and to own property in any pary of the country outside of their regions of origin.[61]

It was not only the constitutional rights of the individuals that had been curtailed by these iron barriers- the constitutional powers of the federal institutions had been so drastically curtailed by entrenched regionalism that they lacked both the power and the legitimacy to enforce compliance with the constitutionally valid pronouncements of the federal role incumbents. The election crisis dramatized the powerlessness of the federal institutions to constrain the regional authorities and compel obedience to its legally binding decisions.

The campaign for the election which was scheduled for December 30, 1964, started with a great deal of confidence and enthusiasm in both the NNA and UPGA circles. But the formation of trans-regional coalition parties and the campaign by the supporters of the two coalitions soon gave rise to inter-regional hostility and recrimination.

Until the 1964 election NCNC and the NPC had a tacit understanding that neither party would invade the territories of the other, but the NPC alliance with the Midwest Democratic Front- in the Midwest- a stronghold of NCNC-ended that agreement. Therefore, the NCNC, with its UPGA allies, was free to give both material and monetary support to the minority parties in the North. As noted earlier, the Bornu Youth Movement had deserted the NCNC because it felt that the NCNC did not give the necessary backing to its supporters in the North. Now with the Action Group contact and its sympathy for minorities in the North and NCNC's open and aggressive moves to assist its allies in the North, the leader of the NPC and its NNA allies were afraid that the outcome of the election might not be in their favor after all. The NNA was more than a little perturbed by the aggressive attempts of UPGA leaders to reach the Northern electorate. In fact, the NNPD organ noted that the UPGA had adopted "a carbon copy of Chief Awolowo's blueprint for the 1959 federal election..."[62] Awolowo's policy of forming coalition parties with minorities in the North (the ag-UMBC) gave the NPC no little trouble in the 1959 election campaign and consequently the NPC swore to destroy the Action Group as a party.

Another reason why the Northern Peoples Congress-NNA alliance, in spite of its apparent lead sought to harass the opposition was that the nature of the political institution in the North fostered the growth of autocratic tendencies both in the region and the regional party(NPC). As Wheare inquiringly suggested:

> ...suppose all the regional governments or a majority of them were dictatorships, what machinery could exist to choose a general government which would be independent of the region governments? No free election by the people of the autocratic regions is to be expected."[63]

As we have noted above each of the regional parties was closely tied to the government and depended on the government for funds. Consequently, none of the regional governments could claim that it did not use its authority to hamper the activities of the opposition in its region in the 1964 election. However, these practices were much more glaring, unabashed and pervasive in the North because the Native Authority institution in the North was highly bureaucratized, and, to say the least, autocratic. There was no doubt that such men as Sir Abubakar Tafawa Balewa nursed marked liberal tendencies. Nonetheless, their subordinates in the Native Authority system showed marked autocratic tendencies. They did not scruple to use force to impress both regional authorities and the party in power (NPC) even when these tactics were not necessary. We have stressed that the Native Authority officials predominated in both the party hierarchy and the regional government and that both party and the regional government in the North could rightly be said to be the Native Authority writ large. These Native Authority officials wore two hats. As Native Authority officials they were bureaucrats. As party members owing their positions to the power of the regional party (NPC) they were politicians. For the most part the lines between the two offices were blurred. This is clearly borne out by the following statement by J.P. Mackintosh:

> Among the Provincial Commissioners, the politicians with ministerial rank in charge of each province, it seems that there was a competion to see who would succeed in having most unopposed returns. A senior minister visited Bauchi and said it would be a disgrace if there were no unopposed returns there. Again in view of the recent trends in Nigerian politics and in particular in the Northern elections of 1961, it was curious that the NPC should have to apply such pressure. Had free elections been held in the North the evidence suggests that the result would have been most exactly the same: the total rejection of the NPF. The explanations cannot be that this was due to fear of opposition victories, as the pressure came almost entirely in NPC strongholds rather that in the few marginal seats.[64]

Fear of the opposition cannot be ruled out; otherwise it would be a case of sheer autocracy to prevent the opposition from contesting an election even where the NPC was sure of victory. According to Mackintosh:

> The sentiments revealed in interviews with the author were the assumption that open opposition was insulting and should be prevented, and the feeling that zeal in preventing opposition candidatures would be regarded with approval in Kaduna.[65]

On the complaint of the opposition, the members of the electoral commission flew to Kano. There, they found that the opposition candidates were virtually prevented from submitting their nomination papers or even entering their constituencies to campaign. All of the 24 opposition candidates in Sokoto province, 12 of the 14 opposition candidates in Katsina, and one candidate from the province of Biu sought refuge in the opposition headquarters in Kano[66] because it was unsafe for them to enter their constituencies, much less to campaign there. Those who dared to file their nomination papers were sent to prison. According to Aminu Kano, the President of the opposition Nigerian People's Front (NPF), as of November 20, 1964 the number of opposition candidates jailed was 26.[67] Even J.S. Tarka, the General President of the United Middle Belt Congress (UMBC), one of the parties that formed the NPF coalition, had been arrested and jailed.[68]

What is perhaps most surprising is that those members of the opposition who were not allowed to submit their nomination papers and 99 percent of those who were arrested an imprisoned were natives of the Northern Region, and a vast majority of them were of the Hause-Fulani ethnic groups. Here the conflict was essentially intraregional, and to a great extent, intra-ethnic in scope. There was no doubt that interethnic overtones exacerbated the conflict. However, of all people jailed in the North, few were Ibo. G.M. Abengowe, an Ibo, one of the lawyers appointed by the UPGA to protect the interests of the coalition, was charged with unlawful assembly[69] by an Alkali Court,[70] tried, and sentenced to nine months imprisonment at hard labor.

The only logical explanation for the victimization of the opposition is that opposition to the region as such. Opposition to the policies and values of the party in power was regarded not as signs of a democratic electoral system, but as treasonable acts to be punished by the regional instruments of power and coercion. As Post and Vickers put it:

> Anxious to defend its values, and jealous of its power, the NPC was accustomed to treat the opposition minority roughly and did not break the habit in 1964. Complaints from UPGA supporters were myriad and often well founded.[71]

In the Western Region where the Nigerian National Democratic Party (NNDP), an ally of the NPC was in power, the victimization of the opposition was both violent and pervasive but not as methodical, systematic or as institutionalized as in the Northern Region. It was not as instutionalized partly because in the Western Region opposition to autocracy was part of the traditional way of life even before the establishment of British authority.[72] Moreover, since the declaration of emergency in 1962, the government had becme increasingly unpopular. The government was, therefore, afraid that in a free election its chances of retaining power were rather slim.

The 1964 election campaign was, therefore, marked with increasingly repressive measures on the part of the NNDP government and the spirited determination of the opposition to resist that oppression. As a result many people on both sides lost their lives.[73] As we noted earlier, since the creation of the Midwest Region, the Western Region became the only ethnically homogenous region in Nigeria. Therefore, the membership of the two parties (NNDP and the Action Group) within the Western Region was made up of people of the same ethnic group (Yoruba). Yet, the feeling of "consciousness of kind", "those congruities of blood, speech and custom"[74] did not exert that "ineffabled and at times overpowering coerciveness"[75] so as to prevent the two parties from resorting to large scale use of force in pursuit of political power.

Although both the Action Group and the Nigerian National Democratic Party were allied to nationwide opposing-coalitions (NNA and UTGA) the causes of the conflict surrounding the 1964 election in the Western Region were intra-ethnic and intra-regional. The conflict assumed crisis portions because the parlimentary system in the Western Region and in Nigeria as a whole had not acquired the necessary legitimacy to mediate effectively electioneering campaigns involving the transfer of political power. Moreover, because of the progressive regionalization of political power and political loyalties, none of the hasty coalitions formed during the 1964 election could acquire a national appeal. Each coalistion was identified with the region which provided the leadership.

The Nigerian National Alliance (NNA) was identified with the Northern Peoples Congress (NPC) which had its base in the Northern Region. The United Progressive Grand Alliance was identified with the National Council of Nigerian Citizens which had its base in the Eastern Region. Because of the low level of legitimacy of both party and parliamentary structures in Nigeria, the lines between these two structures were completely blurred. Therefore, any attempt by the leaders of these two coalitions to campaign for the coalition candidates in regions other than their own was regarded as interference in that other region's affairs.

For example, Dr. Okpara, the leader of the UPGA coalition and deputy leader of the NCNC, was barred from entering Ogbomosho in the Western Region, the home of the leader of the NNDP, when he attempted to campaign for the UPGA coalition candidates in the Western Region.[76] In the North also a team of UPGA leaders consisting of Dr. Okpara, an Ibo, and leader of the UPGA coalition, Chief Adegbenro, a Yoruba, leader of the Action Group party in the Western Region, and Alhaji Aminu Kano, leader of the Northern Elements Progressive Union, a minor party in the Northern Region—all UPGA coalitions menvers—were barred from holding any campaign meetings in the Northern Region.[77] The Northern Region was controlled by the Northern Peoples Congress (NPC) and its alliance in the Nigerian National Alliance (NNA).

It must be observed that all these actions were taken through the governmental institutions of the regions. In the Northern and Western Regions where the Native Authority systems were fully developed, there were special police departments known as Native Authority Police and Special Native Authority Courts known in the Northern Region as Alkali Courts. These courts and Native Authority Police were under the control of regional authorities and in the Nigerian political climate, whatever was under the control of the regional authorities was unter the control of the party in power in that region. Therefore, these governmental institutions (Native Authority Courts and Native Authority Police) were used as effective repressive weapons by the party in power in the regions. In fact, Post and Vickers regarded these institutionalized obstructions ahd harassments as one of the greatest threats to free and fair campaigns for the 1964 elections. They emphasized that, "Much more serious handicaps to the UPGA campaign were the phenomena we have labelled obstruction and punitive control,"[78] that is—blatant "misuse of institutions"[79] by the Native Authority Police and the Native Authority Courts.

Robin Luckman's summary of the situation deserves to be quoted in full. He noted that:

> The 1964 federal election campaign was long and violent. There were riots and clashes between thugs employed by rival political parties. The machinery of local government was used to prevent meetings to intimidate candidates and sometimes to incarcerate them. *These things happened more often in Northern and Western Regions. The Midwest and the East were relatively peaceful, mainly, it should be said, because of each electoral alliance between the contestants in these regions.*[80] (emphasis mine)

It is instructive to note that the Nigerian police force (federal) made efforts to gain control of the Native Authority Police force but were frustrated in their attempt by the Northern and Western Regional government. As early as September, 1964, when violent clashes between opposition parties especially in the Western Region became serious, the Nigerian Police Council headed by the Inspector-General of the Nigerian Police force met in Lagos. This council consisting of the Nigerian Police, the Native Authority Police in the Western and Northern Regions (there was no Native Authority Police in the Eastern Region) invited the Prime Minister and the regional Premiers to the above mention meeting. They concluded an arrangement to place the Native Authority Police under Nigerian (federal) Police control. The Northern Region, although it was party to the agreement, refused to federalize its Native Authority Police. The Western Region federalized the Native Authority Police but later withdrew the order and instructed the Native Authority Police in the Western Region to act independently.[81] The Nigerian (federal) police was in both cases powerless to compel the regional authorities to keep the agreement. The conclusion is inescapable that the federal police as an institution was overawed by the regional authorities and that the federal government did nothing to aid its law enforcement arm to stop the mounting violence.

As part of the arrangement made between the police and the Premiers, it was agreed that a meeting of the Prime Ministers and the regional Premiers would be held on October 22 and 23rd to draw up plans for the "free and peaceful conduct of the forthcoming federal election."[82] The meeting was subsequently held on the agreed dates. But the Prime Minister and the Premier of the Northern Nigeria were conspicuously absent. Both of these men were leaders of the NPC, the party which controlled the Northern Region. The Federal Minister of Defense, and NPC member, was sent to represent both the NPC and the Northern Regional interests. The nine-point plan for free and fair elections worked out by the conference of Premiers was characterized by the Northern Peoples Congress and its ally the Nigerian National Democratic Party (Western Region) as "empty and meaningless phrases."[83]

It is obvious that amidst the mounting violence and the inability or disinclination on the part of some of the regiona Premiers and even the Prime Minister to suppport the Nigerian Police in their effort to make the election free and fair, repression, violence and intimidation were bound to be rampant. Under such conditions, the elections could neither be fair nor free.

The problems of the Nigerian Police (federal) only serve to highlight the problems faced by the Federal Electoral Commission which was mandated by law to arrange and supervise the conduct of elections. The Electoral Commission was established under the Electoral Act of 1962. Its membership reflected the main political division of the country into regions. Each was represented in the commission by a person nominated by that region and appointed to the commission by the President. The North was represented by an official of the Kano Native Administration, the East was represented by a lawyer, the Midwest, by a lawyer, who was, at the same time a son of the King of Benin; the West was represented by a medical doctor, and Lagos, the capital of Nigeria, was represented by an Anglican clergyman. There were also two officials, the chairman and a secretary to the commission. The chairman was appointed by the President on the advice of the Prime Minister. The secratary to the commission was a civil servant from the Northern Region.[84] The commission was, therefore, made up of six voting members and one secretary.

The powers of the commission were elaborated in the Electoral Act of 1962 which was part of the fundamental law of the First Repblic of Nigeria; section 156 (2) of the act states that:

> "If the Electoral Commission is satisfied that there has been a substantial failure to comply with the requirements of this act before the date fixed for holding elections in respect of nominations or otherwise, however, the Electoral Commission may postpone the election until such a time as such requirements are satisfied."

The commission was, therefore, clearly, unequivocally and definitely empowered by the act to postpone elections if there had been a substantial failure to comply with the requirements of the act. The relevant question in this case was whether substantial failure to comply with the provisions of the act and had been proven to exist.

Complaints which reached the commission by telegrams, letters, and personal representation revealed that there had been widespread violations of the electoral provisions. As a result of numerous and serious allegations made by the opposition candidates, especially in the North, the commission flew to Kano in Northern Nigeria to make an on-the-spot verification of the situation on the 18th of December, 1964.[85] In Kano, the commissioners found 25 opposition candidated from Sokoto, 12 candidates from Katsina, and one candidate from Biu, all from Northern Nigeria, who sought shelter in Kano because they were unable to enter their respective constituencies to file nomination papers due to intimidations by supporters of the Northern Peoples Congress, the party in power in the region. In addition to the visit by a team of electoral commissioners, the chairman of the commission, Mr. Esua, investigated the adequacy of the privacy of the erected election booths and sent teams of inspectors to the various regions to supervise voting arrangements and the procedures for the publication of voters lists.

Thise investigations revealed that although the closing date for nomination of candidates for the election was December 19, 1964, the voter registration list was not published until December 17, 1964. According to the requirements, any person wishing to nominate a candidate for an election must prove that he or she was a registered voter. NPC candidates, being the candidates of the party in power, did not find it difficult to file nomination papers. Those who wished to nominate opposition members were unable in the absence of a voters list to prove that they were properly registered as electors and, therefore, entitled to nominate candidates. Complaints were lodged before the commissioners that when opposition candidates had secured valid nomination papers, the Nothern Regional electoral commisioners had devised ingenious ways to dodge the receipt of nomination papers from opposition candidates.[86]

After examining the evidence, the Chairman of the Electoral Commission, Mr. E.

E. Esua, made a radio broadcast to the nation on December 22, 1964. He declared that evidence collected as a result of the investigations has revealed that there was substantial failure to comply with the requirements of the Electoral Acts.[87] As we pointed our earlier, section 156 (2) of the Federal Electoral Act of 1962, gave the commission full power to postpone elections when there had been substantial failure to comply with the requirements of this act. Section 156 (3) of that act also gave the commission the power to postpone elections selectively and only in those areas where there had been substantial failure to comply with the requirements of the Act.

Not only was the commission given ample powers to postpone elections either in selected areas or throughout the federation, its autonomy, tenure and security were specifically guaranteed by the constitution. Section 50 (9) of the Federal Constitution of 1963 guaranteed that "in the exercise of its functions under this constitution, the commission shall not be subject to the direction or control of any person or authority." Section 133 also guaranteed that the salaries and allowances of the electoral commissioners "shall be a charge on the consolidated Revenue of the Federation."

In addition, ethnically and regionally the compositon of the commision was mixed. The Chairman of the Commission, as we have noted, was an Efik (a minor ethnic group in the Eastern Region). None of the major ethnic groups—Hausa-Fulani, Ibos or Yorubas—had an overriding majority in the commission. The issue of one of the ethnic groups dominating the commission was clearly out of the question.

Yet, the commissioners were unable to arrive at any decision regarding the postponement of the election. The crucial question is why. The reasons are clearly evident. As we shall indicate the institution of regional separation by devolutionary method prevented the emergence of federal institutions which are independent of the regional authorities and which have power to mediate effectively political interation between the component units.

The internal operations of the whole electoral commission reveal how the cross pressures of regional loyalties exerted a crippling influence over the corporate responsibility of the commission. In order to carry out their legally assigned duties in the regions, the commissioners had to rely on a cadre of subordinate staff, including regional electoral commissioners. For the most part, these were recruited from the regions in which they were to serve. Because of the intimate knowledge of the election districts which the electoral process demands, these regional officers were fo the most part parmanent staff of the regional governments who were temporaly relieved of their regular duties and assigned to the electoral commision for the duration of the electoral campaign. Being permanent employees of the regional governments which were controlled by the party in power in the regions, they were both by necessity, political pressure, and personal interest contrained to place the interest of the regions above a vague, if not remote, interest and loyalty to the federal government. Hence, we find many of these regional electoral officers inaccurately declaring candidated belonging to the dominant political power in the regions as having been returned unopposed even where valid nomination papers were filed by opposition candidates.

When the chair man of the federal election commission challenged the propriety of the actions of these regional electoral officers, the Premier of the Western Region, Chief Akintola, defended the action of the regional electoral officers in the Western Region.[88] Alhaji Abdul Razaq the NPC National Legal Adviser, issued a statement calling the challenge by the Federal Election Commissioner, Mr. Esua, "unfortunate and preposterous" and declared that the Northern Peoples Congress(NPC) would "challenge in any court any attempt to discourage the Nigerian National Alliance (NPC controlled coalition) candidates from returning unopposed."[89] In the face of these powerful regional oppositions and reactions the federal election commission was unable to assert any authority over the regional electoral officers.

Not only were there high-powered and crippling regional pressures on the federal election commission but the commissioners themselves were not able to transcend the bariers of institutionalized regional pressures and regional loyalties in their own deliberations. It was obvious from subsequent events discussed below that there were deep and disturbing controversies behind closed doors among the members of the electoral commission. After lengthy deliberations the hopes that the electoral commission

107

could put a lid on the conflict by postponing the election and correcting the abuses were shattered by the chairman's announcement over the radio on the evening of December 29, 1964, that voting would start on the following morning, December 30, 1964.

As soon as the announcement was made, three members of the commission, one from the East, one from the Midwest and one from the capital territory of Lagos, resigned. They stated that the announcement was made without the concurrence or knowledge of the members. They issued a statement to the effect that the commission had been stalemated on the issue of postponement.[90] It is interesting to note that all three who resigned came from areas in which the NCNC-UPGA alliance had overwhelming support. Thus, the low institutionalization of the electoral commission as an institution gave full scope to regional and party loyalties and made them prevail over national (federal) interests.

Furthermore, even if the electoral commission had been unanimous in the decision either to postpone the election or to go on with it as scheduled, whatever power the commission had could not be enforced because the commission had no coercive powers to give effect to its decisions. It had to depend ultimately on the Prime Minister. But the Prime Minister had made it perfectly clear on the 28th of December, 1964, (a day before the chairman of the commission made his announcement) that the election must go on as scheduled on the 30th of December, 1964.[91]

The Prime Minister had, in face, pre-empted the power conferred by the constitution on the electoral commission. His total disregard for this exclusive clause of the constitution which gave the commission executive power over the conduct of elections and their postponement can only be understood in terms of the fact that the Prime Minister owed his power to the NPC, the party which was in power in the Northern Region; that the institutionalization of regional separation had made the interest of the North, and loyalty to that interest, supreme in the minds of NPC members. Since the NPC controlled the central cabinet, the interest of the North was ipso facto the interest of the central cabinet of which the Prime Minister was the leader.

As we have noted earlier, most of the irregularities occured in the Northern Region. In the absence of a strong federal government with the ligitimacy and capability to make its decisions effective, respected and binding on the regional government, it is hardly conceivable that a federal Prime Minister who owed his power and position to a regional party would take actions which was seriously prejudicial to the interest of that region and the party in power in that region.

The President of the Federation, on the other hand, who was not a member of the party in power in the Northern Region (NPC), had the institutiona power and authority to preserve the constitution, but did not have the coercive power to back his decidions in the event of a conflict with the Prime Minister. It is with these points in mind that we must understand the conflict and crisis in the 1964 federal election as they revolved around these two powerful political figures.

As far back as December 10, 1964, the President, acting on the Prime Minister's advice, dissolved the Federal Parliament in accordance with constitutional provisions which stipulated that an election shall be held every five years. In the address which stipulated that an election shall be held every five years. In the address which accompanied the formal dissolution, the President informed the nation that already hundreds of telegrams had been sent to him alleging unfair practices in the campaign which was already underway.[92] He detailed the allegations and warned the national politicans that they were courting national disaster in their desire to satisfy "their lust for office."[93]

Events soon drew the President into the conflict. On December 22, 1964, 66 members of the NNA and 15 members of the UPGA were declared unopposed. We have already discussed the circumstances surrounding the conflict over these unopposed returns. On the same day the chairman of the electoral commission made an "emergency" broadcast indicating that some of these candidates were returned unopposed from constituencies in which opposing candidates had filed valid nomination papers.[94]

As a result of these developments, a deputation was sent by UPGA to urge the President to postpone the election. The President, after due deliberation, summoned a conference of regional governors to the State House on December 26, 1964. At the end, the conferees issued a communique deploring the widespread allegations of violence, intimidation, and molestations of political opposition throughout the federation. They urged the public at large to do all in their power to ensure unity and stability and "expressed the wish for a better response from the public and particularly political party supporters, to the apppeals being made by all their leaders for peace and better understanding."[95].

As an instrument of persuasion, the conference was an adroit political ploy. The move was hailed in the *Daily Express* as the "first of its kind."[96] Both the *West African Pilot* and the *Daily Express* wrote editorials in praise of the efforts of the President and the Governors. A mammoth crowd, led by the UPGA politicals and supporters, staged a demonstration in Lagos calling for postponement of the election. The Action Group section of the alliance reminded the demonstrators that the electoral commission had full powers to postpone the election. Therefore, the demonstrators, numbering about 20,000 passed a resoltuion stating that:

> Whereas the Federal Electoral Commission in the Same statement declared some polling booths in Northern Nigeria did not conform to stipulated specifications and that elections would be postponed in the constituencies and those were candidates were wrongfully returned unopposed;
>
> Whereas there are only two days to the election and the Federal Electoral Commission has not announced the number of seats to be contested;
>
> Whereas there had been irregularities in all stages of the elections so far: preliminary voter's lists, claims and objections, appointment of registration, electoral, presiding and polling officers, nominations, etc.;
>
> Whereas NNA has not honored any of the agreements reached at the meeting of political parties to guarantee free and fair elections;
>
> Whereas we have lost faith in the ability of the Federal Electoral Commission to guarantee free and fair elections:
>
> Now be it resolved and it is hereby resolved as follows:
>
> That the Federal election be postponed forthwith.
>
> That the report that 68 NNA candidates are now returned unopposed be rejected. (The exact number of candidates returned unopposed is variously stated in different places.)
>
> That we demand a free and fair election at which electoral officers should be exchanged between the regions and the regions and the army invited to maintain order so that citizens may vote without molestation and that safe conduct of ballot boxes is guaranteed.
>
> That we warn the nation of the disastrous consequences that would result if there is any attempt to impose an unpopular and unacceptable government on the people.[97]

The demonstrators marched to the State House and had an audience with the President. There is not doubt that the President's attempt to influence and persuade the public to express their concern about the travail of the constitution was successful. But, the success was a partial one. The President, as an erstwhile President of the NCNC, was looked upon as favoring his party. As th support of his views came mainly from the South, he was viewed by the North as part of the Southern plot to exclude the

North from power. It did not matter that some of the parties allied with UPGA were from the North. What mattered was that UPGA's top leaders came from the South. Here the struggle had assumed a North-South dimension. Unlike the President of the United States, the President of the First Republic of Nigeria had no patronage to dispense and, therefore, little with which to influence those he wished to persuade. Additionally, he had not national electoriate to which he coulddirect his appeal.

It is under these circumstances that we can understand the factors which led to the confrontation between the President and the Prime Minister. Pressured by a largely Southern demand for postponement, and goaded by the pressures from UPGA Leaders, the President arranged a meeting with the Prime Minister on December 29, 1964. In the course of the meeting the President suggested that the election be postponed for six months, that a United Nations team of observers be invited to supervise the election to ensure a free and fair one. The Prime Minister replied that postponement was not warranted by the circumstances and that it would be both demeaning and humiliating to seek outside assistance.[98]

The disagreement between the two chief officers caused a deadlock. The President is vested with executive authority of the federation, but in order to exercise this authority he must take the advice of the Council of Minister, headed by the Prime Minister. The President was painfully aware that the Prime Minister stood on his constitutional rights. But it was equally clear that the provisions of that constitution had been contrvened and flouted by the various parties during the 1964 election campaign. The only recourse left to the President to keep his oath to defend the constitution was to force the issue with the Prime Minister. But he know only too well that to enforce compliance with his decisions he must have control of the armed forces and the police. However, the constitution placed the ultimate control and disposition of the armed forces and the police under the "overall directions of the Council of Ministers" headed by the Prime Minister.[99]

Nonetheless, legal control of the armed forces and of the forces of coercion is one thing and defacto control is another, depending on the loyalty of the armed forces and the police. The gauge the level of the loyalty of the armed forces and the police to his office, the President called a meeting of the heads of the armed forces and police. He reminded them that the President was the commander-in-chief and that the officers of the armed forces and the police took the oath of allegiance to him as President. The Commander of the Navy, Commodore Wey, told the President in no uncertain terms that they would take orders from the Prime Minister not from the President. This reply only served to drive home to the President that he had neither the legal nor de facto control of the army. Under the Nigerian Constitution, the President as a constitutional head of the state was a Commander-in-Chief without an army and, in this case—without its loyalty.

The Prime Minister, on the other hand, was under no illusion as to his legal control over the armed services and the police and their loyalty to him. He did not, therefore, scruple to show that he was ready to use them. ON December 28, 1964, there was a large demonstration in Lagos in support of the President's positon that the election be postponed. As the crowd of about 20,000 demonstrated in the streets of Lagos, the Prime Minister ordered a military maneuver in which 400 troops took part. It was, indeed, a clear warning to the demonstrators that disorder would not be toleratd. Yet, as the election campaign drew to a close, acts of violence were being perpetrated, especially in the North and the West, without effective action on the part of the Prime Minister to bring the wave of violence under control. Finally, on December 29, 1964, a day before the election, the Prime Minister summond the heads of the armed services and the police to discuss indetail the precautionary measures to be taken on election day.[101]

The fruitless attempt by the President to enlist the help of the armed forces and the police and the military maneuver ordered by the Prime Minister are clear indications that the federal institutions were unable to mediate a peaceful transfer of power within the federation. As the federal institutions became bogged down in the conflict between the President and the Prime Minister, the conflict over the election assumed the character of a trial of political strength between the regions and the political parties which had their bases in these regions.

At this stage, the United Progressive Grand Alliance, controlled by the NCNC with its base in the Eastern Region, decided to boycott the election. The Nigerian National Alliance, controlled by the NPC with its base in the Northern Region, decided to go ahead with the election. The Midwestern Region, controlled by the NCNC with its UPGA alliance, at first decided to boycott the election. But fearing that opposition party would take advantage of the situation, the NCNC, the party in power in the Midwest, decided to lift the boycott and urged its supporters to vote on the 30th of December, 1964, when the election was scheduled. In the Western Region election was held in the areas which supported the Nigerian National Democrats Party (NNDP) which was in alliance with the Northern Peoples Congress (NPC). Those in support of the Action Group which was allied to the NCNC boycotted the election. The boycott was completely effective in the Eastern Region where the NCNC was in power. The election was effectively conducted in the Northern Region NPC power base. The NCNC won the election in the Midwest where the regional NCNC leaders in power changes its mind and mobilized the voters to vote. In the West, the election was partially successful. The supporters of the NNDP came out to vote while the supporters of the Action Group boycotted the election.

Thus, the institution of regional separation and the weakness of the federal institutions led to a situation in which the decision whether to hold or boycott the federal election passed to the regions and the parties in power in those regions. Ethnic factors entered into the conflict because of the provenance of the principal actors and their connection with parties in power in those areas. The fact that the Prime Minister and the leader of the NPC (Sardauna of Sokoto) were Hausa-Fulani, the predominant ethnic group in the Northern Region, led to the association of the activities of the NPC and the Northern Regional government controlled by that party was the Hausa-Fulani. On the other hand, the fact that the President and the leader of NCNC (Dr. Okpara) were Ibos made the acts of the NCNC and its leadership the acts of the Ibos in general. The ensuing conflict thus assumed the character of a confrontation between the Northern Region and the Eastern Region; between the Hausa-Fulani ethnic group and the Ibos. Because of the low legitimacy of the federal institutions, it was assumed that these incumbents were acting in their capacities as Ibos and Hausa-Fulanis from the Eastern and Northern Regions, respectively. The concept of a National President and a National Prime Minister acting in the interest of the nation was not clearly perceived by the people or perhaps by the incumbants themselves.

The crisis surrounding the federal election of 1964 thus developed into a major conflict between the Northern Region and the Eastern Region. The election results reflects this controntation. In the Northern Region where the NPC controlled the government, 162 out of the total 167 seats were won by the NPC. Two seats went to the opposition parties in the North that were allied with NCNC in the UPGA coalition. In the Midwest the NCNC won all the seats. In the Western Region where there was a partial boycott of the election, the Nigerian National Democratic Party allied to the NPC won 36 out of the 57 seats. Thus, the NPC and its ally, the NNDP had a clear Majority. In the Eastern Region, where there was a total boycott, arrangements were made to hold a fresh election on the 18th of March, 1965.

In the meantime, attention centered on whether the President would call on Sir Abubakar Tafawa Balewa to form a government. His party had won a majority of the seats in the election. But the legality of the election was questioned both by the President and the UPGA coalition led by the NCNC. There was also the conflict over the role of the President and the Prime Minister prior to the election and the constitutional question of the role of the President in Nigerian politics in general. Furthermore, an election had not been held in the Eastern Region.

According to Section 43 of the Nigerian Constitution of 1963, "the House of Representatives shall consist of three hundred the twelve members." Also, Section 52 of the constitution states that "every constituency established under Section 51 of this constitution shall return to the House of Representatives, one member who shall be directly elected in such manner as may be prescribed by Parliment."[102] No election was held in 51 constituencies in the East nor in 3 constituencies in Lagos.

Hence, apart from the irregularities in the election campaign itself, two provisions of the constitution - Sections 43 and 52 (1), as we noted above, were not met. Whether the Federal House of Assembly could be legally constituted was highly arguable. What then were the options before the President? The President could, under Section 87 (2) and (8) refuse to reappoint the Prime Minister and so inform him. This he threatened to do and had prepared a broadast to that effect. The broadcast was never officially aired. The Prime Minister's statement that "if we are to go by our constitution, there is nothing to stop the machinery of forming the Government and calling Parliament from being set in motion."[103] could not legally be supported. The President could simply inform the Prime Minister that he had no intention of reappointing him. At that point, that office would become vacant, according to Section 87 (8a). Or the President could delay the summoning of the Parliment for a month under Section 67 of the constitution, and thus paralyze all governmental activities.

The President, however, did not take any of these measures. In his opinion, it was not a question of legal technicalities but essentially a political and moral question. But whether it was a legal, political or moral question, it was certain that the institutional structure of the federation designed to ensure a peaceful transfer of power through election had failed. It was equally clear that the edifice of the federal constitution had been assaulted, battered and rudely shaken.

As the President and the Prime Minister was contemplating what actions to take to salvage the situation, the Chief Justice of the Federation, Sir Adetokumboh Ademola, a Yoruba, and the Chief Justice of the Eastern Region. Sir Louis Mbanefo, an Ibo, headed a team which worked out a compromise solution known as the Zik-Balewa compromise. This six point plan which was accepted by both the President and the Prime Minister stated that the only way to save the constitution, avoid deadlock, and prevent bloodshed and disintegration would be by:

> 1. Reaffirmation of belief in the unity of the Federation in which every citizen shall have equal opportunity and no one shall be oppressed.
>
> 2. Strict observance of the Constitution until it is amended according to the law and the will of the people.
>
> 3. A broad-based government should be formed on the results of the last election so as to avoid chaos.
>
> 4. The legality of the present election should be determined by the courts and the results of the elections should be upheld, except in certain constituencies where the number of voters were rather small as to make a mockery of democracy. In such a case another election should be held.
>
> 5. Arrangements should be made within six months to review the Constitution and machinery for elections. This should be in the form of a Commission of 11, constituted as follows: one to be appointed by the President, two to be appointed by the Prime Minister, and two each by each regional Premier. The Commission should work for one year in order to ascertain the wishes of the people of Nigeria. Then a constituent assembly can take the final decision.
>
> 6. Dissolution of the Government of Western Nigeria to enable the people of the Region to express their will as to who should govern them.[104]

This was at best a reprieve. It did not address itself to the underlying causes of the conflict. To save the constitution, it validated the gross violations of that very constitution. These violations as noted above enabled the NPC to harass and destroy the opposition in the North and thus, win enough seats to gain a controlling majority in the federal legislature. This majority enabled it to dominate the federal institution Once in power, the NPC set about to strenghten its hold on the federation. All talk of a broad-based government was consigned to the scrap heap. Regionalism stood triumphant and hastened the day of reckoning which came with the military coup d'etat of January, 1966. Both the constitution and democracy were drowned in a revolt which resulted in a civil war.

In conclusion, it must be emphasized that the institutional framework—the electoral commision—designed to mediate conflict over succession, utterly failed in its function. The power to use coercive measures to support the decisions of the electoral commission rested squarely with the Prime Minister and his Cabinet. The commission had, by law, full powers and was not subject to any direction or authority from any source. But if it made a decision which the Prime Minister did not approve, it could not compel the Prime Minister to use the coercive powers to support that desicion. The Prime Minister, who owed his power to the NPC could not use the power against the region controlled by his political boss.

Therefore, the electoral commission, as a political institution, was unable to mediate conflict arising out of the election because it had all the legal power but no coercive powers. Moreover, this being its first attempt to manage the electoral machinery since independence, it had not acquired the legitimacy which comes from competence and habit.

On the other hand, the constitution made the President a Commander-in-Chief without an army. He was vested with the executive power of the federation but he had to take the advice of the cabinet of which the Prime Minister was the chief. It was certainly correct that Under Section 93, subsection 3, he could take action without the advice of the cabinet, and, in spite of it. But if he had opted for this coursse of action, he would not kave been able to depend on the Prime Minister to order the police and the army to back his decision, especially when that decision adversely affected the Prime Minister and the regional party which put him in power. It is obvious that the President whipped up tremendous popular support, especially in the South, but popular support had little effect on the Prime Minister. He did not owe his election to the whole people—he owed his position to the NPC and its Northern supporters. As long as the Northern Regioin, the most populous region in Nigeria, was behind him, he had both the manpower and the coercive potential to force any issue with the President.

To quote Kenneth Post and Michael Vickers:

> The basic source of conflict was the mobilization of people, not towards some transcending national loyalty, but rather towards indentification with an intermediate cultural section.[105]

In Nigeria this problem has been compounded by making the regions the focus of political power and political competition. The unique feature of the Nigerian political system is that it was a confederation of autonomous regions, created by progressive devolution of power from a colonial based unitary central government to regional governments with residual powers. As the colonial power waned, the power of the federal government as an independent institution faded accordingly. The federal government became little more than a distributive mechanism, mediating the progressive allocation of power and revenue to the regions.

CONCLUSION

It is the contention of this study that the constitutional development of Nigeria was delimited and structured by the British policy of devolving maximum political power to the component regions of the federation. This devolutionary process culminating in the Federal Constitution of 1954 resulted in the progressive weakening of the central government and the emergence of strong regional centers with power resources and capabilities which dominated the center. Thus, on the attainment of independence in 1960, Nigeria became, as William H. Riker noted, the prime example of a federation in which constituent governments could "overawe the center."[1]

Because of this weakness of the federal government, the withdrawal of the superimposed colonial authority created a power vacuum which turned the federal institutions into an arena where powerful regional groups engaged in a unmitigated competitive struggle for dominance, power and resources. The continuous conflict over revenue allocation, the unresolved conflict and crisis over the census, and the election crisis of 1964, were the eventual outcome of these unmediated struggles. As Huntington aptly observed:

> A society with weak political institutions lacks the ability to curb the excesses of personal and parochial desires. Politics is a Hobbesian world of unrelenting competition among social forces—between man and man, family and family, clan and clan, region and region, class and class—a competition unmediated by more comprehensive political organizationis.[2]

Politics is by nature conflice generating. The problem in Nigeria, therefore, is not the existence of conflict between region and region, between clan and clan, per se, but the absence of a strong central institution which has the legitimacy and independent power base to achieve authoritative and binding allocation of the scarce resources and thereby delimit the conflicts.

The problem has been further complicated by the fact that the emphasis in the Nigerian Federation was not on the surrender of certain powers by the component units to the federal union, but on the devolution of power from the central government. The emphasis was on disengagement, not on the desire for union, and according to C. K. Wheare:

> If states really desire to form an independent general government for some purposes, then they have gone a long way towards being able to work such a government. And the same is true of the desire to remain as independent governments inside the union. A desire for federal union among communities is a first and obvious factor which produces in them the capacity to make and work a federal union.[3]

In Nigeria the existence of the superimposed colonial government at the central level rendered less obvious to Nigerian politicians the absolute necessity for creating a suitable federal structure that would replace the colonial structure on the attainment of idependence. Thus, the emphasis was on the immediately obvious need for regional autonomy. The immediate problem of enhancing regional autonomy tipped the delicate balance between the desire for the union and the desire for regional independence, in favor of regional autonomy. The deisre for regional autonomy gained ascendance as the regions struggled to build a secure and independent power base in their respective areas.

The development of regional autonomy was contingent on the devolution of power and resources from the central government controlled by the colonial powers. As the colonial authority at the central level was gradually deemphasized, the struggle for the control of this source of power and prestige became the preoccupation of the regional authorities.

This struggle was complicated by the fact that the devolution of power to the regions by imperial government coupled with the electoral system established to seek power by constitutional means gave rise to the emergence of regional parties. That fact that these parties almost without exception derived their origin from deveolutionary regionalism and the introduction of electoral procedures to seek the control of the power thus devolved[4] stunted their development as national parties. The competitive struggle to seek and enhance the power of the regions created, on the other hand, what Rivkin called "the constitutional dilemma of the institutional relationship to be established between the state (regional) institutions and party institutions."[5]

The fact that these parties derived their institutional support from their positions as governing parties in the regions complicated the problem of institutional differentiation of both parties and regional parliamentary institutions. Thus, the distinction between regional government and the party in power; between the party in power and the dominant ethnic groups within the various regions became blurred. This close identification of the region with party on the one hand and party with the dominant ethnic group within the region on the other hand, tended to make the party in power intolerant of opposition within the region and at the same time incapable of responding effectively to cross-pressures from other regional parties at the federal level. The lack of responsiveness has, in turn, severely stunted the growth of communication between the regions and reinforced sectionalism. And according to Lipset, "the greater the amount of sectionalism, the greater the danger for political system."[6]

This Lipset thesis supports our major contention that it is the institutionalization of regional separation (sectionalism) which is the principal cause of conflict and crisis in Nigeria. Because of the exaltation of this regional or sectional particularism, Nigerian political parties remained, functionally, the major organizational platform for the promotion and consolidation of regional power both within the regions and at the central level of government. In turn, this preoccupation with the maximization of regional power has had a detrimental effect on the development of political parties as distinct institutions separate from the parliamentary inststitutions of the regions.

The blurring of distinction between party institution and parliamentary institution complicated the competitive struggle for succession to political power both within the regions and within the federation as a whole. Within the regions, electoral contests for the transfer of power came to be viewed, not as competition between the party in power and the opposition party, but as competition between the government in power and the dissident groups. The party in power in the region became in essence an extension of the government in power in that region. Within the federation, the electoral contest between these parties for the control of the federal legislature was confounded by this symbiotic relationship between the parties in power and the regional governments.

Therefore, the inability of these parties to transcend their regional base and their original purpose of enhancing regional autonomy had an equally adverse effect on their levels of institutionalization. As Huntington observed:

> Institutionalization makes an organization more than simply an instrument to achieve certain purposes. Instead its leaders and members come to value it for its own sake, and it develops a life of its own quite apart from the specific functions it may perform at any given time. The organization triumphs over its function.[7]

Mutatis mutandis, the inability of the Nigerian parties to triumph over their functions of ensuring maximum regional autonomy frustrated efforts aimed at the institutionalization of these parties and broadening their base beyond the confines of the regions from which they derived their institutional support and sources of patronage. This was the problem of the Action Group in the 1959 election. It was equally evident in the conflict and crisis surrounding the 1964 election in which both the National Council of Nigerian Citizens (NCNC) and the Northern Peoples Congress (NPC) tried to transcend their regional base and form trans-regional coalitions.

However sincere their motives in forming these coalitions might have been, they were not able to overcome their regional past. These motives were, therefore, associated in the minds of the people with an attempt by the two regional parties (NC-

NC and NPC) to control the federal legislature in the interest of their regions. The pronouncements of the leaders of the various parties seemed to lend weight to this assumption. As far back as 1959, when the last pre-independence election campaign was in progress, the Sardauna of Sokoto, the leader of the NPC predicted that:

> As things stand in the present constitution, the North has half the seats in the House of Representatives. My party might manage to capture these, but it is not very likely for the present to get any others; on the other hand, a sudden grouping of the Eastern and Western parties (with a few members from the North opposed to our pary) might take power and so endanger the North. This would, of course, be utterly disastrous.[8]

The complete identification of the interest of the NPC with the survival of the Northern Region as a political entity is clearly evident from the tenor of this speech. Instances like this find repeated echoes in the speeches of the leaders of the NCNC and the Action Group.

A clear example of this identification of party interest with regional interest and the assumption, largely unwarranted, that what is in the regional interest is ipso facto in the interest of the federation is exemplified by the following statement from Chief Awolowo:

> ...If the Action Group and the NCNC, both of which have a monopoly of the political following in the South and at least one-third of the following in the North could come together, then, they would serve as a catalyst to the political situation in the North, ensure the creation of more states (regions) particularly in the North, entrench liberal democracy in the country and infinitely increase the tempo of progress in the federation as a whole. I hold it as a fact that such a combination is sure to win a landslide victory at a subsequent election.[9]

Several significant points emerge from this statment: (a) while extolling the monopoly of the political following in the South (that is in the Eastern and Western Regions) by the NCNC and the Action Group, he regarded the monopoly of effective political following in the North by the NPC (without specifically mentioning its name) as an evil which must be curbed by the creation or more states (regions) in the North; (b) he cast the struggle as a struggle between the Northern Region and the Southern Region (Eastern and Western Regions). In this statement, as well as in the statement by the leader of the NPC, quoted above, the salient institutional base is regional not ethnic. At a secondary level, the conflict is conceived as a conflict between the Eastern Region and the Western Region or between the Northern Region and the Eastern and Western Regions respectively and severally, but not jointy. But there is no doubt that the underlying cause of conflict in the minds of the Northern elite is the possibility of a combination of the two Southern Regions and consequently a domination of the North by the more economically advanced Southern Regions. The Southern political elites see the domination of the federation by the North as a veritable stumbling block in the attempt to establish a viable and unifed Federation in Nigeria.

It is the institutionalization of regional separation that had made the regions the most effective organizational base for the sturggle for power. As the Willink Commission appointed to inquire into the fears of the minorities has observed:

> It can hardly be said too often that at the moment there is a general struggle for power in Nigeria and that any group with a corporate feeling can be the vehicle by which a politician reaches power; there is, therefore, a tendency on the part of the ambitious to work up party feelings where it was hardly formulated before.[10]

Thus, to sustain the regional parties such factors as ethnic affinity, religions and cultural affinity were called in to bolster regional power in the competitive struggle for power and influence. This point is in consonance with the observation made by Berelson and Steiner to the effect that:

> Regional parties can emerge on economic, social or historical grounds but they typically require additional differences of an ethnic religious, linguistic or cultural character to sustain themselves.[11]

Therefore, the conflict in Nigeria is not due to ethnicity per se. Ethnic cleavage is used to reinforce regional sectionalism when the institutional mechanism designed to mediate inter-regional interaction has failed to stem the tide of rising regional conflict. Ethnic conflict is, therefore, an offshoot of the political competition fostered by the policy of devolutionary regionalism. This point is clearly made by the *International Encyclopedia of Social Sciences* edited by Edward Sills. Paraphrasing Ruth Benedict's statement on race conflict, the encyclopedia noted that:

> It is not race that we need to understand but conflict; so, for on understanding of ethnic groups in a social system, it is not on racial or cultural differences that we need to focus our attention, but on group relations.[12]

This statement is pertinent to the Nigerian situation. It is not so much the ethnic heterogeneity in Nigeria as the conflicts between the regional groups that one must look to for the causes of crises and conflicts. In the present essay, we have endeavored to demonstrate that it is when the regional conflicts reach crisis stage that ethnic factors become salient.

We cannot totally ignore the role of ethnicity in the conflict and crisis that plagued the First Republic in Nigeria. Ethnicity[13] is, certainly, one of those words which have undergone what Lovejoy calls 'semantic transition.'[14] In fact, Glazer and Moynihan asserted that:

> We are suggesting that a new word reflects a new reality and a new usage reflects a change in that reality. The new word is "ethnicity" and the new usage is the steady expansion of the term 'ethnic group' from minority and marginal sub-groups at the edge of a group expected to assimilate, to disapper, to continue as survival exotic or troublesome - to major elements of a society."[15]

With due respect to these two intellectual giants, the expansion of the term ethnicity to include both minority and majority ethnic groups can scarcely be said to endow it with new meaning. What is much more pertinent to this essay is their argument that enthicity has become a source of interest auticulation. But even this is not new. According to Arthur Nussbaum, when the barbarians overran and broke up the Roman Empire, ethnicity became the basis of interest articulation. He observed that:

> The concept known as personality of the law came into existence because of the ethnic bond of the person - then his or her crucial characteristic - determined the laws applicable to his or her legal relations: in important legal transactions the parties by staking their ethnic affiliations would thereby indicate the law to which they were subject (professiones juris). Personality of the law has sporadically survived in colonies and other territories with racially or religiously mixed populations...where, however, ethnic segregation vanished and legal transactions ocurred more indiscriminately among the members of the various ethnic communities new solutions had to be sought. This necessity became urgent as a result of the signal evolution of the Italian city states.[16]

Ethnicity became relevant during this period because it was used as a vehicle for the differential application of the law. It was this differential application of the law which is a means of identification and articulation of the legal rights and interests of the parties. It is also noteworthy that it was at the collapse of the over-arching authority of the Roman Empire that the ethnicity of the individuals became a relevant characteristic.

The rise of ethnic particularism at the break-up of an over-arching authority of an empire is again demonstrated by the break-up of the Czarist Empire in 1917. Between 1917 and 1922, a total of sixteen ethnic groups proclaimed their independence.[17] Lenin and Stalin, recognizing the potential disruptive effect of this reassertion of ethnicity, signed a joint declaration of the rights of the peoples of Russia which recognized the right of ethnic groups to secede from the union and thus allayed the fears of these ethnic groups. Whether Lenin and Stalin would have tolerated the secession of these ethnic groups is outside the ambit of this essay.

The significant fact is that both the collapse of the Roman Empire and the collapse of the Czarist Empire led to the re-emergence of ethnic particularism. This idea that the break-up of a socio-political order fosters the reassertion of sectional feelings and a regrouping under more stable social bonds is discussed by Eisenstadt in his *Political Systems of Empires*.[18] Mannheim, using the anology of the effect of the death of the queen bee on the activities of the hive suggests that a partial or complete collapse of the established order leads to a regression to an earlier stage of behavior on the part of the individuals affected.[19]

It is, therefore, during the period when the props of legitimate or legalized authority of an empire or a polity are withdrawn that ethnicity becomes a possible avenue for the expression of values and interests which determine political interaction. This expression takes on a conflictual connotation when ethnicity becomes the basis for the allocation of political rights and values. Thus, the institutionalization of ethnic differentiation (even within a stable polity) gives rise to ethnic conflict. Whether ethnicity succeeds in canalizing the loyalty and allegiance of the individuals within the groups depends on the presence or absence of a legimate or legalizing authority capable of attracting the transcendental loyalty of the group and able to ensure an equitable and binding allocation of political values within the society.

In Nigeria ethnicity was used as a vehicle by regional authorities to enhance regional loyalty and allegiance. In the process the struggle within the regions between the regional institutions and the ethnic institutions resulted in the increasing autocracy of the regional government. The fact that the dominant ethnic groups within the region constituted a majority of the elites within the regional institution led to the identification of the regions with the dominant ethnic group.

This constant struggle between the regional institutions and the ethnic institutions, especially those of the minorities, was one of the reasons why the ethnic minorities in Nigeria over-whelmingly recommended to the Willink Commission[20] that the only solution to their problems would be the creation of more regions. The attempt by the Action Group to attract a following among the minorities by espousing a policy which favored the creation of more states, complicated the struggle between the regions at the central level. As we noted in Chapter 3, both the NPC and NCNC regarded the Action Group as a threat because by supporting the minorities in the Northern and Eastern Regions, it threatened the regional base of each of these parties. Thus, we can see that every political conflict in Nigeria either stems from rivalry between the regions or is directly or indirectly reinforced by regional cleavages.

In Chapter 4, we analyzed how the unrelenting drive toward regional autarchy warped any objective approach to the census and led to unabashed efforts on the part of regional governments, communities and individuals to outdo each other in inflating the census returns. This census crisis in turn exacerbated the renenue allocation crises. In Chapter 5, we discussed how the emphasis on regional seperation resulted in the attempt by each region to maximize the resources for its separate development. Thus, the emphasis was on sharing of resources. The eventual outcome of this emphasis on sharing was that revenue allocation became essentially a question of financial administration between the regions unencumbered by any thought of interdependence between them and of the viability and strength of the federal structure. The preoccupation of the regions with the desire to maximize their share of the revenue prevented the development of a suitable institutional structure for revenue allocation that would have been flexible enough to handle the problems of building a federation by devolutionary method. No attempt was made to define the long term objective of the federation in the economic sector. Therefore, every approach to revenue allocation was halting, haphazard and hastily contrived. Much time and energy was diverted to the barren contention over which region was receiving 'more or less' in the allocation of revenue. This contention reinforced the struggle for control of the federal power structure by electoral means - as the domination of the center was deemed absolutely necessary for the control of federal resources and its allocation processes.

The struggle for the control of the federal structure was analyzed in Chapter 6 which deals with the election crisis of 1964. In Chapter 6, we discussed how the institutional framework - the federal electoral commission designed to mediate conflict over succession to power-failed to do so. The commission had by law, full powers to organize and supervise the conduct of elections. But the power to use coercive measures to support the decision of the commission rested squarely on the Prime Minister. As most of the complaints regarding the violations of the electoral procedures came from the Northern Region, controlled by the NPC and in the Western Region, controlled by the NPC-NNDP alliance (NNA), the Prime Minister who owed his power to the NPC could not use that power against a region controlled by his political boss. Therefore, the electoral commission was unable to enforce compliance to its directives because it did not have the coercive powers of the Prime Minister.

The President of the Republic of Nigeria, on the other hand, could not come to the aid of the electoral commission because, although he was vested with executive power of the federation, the Prime Minister had the full constitutional powers to control the armed forces and the police. Therefore, in order to back the electoral commission with coercive measures, he had to seek the advice and consent of the Prime Minister. He was, in fact, a Commander-in-Chief without an army to command.

Thus, the conflicts and crisis which plagued the First Republic of Nigeria were the result of the progressive devolution of power from a colonial based central government to regional government without adequate measures to encourage the development of a federal structure independent of the regions and controlled by indigenous elites. As the colonial power waned, there was no indigenous central institution, independent of the regions and capable of mediating, impartially, political interaction between the regions. The federal government became little more than an extention of the Northern Region which had both the size and polulation to exercise effective control over the deliberation of the central government.

The eventual result was that every conflict took on the character of confrontation between the regions. This confrontation made it impossible to resolve any of these conflicts successfully. One unresolved conflict reinforced another and led to the eventual collapse of the federation in 1966. As Dahl remarked:

> The severity of a conflict depends on the way in which one conflict is related to another. A society offers a number of different lines along which cleavages in conflict can take place; differences in geography, ethnic identification, religion, and economic position, for example, all present potential lines of cleavages in conflicts. If all the cleavages occur along the lines, if the same people hold opposing positions in one dispute after another then severity of conflict is likely to increase. The man on the other side is not just an opponent, he soon becomes an enemy.[21]

Chapter 1 Footnotes

S.N. Eisenstadt, *Essays on Sociological Aspects of Political and Economic Developemnt*, (The Hague, Mouton and Co., Ltd., 1961), p. 32

[2] *Report of the Constitutional Conference on the Nigerian Constitution(Lagos: Government Printing Press, 1950), p. 65, held in Ibadan.*

[3] Bertrand de Jouvenel, *Sovereignty*(Chicago: University of Chicago Press, 1963), p. 123.

[4] Heinz Eulau, *The Behavioral Persuasion in Politics*(New York: Randon House, 1967), p. 18.

[5] Ibid.

[6] Ibid.

[7] Samuel P. Huntington, *Political Order in Changing Societies* (New Haven: Yale University Press, 1975), p. 24

[8] Heinz Eulau, *The Behavior Persuasion in Politics*, pp. 4-5.

[9] Talcott Parsons and Edward Shils, *Towards a General Theory of Action* (Cambridge, Massachuetts:Harvard University Press, 1962), pp. 40 and 58.

[10] Heinz Eulau, *The Behavioral Persuasion in Politics, p. 53.*

[11] National Broadcast by His Excellency the Governor, March 1953, quoted in *Nigeria's Constitutional Development: 1861-1960*(Lagos: Federal Ministry of Education, 1960), p.18. It is necessary to point out that throughout the life of the First Republic in Nigeria, the ministers were selected on a regional basis and the Northern Region had the largest number.

[12] Taylor Cole, *Emergent Federalism in Nigeria: Constitutional Problems of the Federation of Nigeria*, Record of the Proceedings of s Seminar held at King's College, Lagos, August 8 to 15, 1960, p. 4.

[13] K.C. Wheare, *Federal Government*(London: Oxford University Press, 1967), p. 29.

[14] Ibid.

[15] John Stuart Mill, *Representative Government,*pp. 367-368, quoted in Wheare, *Federal Government, pp. 50-51.*

[16] Robert Melson and Howard Wolpe(eds.), *Nigeria: Modernization and the Politics of Communalism*(michigan State University Press, 1971), p. vii.

[17] K.C. Wheare, *Federal Government'*(London:Oxford University Press, 1967), p. 49.

[18] *Nigeria's Constitutional Developments: 1861-1960*(Lagos: Federal Ministry of Information, 1960), p. 18.

[19] Joseph LaPalombara, *Politics Within Nations*(Englewood Cliffs, NEW Jersey, Prentice Hall, 1974), p. 74

[20] Peter Waterman. "Structure, Contradiction and the Nigerian Catastrophe: Elements of an Analysis, " *Pressence Africaine*Vol. 77 (1971), p. 192

[21] Ibid.

[22] Walter Schwarz, *Nigeria*(New York: Fredrick A. Praeger, Publishers, 1968), pp. 1-19; John Hatch, *Nigeria: The Seeds of Diaster* (Chicago: Henry Regnary Company, 1970), passim; Ulf Hummelstrand, "Rank Equilibrium, Tribalsim and Nationalsim in Nigeria, " in Melson and Wolpe, *o-. cit., p.*.254.

[23] John Hatch, Nigeria: *The Seeds of Diaster* (Chicago: Henry Regnary Company, 1970), Fly Page.

[24] *Commission Report 505.*Report of Commission appointed to enquire into the fear of minorities and the means of alleying them, July, 1958, p. 87 (Willink Commission, 1958).

[25] Robert Melson and Howard Wolpe, *Nigerian Modernization and the Politics of Communalism*(Michigan State University Press, 1971), passim; Kenneth Post and Michael Vickers, *Structure and Conflict in Nigeria*(Madison: The Univeristy of Wisconsin Press, 1973), passim.

[26] Clifford Geerts(ed.) "The Integrative Revolution, "*Old Societies and New States*

(Glencoe: The Free Press, 1963), p. 109.

[27] Richard L. Sklar, *Nigerian Political Parties*(Princeton, N.J.: Princeton University Press, 1963), p. 203. But a unitary party is not necessarily inconsistent with a federal state. Both the Democratic Party and the Republican Party in the United States are unitary parties in that they each have a countryside following as the National Council of Nigerian Citizens in Nigeria. They each have a national leadership that transcends the state boundaries and speaks for each party on the national level. There is, however, the implication that the federal set-up in Nigeria was inconsistent with the development of a national party. This is because the center of political power in Nigeria lay, not in the center, but in the regions.

[28] John N. Paden, "Communal Competition, Conflict and Violence in Kano," in Robert Melson and Howard Wolpe (eds.), *Nigeria: Modernization and the Politics of Communalism*(Michigan: State University Press, 1971), p. 140

[29] Edward Feit, "Military Coups and Political Development: Some Lessons from Ghana and Nigeria, "*World Politics,* Vol. XX, No. 2, January 1968; Princeton University Press, Princeton, N.J., pp. 179-193.

[30] Samuel P. Huntington, "Political Development and Political Decay,"*World Politics* XVII (April 1965), p. 394.

[31] Edward Feit, "Military Coups and Political Development, " *World Politics,* Vol. XX, No. 2, January 1968; Princeton University Press, Princeton, N.J., PP.179-193.

[32] Keneth Post and Michael Vickers, *Structure and Conflict in Nigeria(*Madison: University of Wisconsin Press, 1973), pp. 6-7.

[33] Walker Connor, "Nation Building or Nation Destroying, " *World Politics* 20 (October 1967), p. 31.

[34] Alexander Hamilton, *The Federalist Papers, No. XV.*

[35] Morton Grodzins, *The Loyal and the Disloyal* (Chicago: The University of Chicago Press, 1956), p.7.

[36] Ibid., pp. 6-7.

[37] *Population Census of Northern Nigeria, 1952* (Lagos: Government Printing Press, 1953), pp. 10-11.

[38] The discussion in this concluding analysis in inspired by P. Selznick, "Foundations of the Theory of Organization, " in F.E. Emery's (editor), *System Thinking* (Baltimore, Md.: Penguin Books, Ltd., 1969), pp.268-269.

Chapter 11

[1] See *British Parliamentary Papers, Colonies Africa, Sessions: 1801-1802* (100), Appendix A.p. 30, where a Select Committee of the British House of Commons advocated a policy of Cultural Imperialism in Africa, London, England, 1802.

[2] Margery Pertham, "Nigerian Civil War, " *African Contemporary Record,* Colin Legum (editor), Africa Research, Ltd., Lonfon, England, p.1.

[3] Papers Relatilng to the Occupation of Lagos, 1862, quoted in *Nigeria's Constitutional Development 1801-1960* (Federal Ministry of Information, Lagos, Nigeria, 1960), p.7.

[4] The meaning of the word "protection" is a matter of scholarly debate since the British Colonial authorities did not observe any perceptible distinction between colonials and British protected persons. The following explanation give to JaJa, an Ibo chief, when he questioned the meaning of protection before he would agree to sign a treaty of protection with the British is a fair sample of African understanding of the word. In 1884 a British consul wrote to JaJa as follows: "Iwrite as you request with reference to the word, 'protection' as used in the proposed treaty that the Queen does not want to take your country or your markets, but at the same time in anxious that no other nation should take them. She undertakes to extend her gracious favour and protection, which will leave your country still under your government," quoted in John Hatch's, *Nigeria, The seed of Disaster,* Henry regnary Co., Chicago, Illinois, 1970.

[5] A.N. cook, *British Enterprise in Nigeria,* University of Pennsylvania Press, Philadelphia, Pennsylvania, 1943.

[6] C.K. Meek, *Law and Authority in a Nigerian Tribe,* Oxford University Press, London, England, 1937, p.x.

[7] F.A. Atanda, "The Changing Status of the Alafin of Oyo under British Rule and Independence" in Michael Crowder and Obara Ikeme (eds), *West African Chiefs* (Africana Publishing Co., 1970), p. 221.

[8] Fredrick D. Lugard, *Annual Report of 1903,* pp. 105-107.

[9] K.C. Wheare, *Federal Government* (New 'York, Oxford University Press, 1963), p. 45.

[10] *Nigeria's Constitutional development 1861-1960,* Published by the federal Ministry of Information, Lagos, 1960, p.8.

[11] *Legislative Council Debates,* Official Report, 1 November, 1923.

[12] John R. Hicks and Sydney Phillipson, *Report of the Commission on Revenue Allocation* (Lagos: Government Printing Press, 1950), p. 69.

[13] Margery Perham, "Nigerian Civil War, " in Colin Legum, in *Africa Contrmporary Record,* 1969, p. 1.

[14] *Nigerian Constitutional Development 1861-1960,* Federal Ministry of Information, Lagos, 1960.

[15] Ibid., p. 8.

[16] *Lagos Weekly Record,* March 1st to May 31st, 1919, Lagos, Nigeria.

[17] *Economic Survey of Nigeria, 1959;* The Federal Government Printing Press, Lagos, 1959, p. 38.

[18] Nigerian Council::Address by the Governor, Nigeria, December 29, 1920, p. 18. See also T.N. Tamuno, *Nigeria and the Elective Representation: 1923-47* (London: Heinemann, 1966), p.26. This is a reference to the formation in 1920 of the National Council of british West Africa at a conference in Accra, Ghana. This conference constituted itself into "a permanent official body for the purpose of representing constitutionally British West African needs politically and otherwise. See Mascaulay Papers, Vol. IV, No. 13.

[19] Legislative Council: Address by the Governor, Nigeria, October 31, 1923, p.1.

[20] Sir Hugh Clifford, Address to the Nigerian Council, december 29, 1920 (typed copy), Macaulay Papers, quoted in James S. Coleman, *Nigeria: Background to Nationalism,* pp. 192-193.

[21] Sir Hugh Clifford, Address to the Nigerian Council, December 20, 1920.

[22] *Ibid.*

[23] *Ibid.*

[24] *IBID.*

[25] *Ibid.*

[26] John P. Mackintosh, *Nigerian Government and Politics* (Evanston, Illinois, Northwestern University Press, 1966), p. 17

[27] The committee stated that "the object of our policy should be to encourage in the natives the exercise of those qualities which may render it possible for us more and more to transfer to them the administration of all the governments, with a view to our ultimate withdrawal from all except probably, Sierra Leone." Report of the Select Committee on West Africa (1865).

[28] *Sir Hugh Clifford, Address to the Nigerian Council. december 29, 1920. For a detailed discussion on British colonial policy, see Lord Lugard's, The Dual Mandate in Tropical Africa*(Edingburgh, 1918); Mary Bull, "Indirect Rule in Northern Nigeria 1906-1911," in Kenneth Robinson and fredrick Madden (eds), *Essays in Imperial Government.*Sir Donald Cammeron, "The Principles of Native Administration, " in "Colonial Policy and Practice, " a very carefully researched and critical work on colonial policy. Rudolf Von Albertini, *Decolonization, The Administration and Future of the Colonies 1919-1960,* Doubleday and Company (New York, 1971), especially Section 1 and 111 - a very incisive, critical and well-documented book. Margery Perham, *Native Administration in Nigeria,* (London, Oxford University Press, 1937). Also by the same author, *Colonial Sequence 1930-1949,* (Methuer and Co., Ltd,), 1967.

[29] *Nigeria's Constitutional developments 1861-1960*, published by the Federal Ministry of Information, Lagos, 1960, p. 9.
[30] *Nigerian Protectorate Order in Council, 1922,* Att. 4
[31] *Ibid.*
[32] *Royal Instructions (protectorate), 1922,* Att. 4
[33] *Royal Instructions (colony), 1922.*
[34] *Nigerian (legislative Council) Order in Council,* 1922, Articles 23 and 25.
[35] *Royal Instructions (Protectorate), 1922,* Article 23.
[36] *Colonial Regulations, 1925,* Col. No. 88 (2), 224.
[37] Ibid. A Crown Colony is a British settlement governed directly by the Crown through Letters Patent and Royal Instructins issued to the Colonial Governors by the British Parliament.
[38] Dame Margery Perham, *Native Administration in Nigeria*(London: Oxford University Press, 1937), p. 326.
[39] Sir Hugh Clifford, Address to the Nigerian Council, December 29, 1920 (typed copy), Macaulay Papers.
[40] *Ibid.*
[41] Sir Bernard Bourdillion, "Nigeria's New Constitution,," *United Empire,* XXXVII, (March-April, 1946), pp. 76-80.
[42] B.J. Dudley, *Parties and Politics in Northern Nigeria,* Frank Cass & Co., Ltd., London, England, 1968, p. 20.
*The Mahdist is an Islamic revivalist sect.
**Satiruy was a Mahdist who raised a revolt against the imposition of British authority in the North.
[43] Margery Perham, *Native Administration in Nigeria,* London: Oxford University Press, 1937), p. 326.
[44] Minutes of February 22, 1873 Kimberley Co. 96 85.
[45] Nigerian Legislative Council Minutes, May 1, 1914.
[46] Sir Donald cameron, *Address to the Legislative Council,* March 6, 1933, quoted in B.J. Dudley, *Parties and Politics in Northern Nigeria,* Frank Cass & co., lts., London, p. 20.
[47] John Stuart Mill, *Representative Government,* Everyman Editions, pp. 367-368.
[48] Sidney R. Waldman, *Foundations of Political Action,* (Little brown and Company, Boston 1972), pp. 178-179.
[49] James S. Coleman, *Nigeria: Background to Nationalsim (Berkely, University of California Press, 1971), p. 50.
[50] *For an excellent analysis of the various factors which impinged on the pattern and pace of political development in Nigeria, see James S. Coleman's Nigeria:: Background to Nationalism,* (Berkely, University of California Press, 1971), Chapters 7,8, 9, 10, and 11.
[1] Even in the army the same differential treatment of Northerners and Southerns which had characterized British policy in Nigeria was visibly in evidence.
[52] James S. Coleman, *Nigeria: Background to Nationalism* (Berkely, California; University of California Press, 1971), p. 254.
[53] Sir John R. Hicks and Sir Sydney Phillipson, *Report of the Commission on Revenue Allocation*(Lagos: Government Printer, 1950), p. 12.
[54] Sir Bernard Bourdillion, "Nigeria's New Constitution," *United Empire* 37 (March-April, 1946): 77.
[55] *Ibid.*
[56] *Ibid.,* p.79
[57] Hicks-Phillipson Report on Revenue Allocation, p. 13.
[58] *Ibid.*
[59] *Ibid.*
[60] Margery Perham, *Native Administration in Nigeria,* Oxford University Press, London, England, 1937, p. 362.
[61] Sir Bernard Bourdillion, "Nigeria's New Constitution," *United Empire* 37 (March-April, 1946), pp.77-78. In actuality the bills to be introduced in the regional legislatures were drafted by the colonial civil servants, and cleared with the Lieutenant

Governor of the region before they could be introduced in the legislature under the Richard Constitution.

⁶²*Ibid.*

⁶³Sabon-Gari: special areas in Northern cities inhabited by non-Northern Nigerians from the Western and Eastern Regions of Nigeria. These groups were regarded as aliens.

⁶⁴Dispatch to the Secretary of State by the Governor, December 6, 1944.

⁶⁵James S. Coleman, *Nigeria: Background to Nationalism*(Berkeley: University of California Press, 1971), p. 254.

⁶⁶Sir Bernard Bourdillion, "Nigeria's New Constitution," *United Empire* 37 (March-April, 1946): 77.

⁶⁷*Ibid.*

⁶⁸*Ibid.*

⁶⁹*Ibid.*

⁷⁰*Ibid.*

⁷¹*Hicks-Phillipson Report on Revenue Allocation,* p.5. For a detailed discussion on Revenue Allocation see Chapter 5 of this study.

⁷²*Ibid.*

⁷³Obafemi Awolowo, *Path to Nigerian Freedon* (London: Faber, 1947) pp. 61-69.

⁷⁴H.O. Davis, "Nigeria's New Constitution," *West African Review* XVI (May 1945), p. 15

⁷⁵Sir Bernard Bourdillion, "Nigeria's New Constitution, "*United Empire* 37 (March-April, 1946), p. 76.

⁷⁶Dame Margery Perham, *Native Administration in Nigeria,* (London, Oxford University Press, 1937), p. 362.

⁷⁷James S. Coleman, *Nigeria: Background to Nationalism* (Berkely, University of California Press, 1971), p. 274.

⁸⁰Richard L. Sklar, *Nigerian Political Parties*(Princeton, New Jersey: Princeton University Press, 1963), p.30.

⁸¹*Proceedings of the General Conference on the Review of the Nigerian Constitution* (Lagos, 1950), p. 17.

⁸²The political controversy surrounding the Richards Constitution gave birth in 1949 to two regionally based parties: the Action group (AG(in the Western Region and the Northern People's Congress (NPC) in the Northern Region. Each of the two parties pledged to work through and with the traditional elite. The two parties together with the National Council of Nigeria and the Cameroons formed the three principal parties in Nigeria. Each was dominant in one of the threee regions into which Nigeria was divided.

⁸³For a detailed account of the 1951 election in the Western Region, see Richard L. Sklar, *Nigerian Political Parties,* (Princeton, New Jersey: Princeton University Press, 1963), p. 115-118

⁸⁴Richard L. Sklar, *Nigerian Political Parties,* pp. 112-118. See also Eme O. Awa, *Federal Government in Nigeria* (University of california Press, 1964), pp. 36-43; James S. Coleman's *Nigeria: Background to Nationalism* (University of California Press, 1958), p. 370

⁸⁵*Ibid.*

⁸⁶Richard L. Sklar, *Nigeria Political Parties,* (Princeton, New Jersey: Princeton University Press, 1963), p. 118.

⁸⁷*Ibid.*

⁸⁸*Ibid.*

⁸⁹*Daily Times,* (Lagos), December 11, 1952.

⁹⁰Three of the members expelled were Ibos, one was from Ekoi, a sub-ethnic group of Ibos. The attacks on Professor Eyo Ita, an Efik, during the conflict, led to ethnic antagonism between the Efiks and the Ibos. This antagonism had far-reaching consequences - it led directly to the Foster-Sutton Enquiry into the conduct of the Premier of the Eastern Region in 1956.

⁹¹Eastern House of Assembly Debates, Second Session, Vols. 1 and 11, January 30 - February 23, 1953. The best account of the events in the Eastern Region at this time is in Sklar, *Nigerian Political Parties,* (Princeton, New Jersey: Princeton University Press,

1963), p. 118-124.

[92]Obafemi Awolowo, *The Autobiography of Chief Obafemi Awolowo* (Cambridge: Cambridge University 'Press, 1960), pp. 227-239. See also Richard L. Sklar, *Nigerian Political Parties* (Princeton: Princeton University Press, 1963),p. 124; and Eme O. Awa, *Federal Government in Nigeria* (berkeley: University of california Press, 1964), pp. 41-43.

[93]Statement of Non-Fraternization with Sir John Macpherson, Action group, Secretarial record, Ibadan, 1952.

[94]House of Representatives Debates, Second Session, March 3, - April 1, 1953, p. 992.

[95]See *Daily Times*, (lagos), May 22, 1953 for full text of the eight-point program.

[96]James S. Coleman, *Nigeria: Background to Nationalism,* (Berkely, University of California Press, 1971), pp. 399-400

[97]*Report of Kano Disturbance,* 16th-19th May, 1953, (Lagos, 1953) Appendix B, p..46

[98]*Report of Kano Disturbance*(Kadkna, 1953), pp. 39-40.

[99]Richard L. Sklar, *Nigerian Political Parties,* (Princeton, New Jersey: Princeton university Press, 1963), p. 131.

[100]Richard L. Sklar, *Nigerian Political Parties,* (Princeton, New Jersey: Princeton University Press, 1963), p. 131.

[101]*Daily Times,* April 9, 1953.

[102]According to Chief Awolowo, the leaders of the Action group: "Five Northern Ministers, three from the region and two from the center, flew to Ibadan to meet the Western Regional and central ministers to discuss ways and means of strengthening Nigerian unity and accelerating its progress and freedom. The meeting decided to establish a coalition between the leaders of Northern and western Legislatures with a view to their pursuing a common policy in the center and in the regions. The first meeting of the coalition will be held in Lagos in March, 1953." *Daily Times,* April 10, 1943.

[103]The Memoirs of Lord Chandos, p. 419, quoted by John P. Mackintosh, *op. cit.,* p. 27.

[104]*British House of Commons Debate,* Statement by Oliver Lyttleton in the British House of Commons, May 21, 1953.

[105]Richard L. Sklar, *Nigerian Political 'Parties,* (princeton, New Jersey: Princeton University Press, 1963), p. 133.

[106]*Ibid.*

[107]L. Brett (ed). *Constitutional Problems of the federation of Nigeria*(Lagos: government Printing Press, 1960), pp. 237-238.

[108]Richard L. Sklar, *Nigerian Political Parties,* (Princeton, New Jersey: Princeton University Press, 1963), p. 30

[109]K.C. Wheare, *Federal Government,'*(New York, Oxford University Press, 1963), p. 45.

[110]*Economic Survey of Nigeria,* (Lagos Government Printing Press, 1959), p. 51.

[111]Proceedings of the Tribunal to inquire into Allegations of Improper Conduct by the Premier of the Eastern Region of Nigeria, in connection with the affairs of the African Continental Bank, Ltd., and other related matters, Command No. 51, p. 42.

[112]Report of the Commission to Enquire into the Fears of Minorities and the Means of Allaying Them, *Command 505* (1958).

[113]*Ibid.,* p. 89.

[114]*Ibid.,* p. 87.

[115]*Ibid.,* p. 87.

[116]*Ibid.,* p. 87.

[117]The provision required a resolution approved (a) by two-thirds majority of both Houses of the Central Legislature and (b) by a resolution of at least two regions including any region comprising any part of Nigeria that would be transferred to the new region. (*Nigerian Constitution,* 1960), Section 4.

[118]For a detailed discussion on the election, see Kenneth W. Post, *The Nigerian Federal Election of 1959,* Oxford University press, London and New York, 1963.

[119]Kenneth W. Post, *op. cit.,* p. 439.

[120]*Ibid.*

[121]This following account by a leader of the Bornu Youth Movement - a Kanuri party.

opposed to the NPC - the regional party shows the extent of the abuse glossed over by the British. "In 1958 my house was attacked by members of the NPC. Five members of the Bornu Youth Movement were killed, one inside my house and four some where else. I made a report to the police. No one was prosecuted for the murders."

CHAPTER III

[1] For a discussion of the division of power under the 1954 Constitution, see Chapter 2 of this dissertation.
[2] Quoted in Walter Schwarz's, *Nigeria,* Fredrick Praeger Co., New York, 1968, p. 127.
[3] Samuel P. Huntington, *Political Order in Changing Societies,* Yale University Press, 1968, p. 24.
[4] *Ibid.*; see also Karl W. Deutsch, et. al., *International Political Communities,* Doubleday, Anchor Originals, New York, 1966, pp. 2-3.
[5] James O'Connell, "Political Integration: The Nigerian Case," in Arthur Hazlewood's (editor), *African Integration and Disintegration,* Oxford University Press, 1967, p. 159.
[6] C.O. Ojukwu, statement by Lt. Col. Ojikwu, Addis Ababa, August 5, 1968, in Colin Legum (editor), *Africa Contemporary Record,* African Research, Ltd., London, 1969, p. 655.
[7] Paul O. Proehl, *Foreign Enterprise in Nigeria,* University of North Carolina, Chapel Hill, North Carolina, 1965, p. 176.
[8] For a discussion of the *Willink Commission,* see Chapter 2 of this dissertation.
[9] The Tiv people expressed resistance to this incorporation in violent protests in 1929, 1939, 1960 and 1964. See Walter Schwarz's, *Nigeria,* Fredrick Praeger, 1968, p. 242.
[10] Fredrick A.O. Schwarz, Jr., *Nigeria: The Tribe, The Nation, or The Race - The Politics of Independence.* MIT Press, 1965, p. 124.
[11] *Ibid.*, p. 124. Very little attention has been given to the Tiv riot as one of the main causes of the politicization of the military which eventually led to the 1966 coup d'etat. It was actually an internal war in which the Nigerian soldiers played a creditable role of mediators between the government and the people. See Chapter 6 of this essay for further details.
[12] See the discussion of the crisis below, in this chapter.
[13] James O'Connell, "Political Integration: The Nigerian Case," in Arthur Hazlewood' (editor) *African Integration and Disintegration,* Oxford University Press, 1967, p. 162.
[14] John P. Mackintosh, *Nigerian Government and Politics,* Northwestern University City Press, Evanston, Ill., 1960, p. 441.
[15] In 1953 when the Executive of the NCNC and Eastern Regional Cabinet controlled by the NCNC were in different hands, a crisis occurred over the power of the Party Executive to discipline disobedient members of the cabinet. See Chapter 2 of the essay, p.
[16] James O'Connell, "Political Integration: The Nigerian Case," in Arthur Hazlewood's (ed) *African Integration and Distegration,* Oxford University Press, 1967, p. 163. Professor O'Connell noted that the decision to unseat Premier Akintola was made after much "maneuverings in which a substantial sum of money was said to have changed hands."
[17] Emergency Powers (General) Regulation, Section 4.
[18] Federation of Nigeria, Official Gazette, Supplement to No. 36, Vol. 48, May 18, 1962.
[19] John P. Mackintosh, *Nigerian Government and Politics,* Northwestern university City Press, Evanston, Illinois, 1960, pp. 450-451.
[20] John P. Mackintosh, *Nigerian Government and Politics,* Northwestern University Press, Evanston, Illinois, 1960, p. 456.
[21] Constitution of the Federation of Nigeria, 1960.
[22] Daily Service, May 4, 1962. See also O. Adumosu, *The Nigerian Constitution,* (London: Sweet and Maxwell, 1968), p. 301.

[23] Senator Chief T. Adebayo Doherty vs. the Prime Minister and Others. Federal Supreme Court, All Nigerian Law Report 604.
[24] J.P. Mackintosh, *Nigerian Government and Politics,* Northwestern University Press, 1966, Evanston, Illinois, p. 454.
[25] Federal House (Parliamentary) Debates, May 29, 1962, Col. 2171.
[26] *Nigerian Tribune,* May 29, 1962.
[27] J.P. Mackintosh, *Nigerian Government and Politics,* Northwestern University Press, 1966, Evanston, Illinois, p. 448.
[28] *The Daily Express,* May 25, 1962.
[29] *The West African Pilot,* June 4, 1962.
[30] *The West African Pilot,* June 5, 1962.
[31] Kenneth Post and Michael Vickers, *Structure and Conflict in Nigeria 1960-1966,* (Madison: The University of Wisconsin Press, 1973), p. 88.
[32] See Chapter 6 of the present essay for an analysis of political struggle in the Western Region during the federal elections of 1964.
[33] See the section dealing with the 1964 crisis for a full discussion.
[34] *The Daily Express,* January 5, 1965.
[35] Kenneth Post and Michael Vickers, *Structure and Conflict in Nigeria, 1960-1966;* (Madison: The University of Wisconsin Press, 1973), p. 219.
[36] Ben O. Nwabueze, *Constitutionalism in the Emergent States* (Rutherford, New Jersey: Fairleigh Dickinson University Press, 1973), pp. 149-150.

CHAPTER IV

[1] For a discussion on the problem of revenue allocation in Nigeria, see Chapter 5.
[2] K.C. Wheare, *Federal Government,* Oxford University Press, 1967, p. 51.
[3] Charles D. Tarlton, "Symmetry and Assymetary as an Element of Federalism: A Theoretical Speculation," *Journal of Politics,* Vol. 27, 1965, pp. 861-874.
[4] Quoted in Thomas N. Frank's (editor), *Why Federations Fail?,* New York University Press, New York, 1968, p. 181.
[5] Sir Bryan Sherwood Smith, Letter to Mallam Tafawa Balewa, August, 1956, quoted in J.P. Mackintosh's, *Nigerian Government and Politics,* Northwestern University Press, 1956, Evanston, Illinois, p. 33.
[6] *Ibid.,* p. 33.
[7] J.S. Mill, *Representative Government,* Everyman Editions, pp. 367-368.
[8] Robin Luckman, *The Nigerian Military 1960-1967,* Cambridge University Press, 1971, p. 208.
[9] The Northern Peoples Congress Constitution, reproduced in B.J. Dudley's *Parties and Politics in Northern Nigeria,* Frank Cass and Co., Ltd., London, 1968, pp. 314-315.
[10] *Hicks-Phillipson, Report on Revenue Allocation,* (Lagos Government Printing Press, Lagos, 1954), p. 97.
[11] S.A. Aluko, "How Many Nigerians? An Analysis of Nigerian Census Problems, 1901-1963" *Journal of Modern African Studies,* 3,3, 1965; pp. 371-391.
[12] *Ibid.*
[13] *Ibid.*
[14] *Ibid.,* see also S.M. Jacobs', *Census of Nigeria 1931, (London, 1933; Vol. 1), pp.* 60-63.
[15] G.C.A. Oldendorp, Geschichfe Der Evangelischen Bruder Auf Den Caraibischen Insel S. Thomas, S. Croix und S. Jan.
[16] Africanus J.B. Horton, *West African Countries and Peoples* (W.J. Johnson, London: 1868), p. 172.
[17] D.A.G. Leonard, *Lower Niger and Its Tribes* (Frank Cass & Co., Ltd., London, 1968), p. 42.
[18] P.A. Talbot, *Southern Nigeria* (Frank Cass & Co., Ltd., London, 1926), Vol. 1, p. 251.

[19] *Eastern Region Census: Administrative Report,* 1953, p. 2.
[20] *Western Region Census: Administrative Report,* 1952, p. 2.
[21] *Northern Region Census: Administrative Report,* 1952, p. 2. The population of Northern Nigeria was estimated as 10 million in 1901, 8.8 million in 1906, and 7.16 million in 1907.
[22] S.A. Aluko, "How Many Nigerians?" *Journal of Modern African Studies,* 3, 3, (1965), pp. 371-392. It should be noted that the Northern figures were revised upwards while the Eastern estimate noted previously was revised downwards.
[23] Amaury Talbot, *The Peoples of Southern Nigeria,* (Frank Cass & Co., Ltd., 1969), Reprint, Vo., IV, p. 145.
[24] Aluko, "How Many Nigerians?", *Journal of Modern African Studies,* 3,3, (1965), p. 375. Also see *Census of Nigeria,* (London, 1931), Vol. 111.
[25] *Ibid.*
[26] *Northern Region Census: Administrative Report,* 1952, p. 2.
[27] *Ibid.*
[28] *Census of Nigeria,* Vol. 111, pp. 1-2.
[29] John R. Hicks and Sydney Phillipson, *Report of the Commission on Revenue Allocation,* (Lagos: Government Printing Press, 1951), p. 97.
[30] *Proceedings of the General Conference on Review of the Constitution, 1950* (Lagos: Government Printing Press, 1950), p. 108.
[31] *Ibid.*
[32] *Proceedings of the General Conference on Review of the Constitution, 1950* (Lagos: Government Printing Press, 1950), p. 64.
[33] *Ibid.,* p. 103.
[34] *Ibid.*
[36] *Administrative Report of the 1952 Census,* Northern Region, p. 2; Eastern Region, p. 2; Western Region, p. 2.
[37] *Administrative Report, Northern Region,* p. 2.
[38] *Nigerian Census, 1931,* (London, 1933), pp. 1-2.
[39] *Western Nigeria Census: Administrative Report,* 1952, p. 3.
[40] *Eastern Nigeria Census: Administrative Report,* 1952, p.3.
[41] *Northern Nigeria Census: Administrative Report,* 1952, p.2.
[42] *Eastern Region Census: Administrative Report,* 1952, p. 5.
[43] *Western Region Census: Administrative Report,* 1952, p. 4.
[44] An Oba is a powerful chief or king of a Yoruba kingdom.
[45] *Eastern Region Administrative Report,* 1952, p. 3.
[46] *Eastern Region Census: Administrative Report,* 1952, p. 4.
[47] *Ibid.,* p. 7.
[48] *Eastern Region Census: Administrative Report,* 1952, p. 7.
[49] *Ibid.*
[50] *Ibid.*
[51] *Ibid.*
[52] *Enugu Township Report for 1951,* Eastern Region Archives, SME 467/263A. See Mackintosh, *op. cit., pp.* 292-293.
[53] *Western Region Census: Administrative Report,* 1952, p. 4.
[54] *Ibid.*
[55] *Northern Region Census: Administrative Report,* 1952, p. 4.
[56] *Eastern Region Census: Administrative Report,* 1952, p.3.
[57] *Northern Region Census: Administrative Report,* 1952, p. 7.
[58] *Administrative Report, 1952 Census: Eastern Region,* pp. 3,9, and 10; *Western Region,* p. 4.
[59] *Northern Region Census: Administrative Report,* 1952, p. 5.
[60] *Ibid.*
[61] *Ibid.*
[62] *Eastern Region Census; Administrative Report,* 1953, pp. 8-9.
[63] *Eastern Region Census: Administrative Report,* 1953, pp. 8-9
[64] *Western Region Census: Administrative Report,* 1953, pp. 8-9.

[65] *Eastern Region Census: Administrative Report,* 1953, p. 15.
[69] *Ibid.*
[70] *Northern Nigeria Census: Administrative Report, 1952,* p. 3.
[71] *Ibid.*
[72] *Census of Nigeria, 1931,* Vol.1, pp. 4-6. See also Aluko, "How Many Nigerians?", *Journal of Modern African Studies,* 3,3, (1965), pp. 371-392.
[73] Aluki, "How Many Nigerians?", *Journal of Modern African Studies,* 3,3 (1965), pp. 371-392.
[74] *Northern Nigeria Census: Administrative Report, 1952,* p. 3.
[75] *Western Nigeria Census: Administrative Report, 1952,* p. 4.
[76] Aluko, "How Many Nigerians?", *Journal of Modern African Studies,* 3,3(1965), pp. 371-392.
[77] S.A. Aluko, "How Many Nigerians? An Analysis of Nigerian Census Problems, 1901-1963," *Journal of Modern African Studies,* p. 275.
[78] S.A. Aluko, "How Many Nigerians? An Analysis of Nigerian Census Problems, 1901-1963," *Journal of Modern African Studies,* p. 275.
[79] *Constitution of the Federation of Nigeria, 1963,* No. 20, p. 80.
[80] See Chapter 5 for a discussion of the use of population as an indicator of need in revenue allocation.
[81] S.A. Aluko, "How Many Nigerians? An Analysis of Nigerian Census Problems, 1901-1963," *Journal of Modern African Studies,* p. 378.
[82] Quoted in the Debates of the House of Representatives, December 5, 1963. This report was never published officially. See Aluko, "How Many Nigerians? An Analysis of Nigeria Census Problems, 1901-1963," *Journal of Modern African Studies,* p. 387.
[83] Kenneth Post and Michael Vickers, *Structure and Conflict in Nigeria,* (Madison, Wisconsin: The University of Wisconsin Press, 1973), p. 80.
[84] House of Representatives Debate, December 5, 1963. Quoted in S.A. Aluko's, "How Many Nigerians? An Analysis of Nigerian Census Problems, 1901-1963," *Journal of Modern African Studies,* p.381
[85] See the section on *Constitutional Development in Nigeria.*
[86] S.A. Aluko, *op. cit.,* p. 382.
[87] J.P. Mackintosh, *Nigerian Federal Government,* (Evanston, Illinois: Northwestern University Press, 1966), p. 548.
[88] *Eastern House of Assembly Debates* (Enugu), November 16, 1962.
[89] *The Daily Times,* November 17, 1962.
[90] S.A.Aluko's, "How Many Nigerians? An Analysis of Nigerian Census Problems, 1901-1963," *Journal of Modern African Studies,* p. 383. See also *The Daily Times,* December 6 and 7, 1962.
[91] *The Daily Times,* December 11, 1962.
[92] *Ibid.*
[93] Federation of Nigeria, House of Representatives (Lagos), *Parliamentary Debates,* December 5, 1962.
[94] J.P. Mackintosh, *Nigerian Government and Politics,* Northwestern University Press, 1956, Evanston, Illinois, p. 548.
[95] S.A. Aluko, "How Many Nigerians? An Analysis of Nigerian Census Problems, 1901-1963," *Journal of Modern African Studies,* p. 383.
[96] *Ibid.*
[97] At this time, the Western Region included the Midwest which was created in 1963.
[98] *The Daily Times,* February 20, 1963.
[99] James O'Connell, "Political Integration, the Nigerian Case," in Arthur 'Hazlewood's (editor), *African Integration and Disintegration,* Oxford University Press, 1967, p. 169.
[100] Alhaji Waziri Ibrahim, Speech made in the Federal House of Representatives, Federation of Nigeria, *Parliamentary Debates* (Lagos), August 18, 1962.
[101] For proof that the figure in the North was also inflated, see the figures from the demographic checks made in the 1963 census figures which are similar to the revised figures for 1962.

[102] *The Daily Times,* December 6 and 8, 1962.
[103] *The Daily Times,* February 20, 1963.
[104] J.P. Mackintosh, *Nigerian Federal Government,* (Evanston, Illinois: Northwestern University Press, 1966), pp. 551-552. See also S.A. Aluko's, "How Many Nigerians? An Analysis of Nigerian Census Problems, 1901-1963," *Journal of Modern African Studies,* 3,3 (1965), pp. 372-392.
[105] Dr. Okpara, the Premier of the Eastern Region, characterized the result as "worse than useless," in a News Conference which he held on February 28, 1963. The East, the Midwest and the Lagos City Council rejected the results; the Midwest later withdrew its protest and accepted the census results. See J.P. Mackintosh, *op. cit.,* p. 554.
[106] J.P. Mackintosh, *op. cit.,* p. 554.
[107] Federation of Nigeria, *House of Representatives Debate,* December 5, 1962. This report was written in July, yet it was read on December 1, 1962, without being updated.
[108] J.P. Mackintosh, *Nigerian Government and Politics,* Northwestern University Press, 1956, Evanston, Illinois, p. 554.
[109] *The West African Pilot,* February 29, 1964.
[110] *Ibid.*
[111] *The West African Pilot,* February 29, 1964.
[112] *The Morning Post,* March 4, 1964.
[113] For full details of this conflict, see J.P. Mackintosh's, *Nigerian Government and Politics,* Northwestern University Press, 1956, Evanston, Illinois, pp. 551-556.
[114] Kenneth Post and Michael Vickers, *Structure and Conflict in Nigeria,* (Madison, Wisconsin: The University of Wisconsin Press, 1973), pp. 80-81.
[116] *The Daily Express,* December 18, 1963.
[117] *The Morning Post,* March 4, 1964.
[118] J.P. Mackintosh, *Nigerian Government and Politics,* Northwestern University Press, 1956, Evanston, Illinois, p. 556. Also, *Northern House of Assembly Debate,* March 12, 1964.
[119] *Northern House of Assembly Debates,* March 12, 1964.
[120] J.P. Mackintosh, *Nigerian Government and Politics,* Northwestern University Press, 1956, Evanston, Illinois, p. 557.
[122] Non-declared revenue is the revenue allocated to the regions by the federal government from revenue which is not declared to be regional, such as revenue from customs duties.
[123] *Hicks-Phillipson Report on Revenue Allocation,* (Lagos Government Printing Press, Lagos, 1954), p. 10.
[121] B.J. Dudley, *Parties and Politics in Northern Nigeria* (London: Frank Cass and Company, Ltd., 1968), p. 267.
[124] K.J. Binns, *Report of the Fiscal Review Commission* (Lagos: Federal Ministry of Information. 1964). For alternative recommendation by the Commissioner, see pp. 20-22. See also Adedeji, *Nigerian Federal Finance,* Africana Publishing Corporation, New 'York, N.Y., pp. 232-244 for a full description.
*For events leading to the creation of the Midwest Region, please see Chapter 3.

CHAPTER V

[1] Aaron Wildavsky, *The Politics of the Budgetary Process,* 2nd edition, Little Brown and Company, Boston Massachusetts, 1974, p. 5.
[2] Charles A. beard, *An Economic Interpretation of the Constitution of the United States,* The Macmillan Company, New York, New York, p. 180.
[3] K.W. Deutsch, *op. cit.,* pp. 18-26.
[4] K.C. Wheare, *Federal Government,* 4th edition, Oxford University Press, London, England, 1967, p. 45.
[5] Dispatch to the Secretary of States by the Governor, Sir Arthur Richards, december 6, 1944.
Margery Pertham, "Nigeria's Civil War, " in Colin Legum, *Africa Contemporary Record,* Africa Research Ltd., London, 1969, p. 4.

[7] Deutsch, *op. cit.*, p. 39.

[8] Introduction to Hick-Phillipson Commission *Report on Revenue Allocation* (Lagos Government Printing Press, 1951), p. 151-152. This introduction was written and signed by Sir Phillipson.

[9] Australian Grant Commission, *Report on the Application made by the States of Australia, Western Australia and Tanzania for Financial Assistance from the Commonwealth* under Section 96 of the Constitution (First report 1934), p. 15. See also Adebayo Adedeji, *Nigeria Federal Finance* Africana Publishing Corporation, New York, 1969, pp. 10-12.

[10] J.R. Hicks and Sydney Phillipson, *Report of the Commission on revenue Allocation* (lagos: Government Printing Press, 1951), pp. 151-152. The section of the report quoted was written and signed by J.R. Hicks alone.

[11] Raisman Report of revenue Allocation, *Report of the Commission on revenue Allocation*(lagos: Government Printing Press, 1953), p. 1

[12] *Nigerian Legislative Council Debate,* Official Report, November 1, 1923.

For a detailed discussion of the problems of revenue allocation between 1914 and 1946 see Adebayo Adedeji's *Nigerian Federal Finance,* Africana Publication, New York, 1969; P.N.C. Okigbo, *Nigerian Public Finance,* Longmans, green and Company. Ltd., London, 1965; A. Hazelwood, *The Finances of Nigerian federation* (London: Oxford University Press, 1956).

[13a] Sir Bernard Bourdillion, Appointment of Revenue and Duties as between the central government and native administrations. Minutes by the Governor (Lagos: Government Printing Press, 1939).

[14] Sessional Paper No. 4 of 1945; *Political and Constitutional Future of Nigeria,* Government Printing Press, Lagos, Nigeria.

[15] Phillipson Report (Lagos: Government Printing Press, 1947) paragraph 22.

[16] *Ibid., paragraph 24-29.*

[17] *Ibid.*

[18] Phillipson Report, p. 10.

[19] Dispatch to the secretary of States by the Governor Sir Arthur Richards, december 6, 1944.

[20] Phillipson Report, p. 20.

[21] Phillipson Report, paragraph 59.

[22] The merits and demerits of this formula has been the subject of scholarly debate. For a detailed discussion, see Adebayo Adedeji's *Nigerian federal Finance, pp.* 54-67 and P.N.C. Akigbo's, *Nigerian Public Finance,* Longmans, green and co., Ltd., London, England, 1967, pp. 44-48.

[23] Phillipson Report, p. 25.

[24] *Ibid. pp. 26-27.*

[25] *Ibid.,* pp. 26-27

[26] R.J. May, *Federalism and Financial Adjustment,* (Oxford at the Clarendon Press, 1969), p. 135.

[27] Adebayo Adedeji, *Nigerian Federal Finance,* Africana Publication, New York, New

[28] P.N.C. Okigbo, *Nigerian Public Finance,* Longmans, Green & Co., Ltd., London, England, 1965, p. 21.

[29] *Ibid.,* pp. 22-23.

[30] Adebayo Adedeji, *op. cit.,* p. 69.

'York, 1969, p. 52.

[31] Dispatch to the Secretary of State by the Governor, Sir Arthur Richards, december 6, 1944.

[32] Proceedings of the General Conference on the review of the Constitution (lagos: Government Printing Press, 1950), p. 165.

[32] Proceedings of the general Conference on the review of the Constitution (Lagos: Government Printing Press, 1950), p. 165.

[33] Address by His Excellency, Sir Arthur Richards, C.M.G. Governor and Commander in Chief of Nigeria at a meeting of the Colonial Affairs Study Group of the Empire Parliamentary Association, January 28, 1947, issued under the authority of the empire and Parliamentary Association, United Kingdom branch, pp. 10-11.

³⁴K.W. Deutsch, et al., International Political Community (New York: Doubleday and Company, 1966), p. 29.
³⁵Proceedings of the General Conference on the review of the Constitution, 1950 (lagos Government Printing Press, 1950), p. 165.
³⁶R.H. Green and K.G. V. Krish, *Economic Cooperation in Africa: Retrospect and Prospects* (Oxford University Press, London 1967), p. 52.
³⁷Proceedings of the General Conference on the *Review of the Constitution* (Lagos: Government Printing Press, 1950), p. 98.
³⁸Dispatch to the Secretary of State by the Governor, Sir Arthur Richards, december 6, 1944.
³⁹Hicks-Phillipson *Report of the Commission on Revenue Allocation,* 1951 (Lagos: Government Printing Press), p. 152.
⁴⁰*Ibid.*
⁴¹Proceedings of the General Conference on the *Review of the Constitution* (lagos: Government Printing Press, 1950), p. 239.
⁴²Hicks-Phillipson *Report of the Commission on revenue Allocation,* 1951 (lagos: Government Printing Press), p. 7.
⁴³*Ibid.*
⁴⁴R.H. Green and K.G.V. Krishna, *Economic Cooperation in Africa: Retrospect and Prospect*(Oxford University Press, London, 1967), p. 50.
⁴⁵*Ibid.*
⁴⁶Hicks-Phillipson *Report of the Commiion on Revenue Allocation,* 1951, (lagos: Government Printing Press), p. 6. In fact, the commissioners emphasized that their proposals are "entitled to carry some of the weight of an arbitrary award." (p.9) It must be pointed out that the commission carried out an exhaustive highly analytical research into the problem of economic and political conflict in Nigeria. The report presaged most of the problems that eventually caused the collapse of the Nigerian civilian regimes.
⁴⁷R.J. May, in his *Federalism and Fiscal Adjustment* (London, Oxford University at the Clarendon Press, 1969), pp. 136-137 in which he discussed the federal financial arrangements in 12 states called the Hicks-Phillipson Report the most substantial discussion of the topic since the first three reports of the Commonwealth grant Commission in 1930.
⁴⁸R.J. May, *Federalism and Fiscal Adjustment,* (London: Oxford University Press, 1969), pp. 156-157.
⁴⁹Hicks-Phillipson *Report of the Commission on Revenue Allocation,* 1951, (lagos: government Printing Press), p. 13.
⁵¹*Ibid.*
⁵²*Ibid.,* p.8
⁵³Hicks-Phillipson *Report of the Commission on Revenue Allocation,* 1951 (Lagos: Government Printing Press), p. 12. This is a reference to the size and population of Northern Nigeria which is greater than that of the other two southern regions combined.
⁵⁴This principle has been defined earlier in this chapter.
⁵⁵*Ibid.,* pp. 54-58.
⁵⁶*Ibid.,* p. 53.
⁵⁷The definition on 'non-declared revenue' is given one page of this dissertation.
⁵⁸Hicks-Phillipson *Report of the Commission on Revenue Allocation,* 1951 (Lagos: Government Printing Press), p. 22
⁵⁹*Ibid.,* p. 21.
⁶⁰Hicks-Phillipson *Report of the Commission on Revenue Allocation,* 1951 (Lagos: Government Printing Press), p. 156-157.
⁶¹*Ibid.,* p. 77.
⁶²Hicks-Phillipson *Report of the Commission on Revenue Allocation,* 1951, (Lagos: Government Printing Press), pp. 77-78.
⁶³*Ibid.*
⁶⁴*Ibid.,* pp. 158-159.
⁶⁵Hicks-Phillipson *Report of the Commission on Revenue Allocation,* 1951, (lagos: Government Printing Press), Table XXVI, p. 142.
⁶⁶*Ibid.,* pp. 158-159.

[67] *Ibid.*, p. 152.
[68] Hicks-Phillipson *Report of the Commission on Revenue Allocation,* 1951, (Lagos: Government Printing Press), p. 159.
[69] *Ibid.*, pp. 58-59.
[70] *Ibid.*, much of the conflict that developed between the North and East is in part due to the feeling of the Northedrner that they were cheated in favor of the Eastern.
[71] *Ibid.*, p. 59.
[72] Hicks-Phillipson *Report of the Commission on Revenue Allocation,* 1951, (Lagos : Government Printing Press), p. 59.
[73] *Ibid.*, p. 82. The term under-equipment means that the North in comparison with the other two regions is deficient in equipment for public services. It is hard to reconcile this grant with the statement made by the commissioners on page 82 of the report to the effect that: "The North has already been receiving some special assistance to meet its most striking deficiency in eqipment for public services, in the form of 'special purposes' grants to the other regions. Thus in 1950-1951 estimates for the Northern 'Special Purposes' grant is 177,000 pounds against a Western grant of 25,775 pounds and an Eastern grant of 30,000 pounds. These grants under the existing system are part of the general allocation from non-declared revenue ... and will continue to be taken into account in any calculations which follow."
[74] *Ibid.*, p. 82.
[75] *Ibid.*, p. 83.
[76] Address by His Excellency Sir Arthur Richards, GCMG Governor and Commander in Chief of Nigeria at a meeting of the Colonial Affairs Study Group of the Empire Parliamentary Association, January, 1947, pp. 10-11.
[77] Adebayo Adedeji, *Nigerian Federal Finance,* Africana Publication, New York, 1969, pp. 84-85.
[78] For a discussion of the crisis surrounding the independence motion which led to the Kano riots, see Chapter 2 of this dissertation.
[79] Report of the Conference on the review of the Nigerian Constitution, 1953, Command 8934, p. 7.
[80] Chick Commission Report, Command 9026, p. 13.
[81] *Ibid.*
[82] *Ibid.*
[83] *Ibid.*
[84] *Ibid.*
[85] Chick Commission Report, Command 9026, p. 21.
[86] *Ibid.*

[88] *Ibid.*, p. 22.
[89] *Ibid., p.* 21
[90] *Ibid., p.* 22
[91] For the political crisis in the Eastern region in 1953, please see Chapter 2 of this discussion, pp.
[92] Federation of Nigeria, *Accountant General's Report, Annual 1953-54.*
[93] Chick Commission Report, Commany 9026, p. 14.
[94] *Ibid.*
[95] Chick Commission Report, Command 9026, p. 23.
[96] Report of the Conference on the Nigerian Constitution held in London in July and August, 1953, Cond. 9059, 1954.
[97] Chick Commission Report, Command 9026, p. 26.
[98] *Ibid.*
[99] *Ibid.*
[100] *Ibid.*, p. 27
[101] *Ibid.*, pp. 26-27
[102] *Ibid.*, p. 27
[103] *Ibid.*, p. 26.
[104] Adebayo Adedeji, *Nigerian federal Finance,* Africana Publication, New York, 1069, pp. 84-85.

[105] Hicks-Phillpson *Report of the Commission on Revenue Allocation,* 1951 (Lagos: Government Printing Press), p. 28.

[106] *Ibid.*

[107] Charlotte Leubusher, *Bulk Buying from the Colonies* (London, Oxford University Press, 1966), p. 11.

[108] Hicks-Phillipson Report, 1951, p. 28.

[109] Hicks-Phillipson *Report on Revenue Allocation,* p. 28. For a fuller discussion of the Marketing Board see G.H. Hellemer, "The Fiscal Role of the Marketing Boards in Nigerian Economic developemtn, 1947-1961", *Economic Journal,* September, 1964.

[110] A.R.O. Teriba, Nigerian Revenue Allocation Experience 1952-1965; a study in Inter-Governmental Fiscal and Financial relations, *The Nigerian Journal of Economic and Social Studies,* Volume 8, No. 3 (November 1966), pp. 361-382.

[111] The southern cameroons received 1.2 millions pounds. But since the southern Cameroons is outside the scope of this research, discussion on the Cameroons has been excluded.

[112] Adebayo Adedeji, *Nigerian Public Finance,* Africana Publications, New York, N.Y., 1969, p. 111.

[113] See the Coker Commission of Enquiry discussed briefly in Chapter 3 of this research. p.

[114] Hicks-Phillipson Report, 1951, p. 150. This assessment proved to be true when oil was discovered in commercial quantity in the Eastern Region.

[115] At the Constitutional Conference of 1953, the North has specifically called for a customs union, the West had threatened to secede and the colonial secretary had called for a loose federation because he felt that Nigerians could not work together in a tight federation. For a full account, see the Report of the Conference on Nigerian Constitution held in London in 1952, Command 8934.

[116] Hicks-Phillipson Report, 1951, p. 53.

[117] P.N.C. Okigbo, *Nigeria Public Finance,* Longmans, green and Company, Ltd., London, 1965, p. 43.

[118] James S. Coleman, *Nigeria Background to Nationalism* (Berkeley: University of California, 1971), p. 371.

[119] Chick Commission Report, 195l, p. 21.

[120] Adebayo Adedeji, *Nigerian Federal Finance,* Africana Publications, New 'York, 1969, p. 121.

[121] Report of the Fiscal Commission, Command 481, 1958, p. 6.

[122] *Ibid.*, p. 55

[123] *Ibid.*, p. 50.

[124] Report of the Fiscal Commission, Command 481, p. 1

[125] *Ibid.*, p. 8.

[126] *Ibid.*

[127] *Hicks-Phillipson Report of the Commission on Revenue Allocation,* 1951 (Lagos: Government Printing Press), p. 83.

[128] Hicks-Phillipson *Report of the Commission on Revenue Allocation,* 1951 (lagos: Government Printing Press), p. 83.

[129] Chick Commission *Report of the Commission on Revenue Allocation,* Command 9026, p. 19.

[130] Report of the Fiscal Commission, Command 482, p. 24.

[131] Report of the Fiscal Commission, Command 481, p. 32.

[132] Total revenue collected by the federal and regional governments for 1958-1959 was 92 million pounds. The federal government retained 51 per cent; the regions shared 49 per cent.

[133] Report of the Fiscal Commission, Command 481, p. 31.

[134] Report of the Fiscal Commission, Command 481, p. 32.

[135] Eme O. Awa,*Federal Government in Nigeria* (California: University of California Press, 1964), p. 208.

[136] Adebayo Adedeji, *Nigerian Federal Finance,* Africana Publication, New York, 1969, p. 133.

[137] Adebayo Adedeji, *Nigerian Federal Finance,* Africana Publications, New York,

1969, p. 230.

[138] Report of the Fiscal Commission, Command 481, 1958, p. 28.

[139] The Raisman Commission Proposals came into operation in Nigeria on April 1, 1959.

[140] The other three were Phillipson Commission of 1946; Hicks-'phillipson Commission of 1950-1951; and the Chick Commission of 1953.

[141] The Cameroons (north and South) were former German Colonies attached to Nigeria after World War 1 as mandated territories. In 1960, the United Nations decided as a result of the approaching independence of Nigeria to hold a plebiscite in the Cameroons toascertain whether the people of the Cameroons wanted to join Nigeria or the French Cameroons. The Northern Cameroons voted to join the Northern Region while the Southern Camerons voted to join the french Cameroons.

[142] Mr. K.J. Binns was an Under-Treasurer and State Commissioner of Taxes in the State of Tasmania, Australia.

[143] *Official Gazette of the Federal Republic of Nigeria,* Vol. 51, p. 911, Government Notice No. 1072.

[144] For a Survey of Revenue Allocation and Fiscal Adjustment in Other federations, see R.J. MAY, *Federalism and Fiscal Adjustment* (london: Oxford University at the Clarendon Press, 1969).

[145] P.N.C. Okigbo, *Nigerian Public Finance,* Longmans, Green and Company, Ltd., London, 1965, p.

[146] See K.C. Wheare, *Federal Government*, 4th edition Oxford University Press, 1967 pp. 117-118. Wheare notes that in Switzerland reallocation of revenue was the result of the redistribution of burdens between the federal government and the Cantons; in India the reallocation is done after the recommendation of a constitutionally established fiscal commission which takes the fiscal needs of the states into consideration in making recommendations; in Australia, a permanent Commonwealth Grant Commission takes into account the needs of the states in making recommendations to the federal government.

[147] C.J. May, *Federalism and Fiscal Adjustment, op. cit.,* p. 56.

[148] J.P. Mackintosh, *Nigerian Government and Politics,* Northwestern University, Evanston, Illinois, 1966.

[149] Adedeji Adebsayo, *Nigerian Federal Finance,* Africana Publication, New York, NY., 1969, p. 229 (footnote).

[150] K.J. Binns, *Report of the Fiscal review Commission,* (lagos: Government Printing Press, 1964), p. 13.

[151] *Ibid., p.* 13.

[152] K.J. Binns, *Report of the Fiscal review Commission* (Lagos: Government Printing Press, 1964), p. 14

[153] J.P. Mackintosh, *Nigerian Government and Politics,* Northwestern University, Evanston, Illinois, 1966.

[154] Binns suggested that the principle of derivation would eventually weaken the federation, that the principle of need was ill-suited to the Nigerian situation because of the gross inequalities in the level of regional economic development. He then concluded that "particular weight must be given to the necessity to preserve continuity, including the provision of funds sufficient to meet the minimum responsiblilties of governmnent." (p.24) He recommended a fixed annual grant from the center to the regions to ensure that each regional government should be placed in approximately a comparable financial position to enable it to make comparable contribution from its recurrent budget towards financing its capital developement projects. As an alternative policy, he recommended that the Distributalbe Pool be increased by 35 percent of revenue from customs duties and 35 percent of the revenues from mineral rents and royalties. The total revenue should then be divided as follows:
42 percent to the North, 30 percent to the East and 20 percent to the West and 8 percent to the Midwest. The annual grant he recommended was 2.0 million pounds to the North, 0.8 million to the East and 0.6 million pounds to the West; and 0.35 million pounds to the Mid-West. With respect to the North, he noted that the North must be helped to the fullest extent possible to bring it to the same level of development with the othr regions. (p. 34).

[155]R.J. May, *Federalism and Fiscal Adjustment*, (Oxford University Press at Alarendon, 1969, p. 142.)
[156]Hicks - Phillipson *Report of the Commission on Revenue Allocation*, 1951, Government Printing Press, p. 8.
[157]R.H. Green and K.G.V. Krishana, *Economic Cooperation in Africa* (London: Oxford University Press, 1967) pp. 49-50
[158]Hicks-Phillipson *Report of the Commission on Revenue Allocation*, 1951, Government Printing Press, p. 152.
[159]R.J. May, *Federalism and Fiscal Adjustment*, (Oxford University Press at Clarendon, 1969), p. 56.

CHAPTER VI

[1]Jean Blondel, *An Introduction to Comparative Government*, Fredrick A. Praeger Publishing Co., New York, New York, 1969, p. 336.
[2]Robert A. Dahl, *Political Opposition in Western Democracies*, Yale University Press, New Haven, Connecticut, 1966, p. 350.
[3]In 1962 a fourth region known as the Midwest Region was carved out of the Western Region and was controlled by the National Council of Nigerian Citizens which also controlled the Eastern Region.
[4]For the situation of the parties in the Western Region, after 1962, see Chapter 3.
[5]When Southern Cameroon became part of the Cameroon Federation and Northern Cameroon was merged with Northern Nigeria in 1961, the party changed its name to the National Council of Nigerian Citizens.
[6]For detailed discussion on the nature and type of political parties, see M. Duverger's *Political Parties*, (Methuen, 1955). Jospeh LaPalombara and Myron Weiner, *Political Parties and Political Development*, Princeton University Press, Princeton, New Jersey, 1972. M.I. Ostrogorski, *Democracy and the Organization of Political Parties in the United States and Great Britain*, Doubleday Anchor, 1964, Garden City, New York.
[7]It is not unlikely that the criticism of the proposals of the Richards Constitution in 1945 by the Ziks (Ibos) group on newspapers had a direct bearing on the first anti-Ibo riot in Jos, in the Northern Region in 1945. Jos was a mining center and stronghold of the colonial elite. It was the only town in Nigeria with an all volunteer European (English) Army.
[8]For a discussion of the Richards Constitution see Chapter 2.
[9]Richard L. Sklar, "Nigeria," in James Coleman and Carl G. Rosenberg's Jr. (editors), *Political Parties and National Integration in Tropical Africa*, University of California Press, berkeley, California, 1970, p. 599.
[10]James Coleman and Carl Rosenberg observed that African political parties were formed because of imperial constitutional reform and the introduction of electoral institutions; the Action Group is a prime example of this. See James S. Coleman and Carl G. Rosenberg, *op. cit.*, p. 3.
[11]There was a sizeable minority of Ibos in the Western Region until the creation of the Midwest State in 1962.
[12]See Chapter 3 for further details.
[13]In a convention held in Jos in December, 1950, the radical wing of the NPC urged that the organization be converted into an active political party to be used as a party platform for the 1951 election; see B.J. Dudley's *Parties and Politics in Northern Nigeria*, Frank cass & Co., Ltd., London, England, 1968, p. 80.
[14]James S. Coleman, *Nigeria: Background to Nationalism*, University of California Press, Berkeley, California, 1971, p. 363.
[15]B.J. Dudley, *Parties and Politics in Northern Nigeria*, Frank Cass & Co., Ltd., London, 1968, p. 139.
[16]B.J. KDudley, *Parties and Politics in Northern Nigeria*, Frank Cass & Co., Ltd., London, 1968, p. 143.
[17]The Western Region became ethnically homogeneous only in 1962 when the Midwest State was created.
[18]James S. Coleman, *Nigeria: Background to Nationalism*, University of California

Press, Berkeley, California, 1971, p. 20

[19] Ibid.

[20] For the Eastern Regional crisis of 1953, see Chapter 2.

[21] For a discussion of the Western Regional crisis of 1962, see Chapter 3.

[22] Richard L. Sklar and C.S. Whitaker, Jr.; "Nigeria," in James S. Coleman and Carl L. Rosenberg, Jr's., (editors); *Political Parties and National Integration in Tropical Africa*, University of California Press, Berkeley, California, 1970, p. 604.

[23] Thomas Hodgkin, *Nationalism in Colonial Africa*, New York University Press, New York, New York, 1957, p. 138. Ruth Schacter Morgenthau follows Hodgkin in analysis of *African Political Parties*, APSR, Vol. 55, No. 2, 1961.

[24] Rhomas Hodgkin, *Nationalism in Colonial Africa*, New York University press, New York, N.Y., 1957, pp. 159-160.

[25] Thomas Hodgkin, *African Political Parties*, Penguin Books, 1961, passim.

[26] Ruth Schacter-Morgenthau, "Single Party Systems in West Africa," *The American Political Science Review*, Vol. 55, No. 2, June, 1961.

[27] K.W. Post, *Nigerian Federal Election of 1959*, Oxford University Press, 1963, passim.

[28] Sigmund Newmann, "Toward a Comparative Study of Political Parties in S. Newmann's (editor), *Modern Political Parties*, Chicago University Press, Chicago, Illinois, 1956.

[29] For the most recent discussion of the command base of Nigerian political parties see Robert Melson and Howard Wolpe's, *Nigeria: Modernization and the Politics of Communalism*. (Michigan State University Press, 1971); in it, communalism is defined as political assertiveness of groups which have three distinguishing characteristics: first, their membership is comprised of persons who share in culture and identity ... second, they emcompass the full range of demographic divisions within the wider society ... and third, like the wider society in which they exist they tend to be differentiated by wealth, status and power, pp. 1-2.

[30] Richard L. Sklar and C.S. Whitaker, Jr., "Nigeria" in James S. Coleman and Carl G. Rosenberg Jr's., *Political and National Integration in Tropical Africa*, University of California Press, Berkeley, California, 1970, pp. 619-620.

[31] B.J. Dudley, *Parties and Politics in Northern Nigeria*, Frank cass & Co., Ltd., 1968, Appendix 1, p. 320

[32] The regional distribution of seats at the central legislature during the First Republic, in 1964, elections were as follows: Northern Peoples Congress (NPC) 167, Eastern Region 70, the Western Region 57, and the Midwest 14; and Lagos (the Capital) 4 seats. The number required to gain a majority was 167.

[33] Space does not permit us to discuss the minority parties in the regions. However, as we discuss the coalition of the major parties with these minority parties, we shall attempt to place them in proper perspective. For a detailed discussion of the various minority parties in Nigeria see Richard L. Sklar, *Nigerian Political Parties*, Princeton University Press, Princeton, N.J., 1963.

[34] The Action Group was the governing party in the Western Region, the National Council of Nigerian Citizens was the governing party in the Eastern Region and also formed the opposition party in the Western Region. The Northern People's Congress was in control of the government of the Northern Region.

[35] For further details on the Western Regional Crisis of 1962, see Chapter 3 of this dissertation.

[36] The formation on a coalition government between the UPP and the NCNC in the Western Region enabled the Midwesterners to cut through the complicated legal procedure for the creation of a new state.

[37] Kenneth Post and Michael Vickers, *Structure and Conflict in Nigeria*, University of Wisconsin Press, Madison, Wisconsin, 1972, p. 92.

[38] The Sunday Express, December 1, 1963. See also Kenneth Post and Michael Vickers, *op. cit.,* p. 93.

[39] *The Daily Times*, December 18, 1963, quoted in Kenneth Post and Michael Vickers, *op. cit.,* p. 93

⁴⁰*The Daily Express* (Nigeria), December 5, 1964.
⁴¹*The Daily Express*)Nigeria), December 5, 1964.
⁴²*The Sunday Express,* July 15, 1962. See also Kenneth Post and Michael Vickers,*op. cit.,* p. 97.
⁴³Kenneth Post and Michael Vickers, *Structure and Conflict in Nigeria,* University of Wisconsin Press, Madison, Wisconsin, 1972, p. 102.
⁴⁴Richard L. Sklar, *Nigerian Political Parties,* (Princeton: Princeton University Press, 1963), pp. 323-327.
⁴⁵Richard L. Sklar, *Nigerian Political Parties,* (Princeton: Princeton University Press, 1963), pp. 323-338.
⁴⁶*The Bornu Youth Movement, Constitution and Regulations,* July 14, 1954.
⁴⁷Richard L. Sklar, *Nigerian Political Parties,* (Princeton: Princeton University Press, 1963), p. 350.
⁴⁸For a discussion of the Tiv riot of 1960, see Chapter 3.
⁴⁹John P. Mackintos, *Nigerian Government and Politics,* Northwestern University City Press, Evanston, Illinois, 1960,p. 498.
⁴⁹ᵃ J.P. Mackintosh, *op. cit.,* p. 504.
⁵⁰James O'Connell, "Political Integration: The Nigerian Case, " in Arthur Hazlewood's (editor), *African Integration and Disintegration,* London: Oxford University Press, 1967, p. 161.
⁵¹M.J. Dent, "Tarka and the Tiv: A Perspective on Nigerian Federation in Robert Melson and Howard A. Wolpe's (editors), *Nigeria: Modernization and the Politics of Communalism,* Michigan State University, 1971, p. 454.
⁵²Instrument Establishing the Northern Peoples Front reproduced in Appendix 5 of *Parties and Politics in Northern Nigeria* by B.J. Dudley, (Frank Cass & Co., Ltd., 1968), pp. 324-325.
⁵³*The West African Pilot,* December 4, 1963.
⁵⁴Odumosu I. Oluwole, *Constitutional Crisis: Legality and the President's Conscience.*
⁵⁵Kenneth Post and Michael Vickers, *Structure and Conflict in Nigeria,* University of Wisconsin Press, Madison, Wisconsin, 1972, p. 100.
⁵⁶*Manifesto of the Nigerian National Alliance,* 1964, n.p. Quoted in Kenneth Post and Michael Vickers, *Structure and Conflict in Nigeria,* University of Wisconsin Press, Madison, Wisconsin, 1972, p. 113.
⁵⁷*Forward with UPGA to Unity and Progress, Manifesto of the UPCA,* (Lagos: United Nigerian Press, Ltd., 1964), p. 15.
⁵⁸Robert A. Dahl (editor), *Political Opposition in Western Democracies* (New Haven: Yale University Press, 1966), p. 344.
⁵⁹*The Morning Post,* December 3, 1963
⁶⁰Bernard Berelson and Gary Steiner, *Human Behavior, An Inventory of Scientific Findings* New York: Harcourt, Brace and World, Inc., 1964), p. 575.
⁶¹*The Manifesto of the United Progressive Grand Alliance* (Yaba, Lagos: United Nigerian Press, Ltd., 1964), p. 2.
⁶²*The Morning Post,* December 8, 1964.
⁶³K.C. Wheare, *Federal Government* (London: Oxford University Press, 1967), p. 46.
⁶⁴J.P. Mackintosh, *Nigerian Government and Policies,* Northwestern University Press, 1956, Evanston, Illinois, p. 33.
⁶⁵J.P. Mackintosh, *Nigerian Government and Politics,* Northwestern University Press, 1956, Evanston, Illinois, p. 584.
⁶⁶*Ibid.,* p. 583.
⁶⁷*The West African Pilot,* November 21, 1964. See also J.P. Mackintosh. *op. cit., p.*579.
⁶⁸*The West African Pilot,* November 18 and 19, 1964.
⁶⁹*The West African Pilot,* October 21, 1964. See also *The Daily Express,* October 16, 17, 22, and 23, 1964.
⁷⁰The Alkali Court is a special arm of the Northern Native Authority system. The law which operates within it is the Koranic law and the accused is not allowed any al represer tation.
⁷¹Kenneth Post and Michael Vickers, *Structure and Conflict,* University of Wisconsin

Press, Madison, Wisconsin, 1972, p.

[72] Peter Cl. Lloyds, "The Traditional Political System of the Yoruba," in Ronald Cohen and John Middleton (editors), *Comparative Political Systems,* The Natural History Press, New York, 1967, pp.

[73] J.P. Mackintosh, *op. cit.,* p. 577.

[74] Clifford Geertz, "The Integrative Revolution", in Clifford Geertz (editor), *Old Societies and New Stages,* The Free Press of Glencoe, N.Y., 1963, pp. 108-109.

[75] *Ibid.*

[76] *The West African Pilot,* October 27, 1964.

[77] *The Daily Service,* November 7 and 8, 1964.

[78] Kenneth Post and Michael Vickers, *Structure and Conflict in Nigeria 1960-1966;* The University of Wisconsin Press, Madison, Wisconsin, 1973, p. 148.

[79] *Ibid.,* p. 152.

[80] Robin Luckman, *The Nigerian Military,* Cambridge University Press, London, 1971, p. 215. It must not be supposed that there were no harassments of the opposition in the East and Midwest. But these were minor.

[81] Kenneth Post and Michael Vickers, *Structure and Conflict in Nigeria,* The University of Wisconsin Press, Madison, Wisconsin, 1973, pp. 151-154.

[82] *The Daily Press,* October 24, 1964.

[83] *The West African Pilot,* October 27, 1974.

[90] *The Morning Post,* January 1, 1965.

[91] *The Daily Express,* December 30, 1964.

[92] *The West African Pilot,* December 11, 1964.

[93] *The West African Pilot,* December 11, 1964. This speech known as the "Dawn Address" was published in full by the *West African Pilot.*

[94] *Ibid.,* December 24, 1964.

[95] *The Sunday Expres,* December 24, 1964.

[96] *The West African Pilot,* December 29, 1964.

[97] *The Daily Express,* December 28, 1964.

[98] Kenneth Post and Michael Vickers, *Structure and Conflict in Nigeria* (Madison, Wisconsin: University of Wisconsin Press, 1973), pp. 176-178.

[99] Section 106 (3) gave the Prime Minister power to give the Inspector-General of the Police directions "with respect to the maintaining and securing of public safety and public order as he may consider necessary. The Navy and Army Act of the Republication Constitution of 1963 placed the Army and Navy under the overall direction of the Council of Ministers.

[100] J.P. Mackintosh, *Nigerian Government and Politics,* Northwestern University Press, Evanston, Illinois, 1966, pp. 590-591.

[101] It can be seen from the above discussion that before the military coup d'etat of January, 1966, the politicans had continually drawn the armed forces and the police into the political controversy. We have noted how the army was used to quell the Tiv Riots of 1960 (Chapter 3, above). in fact, from 1960 to 1964, there was an undeclared state of emergency in the Tiv area in which the army played a crucial role in restoring peace. In the Western Region in 1962, "the police, acting on the orders of Sir Abubakar (the Prime Minister), had prevented the Western Region Assembly from voting on the question of Akintola's right to continue to be Premier." (N.J. Miners, *The Nigerian Army, 1956-1966,* Methuen & Co., Ltd., London, p. 143). The army was also called into alert during the emergency in the Western Region in 1962. Even as far back as 1960, a member of the Federal House of Representatives from the North had called for the equalization of officers from each region, "so that the officers in the Eastern Region, the Northern Region and the Western Region are equalized." *House of Representative Debate,* April 14, 1960, quoted in N.J. Miners, *op. cit.,* p. 53. Thus, we can see that regionalization also affected the composition of the officer corps of the Nigerian Armed Forces.

[102] I.O. Odumosu, *Constitutional Crisis: Legality and the President's Conscience* (N.P.), pp. 31-32.

[103] *The Sunday Express,* January 3, 1965.

[104] *The Daily Express,* January 5, 1965.

139

[105] *The Constitution of the Federation*, 1963, No. 20, p. 45.

CONCLUSION

[1] William H. Riker, *Federalism, Origin, Operation and Significance: Basic Studies in Politics*, "Little Brown & Co., 1964, p. 48.
[2] Samuel P. Huntington, *Political Order in Changing Societies*, Yale University Press, 1975, p. 24.
[3] K.C. Wheare, *Federal Government*, Oxford University Press, London, England, 1967, p. 44.
[4] The only party organized on a national basis primarily to protest colonial oppression is the National Council of Nigeria and the Cameroons (NCNC). It started as a Nigerian-wide protest movement but was forced to seek a regional base because the regions became by constitutional arrangement the only avenue for effective organization of political power.
[5] Arnold Rivkin (editor), *Nations by Design*, Doubleday and Co., Inc. New York, New York, 1968, p. 16.
[6] Seymour Martin Lipset, *Political Man*, Doubleday and Company, New York, New York, 1963, pp. 77-92. See also Jean Blondel, *An Introduction to Comparative Government*, Fredrick Praeger Publishing Co., Inc., New 'York, New York, 1969, pp. 52-58, for a detailed study of the effects of sectionalism on the political system.
[6] Seymour Martin Lipset, *Political Man*, Doubleday and Company, New York, New York, 1963, pp. 77-92. See also Jean Blondel, *An Introduction to Comparative Government*, Fredrick Praeger Publishing Co., Inc., New York, New York, 1969, pp. 52-58, for a detailed analysis of the effects of sectionalism on the political system.
[7] Samuel P. Huntington, *Political Order in Changing Societies*, Yales University, Yale University Press; New Haven, Connecticut, 1975, p. 15.
[8] Statement by the Sardauna of Sokoto quoted in Walter Schwartz's *Nigeria*, Fredrick A. Praeger, New York, N.Y., 1968, p. 152.
[9] L.K. Jakande, *The Autobiography of Obafemi Awolowo*, Secker and Warburg, London, England, 1966; pp. 172-173; see also Walter Schwarz's *Nigeria*, F.A. Praeger Publishers, Inc., New York, New York, 1968, p. 152.
[10] Report of the commission appointed to inquire into the fears of the minorities and the means of alleying them. Command no. 505, London, Her Majesties Stationaries, 1958, p. 26.
[11] Bernard Berelson and Gary A. Steiner, *Human Behavior*, Harcourt, Bruce and World, Inc., New York, New York, 1964, p. 418.
[12] David Sills (editor), *International Encyclopedia of Social Sciences*, The MacMillan Company and The Free Press, New York, New York, Vol. 5, p. 167.
[13] Ethnic group is defined in this essay as a group with a distinct cultural tradition and origin who perceive themselves and are perceived by others as a differentiated group with a common identity. Perception of the separate identity of the group is the crucial factor. As Hunt and Walker pointed out, "the test of difference in physical appearance (frequently referred to as racial), national origin, or religion is not the difference per se, but whether this difference is considered socially significant." (Chester Hunt and Lewis Walker, *Ethnic Dynamics*, The Dorsey Press, 1974, p. 3. Homewood, Illinois, 1974). Cynthia H. Enloe, considers the expression of commonal distinctiveness as one of the characteristics of a ethnic group. Among the characteristics of ethnicity which she mentioned are: a shared sluster of beliefs and values expressed "through associational forms, the possession of communal institutions, internal differentiation. She also maintains that "ethnic group is biologically self-perpetuating." (Cynthia H. Enloe, *Ethnic Conflict and Political Development*, Little Brown and Company, Boston, Massachusetts, 1973, pp. 16-18). Fredrick Barth, *Ethnic Groups and Boundaries*, Little Brown series in Anthropology, Little Brown and Company, Inc., Boston, Massachusetts, 1969, pp. 11-12.
[14] Arthur O. Lovejoy, *Essays in the History of Ideas*, Capricorn Books, New York, New York, 1960, p. xx.

[15] Nathan Glazer and Moynihan, Daniel P.; *Ethnicity,* Harvard University Press, Cambridge, Massachusetts, 1975, p. 5.
[16] Arthur Nussbaum, *A Concise History of the Law of Nations,* The MacMillan Company, New York, New York, 1958, p. 41.
[17] Cynthia H. Enloe, *Ethnic Conflict and Political Development,* Little Brown and Company, Boston, Massachusetts, 1973, pp. 40-44; see also Alfred C. Meyer's, *Leninism,* Fredrick Praeger Publishing Company, Inc., New York, New York, 1957, pp. 147-148.
[18] S.N. Eisenstadt, *The Political Systems of Empires,* The Free Press, New York, New York, 1969, p. 29.
[19] Karl Mannheim, *Man and Society in the Age of Reconstruction,* Paul Kegan Publishers, London, England, pp. 126-127.
[20] For a discussion on the Willink Commission, see Chapter 3.
[21] Robert A. Dahl, *Pluralist Democracy in the United States,* Rand McNally; Chicago, Illinois, 1967, p. 277.

COMPLETE BIBLIOGRAPHY AND REFERENCES

Adepayo Adedji, *Nigeria Federal Finance,* Africana Publishing Corporation, New York, New York, 1969.

O. Adumosu, *The Nigerian Constitution,* Sweet and Maxwell, London, England; 1968.

S.A. Aluko, "How Many Nigerians? An Analysis of Nigerian Census Problems, 1901-1963;" *Journal of Modern African Studies,* Vol. 3 section 3.

Eme O. Awa, *Federal Government in Nigeria,* Unviersity of California Press, Berkeley, California, 1964.

Obafemi Awolowo, *Path to Nigerian Freedom,* Faber, London, England, 1947.

, *The Autobiography of Chief Obafemi Awolowo,* Cambridge University Press; Cambridge, England, 1960.

Frederick Barth, *Ethnic Groups and Boundaries,* Little Brown series in Anthropology, Little Brown and Co., Inc., Boston, Massachusetts, 1969.

Charles A. Beard, *An Economic Interpretation of the Constitution of the United States.* The Macmillan Company and The Free Press, New York, N.Y. 1963.

Bernard Berelson and Gary kA. Steiner, *Human Behavior,* Harcourt, Bruce and World, Inc., New York, New York, 1964.

Jean Blondel, *An Introduction to Comparative Government,* Frederick A. Praeger Publishing Co., New York, New York 1969.

Bernard Bourdillon, "Nigeria's New Constitution, *United Empire* 37 (March-April, 1946).

L. Brett (editor), *Constitutional Problems of the Federation of Nigeria,* Government Printing Press, Lagos, Nigeria, 1960.

Ronald Cohen and John Middleton (editors); *Comparative Political Systems:* The Natural History Press, New York, New York 1967.

Taylor Cole, *Emergent Federalism in Nigeria: Constitutional Problems of the Federation of Nigeria* (Record of the Proceedings of a seminar held at Kings College, Lagos, Nigeria), August 8 through 15, 1960.

James S. Coelman, *Nigeria: Background to Nationalism,* University of California Press, Berkeley, California, 1971.

James S. Coleman and Carl G. Rosenberg, Jr. (editors); *Political Parties and National Integration in Tropical Africa;* University of California Press, Berkeley, California, 1970.

Walker Connor, "Nation Building or Nation Destroying," *World Politics* Vol. 20 (October 1967).

A.N. Cook, *British Enterprise in Nigeria,* University of Pennsylvania Press, Philadelphia, Pennsylvania, 1937.

Michael Crowder and Obaro Ikeme (editors), *West African Chiefs,* Africana Publishing Corporation, 1970.

Robert A. Dahl, *Political Opposition in Western Democracies,* Yale University Press; New Haven, Connecticut, 1966.

_____, *Pluralist Democracy in the United States,* Rand McNally; Chicago, Illinois, 1967.

H.O. Davis, "Nigeria's New Constitution," *West African Review,* 16 (May, 1945).

Bertrand de Jouvenel, *Sovereignty,* University of Chicago Press; Chicago, Illinois, 1963.

K.W. DEUTSCH, "The Growth of Nations," *World Politics,* V (January 1953), pp. 168-196.

_____, *International Political Communities,* Doubleday; Anchor Originals; New York, New York, 1966.

B.J. Dudley, *Parties and Politics in Northern Nigeria,* Frank Cass & Co., Ltd.; London, England, 1968.

S.N. Eisenstadt, *Essays on Sociological Aspects of Political and Economic Development,* Mouton and Co., Ltd.; The Hague, 1961.

_____, *The Political Systems of Empires,* The Free Press, New York, New York, 1969.

F.E. Emergy (editor), *System Thinking,* Penguine Books, Ltd.; Baltimore, Maryland; 1969.

Cynthia H. Enloe, *Ethnic Conflict and Political development,* Little Brown & Company; Boston, Massachusetts, 1973.

Heinz Eulau, *The Behavioral Persuasion in Politics,* Random House; New York, New York, 1967.

Edward Feit, "Militray Coups and Political Development," *World Politics* Vol. XX, No. 2 (January 1968), Princeton University Press; Princeton, New Jersey.

Thomas N. Frank (editor), *Why Federations Fail?,* New York University Press; New York, New York, 1968.

J.S. Furnivall, *Colonial Policy and Practice,* New York University Press; New York, New York, 1948.

Clifford Geerts (editor), "The Integrative Revolution," *Old Societies and New States,* The Free Press, Glencoe, New York, 1963.

Nathan Glazer and Daniel P. Moynihan, *Ethnicity,* Harvard University Press; Cambridge, Massachusetts, 1975.

R.H. Green and K.G.V. Krish, *Economic Cooperation in Africa:* Restrospect and Prospects, Oxford University Press; London, England, 1967.

Morton Grodzins, *The Loyal and the Disloyal,* The University of Chicago Press; Chicago, Illinois, 1956.

Lord Hailey, *An African Survery* (revised), London University Press, London, England, 1958.

Alexander Hamilton, *The Federalist Papers;* XV. Mentor Books, The New York American Library, New York, New York, 1971.

John Htch, *Nigeria: Seeds of Disaster,* Henry Regnary Co.; Chicago, illinois, 1970.

A. Hazelwood, *The Finances of Nigerian Federation,* Oxford University Press; London, England, 1956.

――――, (editor); *African Integration and Disintegration,* Oxford University Press; London, England, 1967.

Thomas Hodgkin, *Nationalism in colonial Africa,* New York University Press; New York, New York, 1957.

Africanus J.B. Horton, *West African Countries and Peoples,* W.J. Johnson; London, England, 1868.

Chester Hunt and Lewis Walker, *Ethnic Dynamics,* The Dorsey Press; Homewood, Illinois, 1974.

Samuel P. Huntington, *Political Order in Changing Societies,* Yale University Press; New Haven, Connecticut, 1968.

――――, "Political Developoment and Political Decay," *World Politics,* XVII (April 1965).

S.M. Jacobs, *Census of Nigeria, 1931;*London University Press;London, England, London, England, 1933.

L.K. Jakande, *The Autobiography of Obeyfemi Awolowo,*Seeker and Warburn; London, England, 1966.

Joseph LaPalombara,*Politics Within Nations,*Prentice-Hall;Englewood Cliffs, New Jersey, 1974.

Joseph LaPalombara and Myron Weiner, *Political Parties and Political Development,* Princeton University Press; Princeton, New Jersey, 1972.

Colin Legum(editor),*Africa Contemporary Record,*Africa Research,Ltd.;London, England, 1969, p.655.

A.G.Leonard,*Lower Niger and Its Tribes,*Frank Cass & Co.,Ltd.; London, England, 1968.

Charlotte Leubuscher, *Bulk Buying From the Colonies,*Oxford University Press;London, England, 1966.

Arthur O. Lovejoy,*Essays in the History of Ideas,*Capricorn Books;New York, New York, 1960.

Robin Luckman,*The Nigerian Military 1960-1967,*Cambridge University Press;London, England,1971.

Frederick Lugard,*The Dual Mandate in Tropical Africa,*Blackwood & Sons; Edinburgh, England, 1918.

J.P. Mackintosh,*Nigerian Government and Politics,*Northerwestern University Evanston, Illinois, 1956.

⎯⎯⎯⎯⎯,*Nigerian Federal Government,*Northwestern University Press, Evanston, Illinois, 1966.

Karl Mannheim,*Man and Society in the Age of Reconstruction,*Paul Kegan Publishers;London, England.

Seymour Martin,*Political Man,*Doubleday and Company; New York, New York, 1963.

R.J. May,*Federalism and Fiscal Adjustment,*Oxford at the Clarendon Press;London, England,.

C.K. Meek,*Law and Authority in a Nigerian Tribe,*Oxford University Press;London, England, 1937.

Robert Melson and Howard Wople(editors),*Nigeria:Modernization and the Politics of Communalism,*, Michigan State University Press; Ann Arbor, Michigan,1971.

Alfred C. Meyer,*Leninism,* Frederick A Praeger Publishing Co.,Inc.;New York, 'New York,1957.

J.S. Mill,*Representative Government,* Everyman Editions;New York, New York, 1953.

Sigmund Newmann(editor),*"Toward a Comparitive Study of Political Parties, " Modern Political Parties,* Chicago University Press; Chicago, Illinois, 1956.

Ben O. Nwabueze, *Constitutionalism in the Emergent States,*Fairleigh Dickinson University Press;Rutherford, New Jersey, 1973.

P.N.C. Okigbo, *Nigerian Public Finance,*Longmans, Green and Company, Ltd., London, England, 1965.

G.C.A. Oldendorp, Geschichfe Der Evangelischen Bruder Auf Den Caraibischen Insel S. Thomas, S. Croic, S. Jan, (Barby, 1777). Translated in *Bulletin of African Churh History,* Vol. 1, 1963; London, England.

Odumosu I. Oluwole, *constitutional Crisis: Legality and the President's Conscience,* University of Nigeria Printing Press; Nuska, Nigeria, 1966.

M.I. Ostrogorski, *Democracy and the Organization of Political Parties in the United States and Great Britain,* Doubleday Anchor; Garden City, New York, 1964.

Talcott Parsons and Edward Shils, *Towards a General Theory of Action,* Harvard University Press; Cambridge, Massachusette, 1962.

Margery Pertham, *Native Administrations in Nigeria,* Oxford University Press; London, England, 1937.

, *"Nigerian Civil War," Africa Contemporary Record;* Colin Legum(editor), African Research, Ltd.; London, England, 1969.

, *Colonial Sequence 1930;1949,* Methuer & Co., Ltd.; London, England, 1967.

Kenneth W. Post, *Nigerian Federal Election of 1959,* Oxford University Press;Lon-England, 1963.

Kenneth W. Post and Michael Vickers, *Structure and Conflict in Nigeria, 1960-1966;* University of Wisconsin Press; Madsison, Wisconsin, 1972.

Paul O. Proehl, *Foreign Enterprises in Nigeria,* University of North Carolina; Chapel Hill, North Carolina, 1965.

William H. Riker, Federalism, Origin, Operation and Significance:Basic Studies in *Politics,* Little Brown & Company;Boston, Massachusetts.

Arnold Rivkin(editor), *Nations by Design,* Doubleday and Company, Inc.;New York, New York, 1968.

Kenneth Robinson and Frederick Madden (editors), *Essays in Imperial Government,* Humanities Press (1963)

Ruth Schacter(Morgenthau), *"African Political Parties,"The American Political Science Review,* Vol. 55.

Walter Schwartz, *Nigeria,* Frederick A. Praeger Publishing Co.; New York, New York, 1968.

Frederick A.O. Schwarz, Jr.; *Nigeria: The Tribe, The Nation, or The Race-The Politics of Independence,* The MIT Press; Cambridge, massachusetts, 1965.

David Sills(editor), *International Encyclopedia of Social Science,* The Macmillan Company and the Free Press, New York, New York.

Richard L. Sklar, *Nigerian Political Parties,* Princeton University Press; Princeton, New Jersey, 1963.

Amaury Talbot, *The Peoples of Southern Nigeria,* Frank Cass & Co., Ltd.;London, England, 1969.

R.A. Talbot, *Southern Nigeria,* Frank Cass and Co., Ltd.; London, England, 1926.

Charles D. Tarlton, *Symmetry and Assymetary as an Element of Federalism: A Theoretical Speculation,"Journal of Politics,* Vol. 27, University of Florida, Gainesville, Florida, 1965.

T.N. Tamuno, *Nigeria and the Elective Representation: 1923-1947*, Heinemann; London, England, 1966.

A.R.O. Teriba, "*Nigerian Revenue Allocation Experiance, 1952-1965: A Study in Inter-Governmental Fiscal and Financial Relations, The Nigerian Journal of Economic and Social Studies,* Vol. 8, No. 3 (November 1966), University of Ibadan, Ibadan, Nigeria.

Rudolf von Albertini, *Decolonization, the Administration and Futute of the Colonies 1919-1960*, Doubleday and Co., New York, New York, 1967.

Sidney R. Waldman, *Foundations of Political Action*, Little Brown and Co.; Boston, Massachusetts, 1972.

K.C. Wheare, *Federal Government*, 4th edition, Oxford University Press; London, England, 1967.

Aaron Wildavsky, *The Politics of the Budgetary Process*, 2nd Edition, Little Brown and Company; Boston, Massachusetts, 1974.

Government Sources

Austrialian Grand Commission, *Report on the Application Made by the States of Austrialia, Western Australia and Tanzania for Financial Assistance from the Commonwealth* under Section 96 of the Constitution. The First Report, 1934.

K.J. Binns, *Report of the Fiscal Review Commission,* Federal Ministry of Information; Government Printing Press, Lagos, Nigeria, 1964.

The Chick Commission Report(Command 9026), Government Printing Office; Lagos, Nigeria.

Commission Report 505, Report of Commission appointed to enquire into the fear of minorities and the means of alleying them, July, 1958(The Willink Commission).

Constitution of the Federation of Nigeria, 1960; Government Printing Press, Lagos, Nigeria, 1963.

Economic Survey of Nigeria, 1959; The Federal Government Printing Press; Lagos, Nigeria.

Emergency Powers (General Regulation); Section 4, Government Printing Press; Lagos, Nigeria, 1963.

Federation of Nigeria, *Accountant General's Report, Annual, 1953;1954;* Government Printing Press; Lagos, Nigeria, 1954.

John R. Hicks and Sidney Phillipson, *Report of the Commission on Revenue Allocation,* Government Printing Press; Lagos, Nigeria, 1950, 1951 and 1954.

Legislative Council Debates, Official Reports, Lagos, Nigeria; November 1, 1923.

Malcaulay Papers, address by the Governor of Nigeria, December 29, 1920, Vol. iv, No. 13; Lagos, Nigeria, 1960.

Nigeria's Constitutional Development 1801-1960, Federal Ministry of Information; Lagos, Nigeria, 1960.

Nigeria's Constitutional Developments: 1864-1960; (Federal Ministry of Information, Government Printing Press); Lagos, Nigeria, 1960.

Nigerian Legislative Council Debate, Official Report, November 1, 1923; Government Printing Press; Lagos, Nigeria.

Nigerian Order in Council(Legislative Council), 1922; Government Printing Press, Lagos, Nigeria.

Population Census of Northern Nigeria, 1952; Government Printing Press; Lagos, Nigeria, 1953.

The Raisman Commission, Report of the Commission on Revenue Allocation, Lagos Government Printing Press; Lagos, Nigeria, 1953.

Report of Kano Disturbance, May 16 through 19, 1953; Kaduna, Nigeria.

Report of Kano Disturbance, May 16 through 19, 1953; Lagos, Nigeria.

Sessional Paper No. 4 of 1945, *Political and Constitutional Future of Nigeria,* Government Printing Press; Lagos, Nigeria, 1945.

Newspapers

The Daily Express: May 25, 1962; December 5,16,17,18,22,23,24, and 30, 1964; January 5, 1965; lagos, Nigeria.

The Daily Service: May 4, 1962; November 7,8, 1964; Lagos, Nigeria.

The Daily Times: December 11, 1952; April 9, 1953; May 23, 1953; November 17, 1962; December 5,6,7,8,11, 1962; February 20, 1963; October 24, 1964; and December 8 and 24, 1964; January 1, 1965; Lagos, Nigeria.

The Lagos Weekly Record: March 1, 1919 through May 31, 1919; Lagos, Nigeria.

The Morning Post: December 3, 1963; March 4, 8, and 24, 1964; January 1, 1965; Lagos, Nigeria.

The Nigerian Tribune: May 29, 1962 and June 4,5, 1962; Lagos, Nigeria.

The West African Pilot: December 4, 1963; February 29, 1964; October 21,27, 1964; and December 11,24,29, 1964.

ABOUT THE AUTHOR

Ekwueme Felix Okoli was born in Akpujiogu Town in South Eastern Nigeria on December 12th, 1929. He was educated at Christ The King College, Onitsha, where he obtained the Cambridge School Certificate in 1947. As an external student of London University, he passed the Intermediate Bachelor of Laws before proceeding to the United States on a Nigerian Federal Government Scholarship in September of 1959. He earned the Bachelor of Arts Degree in Classics from the University of Colorado, Masters Degree in Classics and A Masters Degree in Public Law And Government from Columbia University. In 1978, he received his Doctorate in Political Science from the New School For Social Research in New York. Professor Okoli has had a rich and varied career. In Nigeria, he worked as a Local Purchase Clerk in the Nigerian Railway stores. Between 1957-59, he was History Master at Adventist High School, Ihe and Latin Master at Baptist High School, Port Harcourt. In the summer of 1966, he worked as a Research Fellow at St. Johns University under a Ford Foundation Grant.

In the Fall of 1966, he was employed as an instructor at St. Johns University. In 1967, he joined the staff of the Manpower Career and Development Agency in New York under the Lindsey Administration. His duties included counseling and placing High School graduates and High School Drop-outs in training programs and jobs. He rose to the rank of Supervisor of Counseling before he joined the City University in February 1970. He was appointed Director of Afro-American Studies at New York City Community College of City University of New York. He was responsible for initiating the program and developing courses in African and Afro-American Studies. He taught courses in African History and Government, and served as the Chairman of the Department from 1970 to 1979. Dr. Okoli is the author of a number of articles, including "Reflections on the Rhodesian Crisis", "Technical Education in Nigeria", "The Press and Nationalism in Nigeria" and "The Supernatural in the Tragedies of Seneca."